NEW

Family Handyman is now streaming on your TV!

Hands-on inspiration for making your house a home.

SCAN AND WATCH FREE NOW

A FAMILY HANDYMAN BOOK

Copyright © 2024 Home Services Publications, a subsidiary of Trusted Media Brands, Inc.

2915 Commers Drive, Suite 700
Eagan, MN 55121

Family Handyman is a registered trademark of Trusted Media Brands, Inc.

Hardcover ISBN: 978-1-62145-914-9
Trade ISBN: 979-8-88977-013-8
E-Pub ISBN: 978-1-62145-916-3
Component Number: 116400112H

We are committed to both the quality of our products and the service we provide to our customers. We value your comments, so please feel free to contact us at TMBBookTeam@TrustedMediaBrands.com.

For more *Family Handyman* products and information, visit our website:

www.familyhandyman.com

Printed in China

10 9 8 7 6 5 4 3 2 1

Text, photography and illustrations for *Whole House Budget-Friendly DIY* are based on articles previously published in *Family Handyman* magazine (familyhandyman.com).

Image Credits

5 (r), 46 FSTOP/Getty Images; 12, 14 (br), 30 (tr), 33 (br), 77, 94 (br), 100 (b), 103 (bl, br), 105 (b), 196, 197, 201 (bl), 205, 221 (t), 229, 234, 238 Frank Rohrbach III; 17 (t), 141 Don Mannes; 26 (br) Ron Chamberlain; 104 (br) Brian Dohrwardt; 120 (b) Christopher Mills; 158 (b) LesPalenik/Shutterstock; 159 (cl, cr) Structure Tech; 216, 217 David Radke; 244, 272 Sonja Dahlgren/Getty Images; 245, 263 BanksPhotos/Getty Images; 246 Pattie Stieb/Shutterstock; 247 WoodysPhotos/Shutterstock; 248 Welcomia/Shutterstock; 249 Leonard Zhukovsky/Shutterstock; 250 (t), 254 (b) Tetra Images/Jupiter Images; 256 Steve Bjorkman; 260 AleMoraes244/Getty Images; 262 (b) Black+Decker; 266, 267, 268, 269 Levi Brown; 270 (t) American Standard; 270 (b), 271 Pfister® Brand by Spectrum Brands, Inc.

All other photographs by Trusted Media Brands, Inc.

Electrical consultant: John Williamson

fh **family**
handyman

WHOLE HOUSE
BUDGET-FRIENDLY
DIY

SAFETY FIRST—**ALWAYS!**

Tackling home improvement projects and repairs can be endlessly rewarding. But as most of us know, with the rewards come risks. DIYers use chain saws, climb ladders and tear into walls that can contain big, hazardous surprises.

The good news is that armed with the right knowledge, tools and procedures, homeowners can minimize risk. As you go about your projects and repairs, stay alert for these hazards:

Aluminum wiring

Aluminum wiring, installed in millions of homes between 1965 and 1973, requires special techniques and materials to make safe connections. This wiring is dull gray, not the dull orange characteristic of copper. Hire a licensed electrician certified to work with it. For more information, go to cpsc.gov and search for "aluminum wiring."

Spontaneous combustion

Rags saturated with oil finishes, such as Danish oil and linseed oil, as well as oil-based paints and stains, can spontaneously combust if left bunched up. Always dry the rags outdoors, spread out loosely. When the oil has thoroughly dried, you can safely throw the rags in the trash.

Vision and hearing protection

Safety glasses or goggles should be worn whenever you're working on DIY projects that involve chemicals, dust or anything that could shatter or chip off and hit your eye. Also, sounds louder than 80 decibels (dB) are considered potentially dangerous. For instance, sound levels from a lawn mower can be 90 dB, and levels from shop tools and chain saws can be 90 to 100 dB.

Lead paint

If your home was built before 1979, it may contain lead paint, which is a serious health hazard, especially for children 6 years old or under. Take precautions when you scrape or remove it. Contact your public health department for detailed safety information or call 800-424-LEAD (5323) to receive an information pamphlet. Or visit epa.gov/lead.

Buried utilities

A few days before you dig in your yard, have your underground water, gas and electrical lines marked. Just call 811 or go to call811.com.

Smoke and carbon monoxide (CO) alarms

The risk of dying in a reported home-structure fire is cut in half in homes with working smoke alarms. Test your smoke alarms every month, replace batteries as necessary and replace units that are more than 10 years old. As you make your home more energy efficient and airtight, existing ducts and chimneys can't always successfully vent combustion gases, including potentially deadly carbon monoxide (CO). Install a UL-listed CO detector, and test your CO and smoke alarms at the same time.

Five-gallon buckets and window-covering cords

Anywhere from 10 to 40 children a year drown in 5-gallon buckets, according to the U.S. Consumer Products Safety Commission. Always store empty buckets upside down and ones containing liquid with the covers securely snapped.

According to Parents for Window Blind Safety, hundreds of children in the United States are injured every year after becoming entangled in looped window-treatment cords. For more information, visit pfwbs.org.

Working up high

If you have to get up on your roof to do a repair or installation, always install roof brackets and wear a roof harness.

Asbestos

Texture sprayed on ceilings before 1978, adhesives and tiles for vinyl and asphalt floors before 1980, and vermiculite insulation (with gray granules) all may contain asbestos. Other building materials made between 1940 and 1980 could also contain asbestos. If you suspect that the materials you're removing or working around contain asbestos, contact your health department or visit epa.gov/asbestos for information.

CONTENTS

Chapter One
KITCHEN & BATHROOM

Chapter Two
GARAGE & SHED

Chapter **Three**
WALLS, CEILINGS, WINDOWS & MORE

Chapter **Four**
APPLIANCES & MAINTENANCE

Chapter **Five**
FURNITURE

Chapter **Six**
OUTDOOR

Special **Section**
SAVE BIG ON HOUSEHOLD BILLS

CHAPTER ONE

KITCHEN & BATHROOM

Add Kitchen Outlets

Run new wiring without wrecking walls.

Not that long ago, the average kitchen counter was home to a toaster, a coffee maker and maybe a blender, but things have changed. We now have juicers, bread makers, TVs, gourmet pizza ovens, computers and charging stations for a half dozen mobile gadgets. And it's getting harder to find available outlets to plug all that stuff into. Extension cords and power strips are unsightly and can be dangerous. The only real solution is to add more outlets.

We tracked down an electrician who, not surprisingly, adds kitchen outlets all the time. He showed us how he adds an outlet to a kitchen backsplash by running conduit through the backs of the cabinets. This method is fast, inexpensive and super simple. Best of all, it doesn't require a whole bunch of wall repairs or painting. This article shows how to install one new outlet, but you can add several by following similar steps.

BEFORE YOU GET STARTED

Kitchen receptacle outlets need to be on dedicated 20-amp circuits and require 12-gauge wire. Today, 12-gauge wire is wrapped in a yellow sheath, but your old cable may be white. New circuits in kitchens need both arc-fault and ground-fault circuit-interruption (AFCI, GFCI) protection. In this story, we're adding an outlet to a kitchen that already has GFCI protection, which has been required for many years. If your kitchen is not on a 20-amp circuit or doesn't have GFCI protection, you'll have to install a new circuit or circuit breaker. For more information, go to familyhandyman.com and search for "new circuit." Also, discuss your project with your local electrical inspector when you apply for a permit. If adding a circuit still seems above your pay grade, then call an electrician.

REMOVE THE EXISTING BOX

The first step is to shut off the power. If your breaker panel is poorly labeled, plug a radio into the outlet you plan to pull power from and start shutting down breakers until the music stops. There may also be wires from other circuits in the junction box, so probe the box with a noncontact voltage tester (available at home centers for around $10 and up) before you disconnect any wires. Cover the ends of the

existing wires with wire nuts as an additional precaution. **Caution:** If you discover aluminum wiring, call in a licensed electrician who is certified to work with it. This wiring is dull gray, not the dull orange that is characteristic of copper wire.

It's easier to fish the new cable if you remove the existing box in the wall. Fiberglass boxes can be busted out with a hammer and chisel or a sturdy screwdriver. It's best to cut the nails on plastic boxes with a hacksaw. Start by probing with a screwdriver to find which side of the box the stud is on. Then pry the screwdriver between the stud and the box to make room for the hacksaw blade **(Photo 1)**.

Metal boxes are difficult to remove without creating the need for some drywall repairs. Before you attempt the removal, see if you can fish the cable down through the existing metal box into the hole in the cabinet.

CUT A HOLE FOR THE NEW BOX

There's no rule mandating the height of the new box, so just match the height of the existing one. The code for kitchens states that there must be an outlet within a 2-ft. reach from anywhere along the countertop, excluding those areas where there's a sink or stovetop. This means there should be an outlet every 4 ft. If you're just adding one outlet, you probably won't be subject to this rule, but if you're remodeling the entire kitchen, you probably will. It's best to check with your local electrical inspector.

Before cutting the hole, go to the floor below and, if possible, check to see if there are any pipes or ducts running through the wall you plan to cut into. Or go outside and see if any vents are sticking through the roof in that area. If you're not sure, make a small exploratory hole that can be patched easily.

The new box does not have to be right up against a stud. In fact, it's easier to install if it's not. Trace around the new box, and cut the hole with a jab saw (**Photo 2**). Don't shove the saw all the way into the wall cavity, just in case there's a wire or pipe hidden behind the wall.

If your backsplash is tiled, use a rotary tool fitted with a diamond tile-cutting bit. Set the depth of the bit so it cuts through the tile only. Finish the cut with a jab saw. Whenever possible, use the grout lines for two sides of the hole, because cutting will be much easier. Drill starter holes in two opposite corners with a glass-and-tile drill bit.

DRILL THE HOLES AND FISH THE NEW CABLE

Empty the cabinets, and pull out the drawers to get better access. Lying on your back halfway inside a cabinet is not the most comfortable position, so throw down a couple of couch cushions before you get started. And be sure to wear eye protection. For the new cable, drill 1-in. holes through the backs of the cabinets, near the top (**Photo 3**). Don't let the bit travel too far into the wall cavity—the insulation may twist up like cotton candy on a stick and make it difficult to pull the bit back out. Also drill a hole through the sides of the cabinets, near the back, for the conduit to pass through.

Measure the distance the new cable will travel both horizontally and vertically, and then add several feet before cutting it—it's better to throw out a few feet of cable than end up short. Shove one end of the cable through one hole in the back of the cabinet and up toward the box hole (**Photo 4**). It doesn't matter if you start at the new or the existing outlet side. Our expert puts a slight bend on the end of the cable so that it hugs the back of the drywall. This will help keep it from getting hung up on insulation.

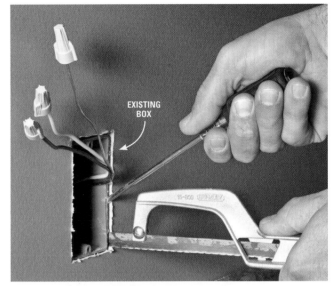

1 CUT OUT THE EXISTING BOX. Cut off the nails on the existing box. Wedge a screwdriver between the stud and the box to make room for the hacksaw blade.

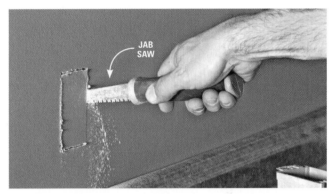

2 CUT A HOLE FOR THE NEW BOX. Trace the outline of the box on the wall at the same height as the existing box, and cut out the drywall with a jab saw. Keep the hole an inch or more away from any studs.

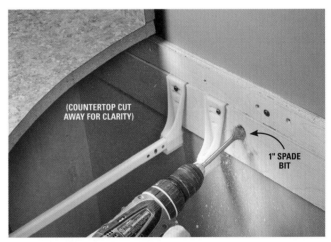

3 DRILL HOLES FOR THE CABLE. Drill 1-in. holes through the backs of the cabinets. Beware of hidden cable, ducts and pipes; when the bit breaks through the drywall, stop. Then drill a hole through the sides of the cabinets.

FIGURE A.
DIAGRAM OF NEW CABLE AND CONDUIT

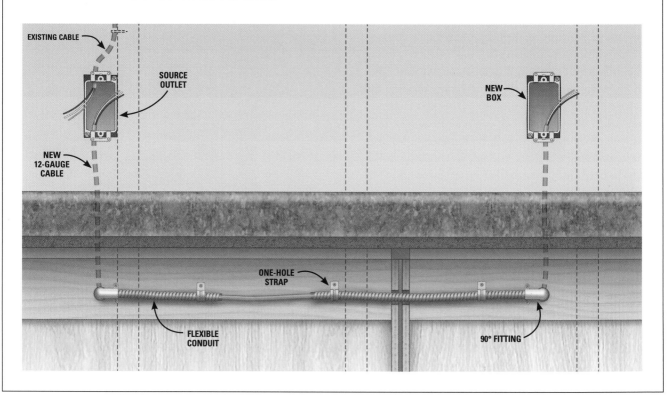

EXISTING CABLE

SOURCE OUTLET

NEW BOX

NEW 12-GAUGE CABLE

ONE-HOLE STRAP

FLEXIBLE CONDUIT

90° FITTING

Following the Electrical Code

For new construction, the National Electrical Code (NEC) requires AFCI protection to be installed where the branch circuit originates in the electrical panel (or at a subpanel). This is meant to protect the entire branch circuit: all the permanent electrical wiring, receptacles, light fixtures, etc., and all equipment and appliances supplied by the branch circuit, whether permanently installed or cord-and-plug connected. The most effective way of doing this is by installing an AFCI circuit breaker. Conversely, GFCI protection is mainly concerned about receptacle outlets and, per the NEC, can be installed at the electrical panel in the form of a circuit breaker, at the end of the branch circuit in the form of a receptacle outlet, or somewhere in between.

Where existing branch circuits are modified, replaced or extended, the NEC requires the circuit to be AFCI protected. To do this, you can install an AFCI circuit breaker in the electrical panel, or a dual function AFCI/GFCI circuit breaker if GFCI protection is also required for the receptacle outlets on that circuit. Another option is to install an outlet branch-circuit-type (OBC) AFCI receptacle outlet like we have shown in this story. The OBC AFCI receptacle outlet must be installed at the first receptacle outlet in the branch circuit.

Dual-Function Breakers

A ground fault can occur if a hot wire accidentally comes in contact with a grounded metal frame of an appliance—or a person standing in a puddle of water. That's why GFCI protection, which has been around for 50 years, is required in kitchens, bathrooms and other potentially wet or damp locations. GFCI devices sense the ground fault and quickly stop the flow of electricity—hopefully before an electrical shock results in a fatality.

An arc fault is an unintended arcing event where electrical current flows through an unplanned path. Common causes include pinched wires, cracked wire insulation, and wires damaged by nails or staples. An arc fault can cause a fire, so AFCI protection is mandated by the electrical code for most of the house.

In the past, the only way to achieve both GFCI and AFCI protection on the same circuit was to install an AFCI circuit breaker in the panel and the GFCI protection at the first available receptacle. Now there are dual-function circuit breakers that offer both AFCI and GFCI protection. Dual-function AFCI/GFCI receptacle outlets are also available for use in limited situations.

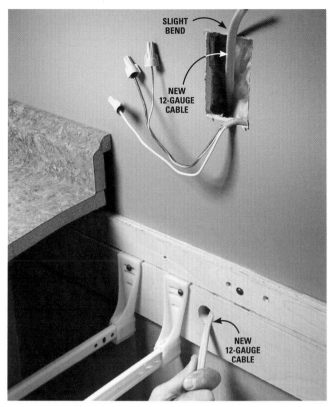

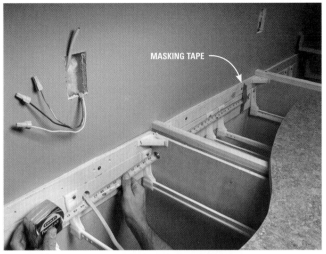

5 **MEASURE FOR THE CONDUIT LENGTH. Stick your** tape measure through the conduit holes to measure the length of the flexible conduit. Have a helper hold the end of the tape, or secure it with masking tape.

4 **FISH IN THE NEW CABLE. Slide the new cable through** the drilled hole, then up and out through the electrical box hole. Put a slight bend on the cable so it hugs the wall and doesn't get hung up on insulation.

INSTALL THE CONDUIT

Measure the length of the flexible conduit by sliding a tape measure through the hole in the sides of the cabinets. Have a friend hold the end of the tape in the hole or secure it with masking tape **(Photo 5)**.

Cut the conduit to length and attach a bushing or fitting to the side you plan to push the wire through. Bushings and fittings protect the cable from getting damaged on the sharp edges of the conduit. Our expert likes the 90-degree fitting because it results in a nice "finished" look with no cable exposed. A standard bushing will result in a small section of exposed cable at the ends, but that's acceptable.

Push the cable through the conduit so that it sticks out a few inches on the other side, and then slide the conduit through the hole in the sides of the cabinets **(Photo 6)**. Once the conduit is through, install the bushing/fitting on the other end of the conduit, and then pull the cable the rest of the way through the conduit.

Push the cable up through the second hole in the wall the same way you did through the first, and then secure both sides of the conduit with straps near the hole **(Photo 7)**. If the conduit travels more than halfway across the length of the cabinet, add another strap halfway between the end of the conduit and the hole in the cabinet.

6 **SLIDE THE CONDUIT INTO PLACE. Feed the new cable** through the conduit, and then push the conduit through the 1-in. hole drilled into the sides of the cabinets.

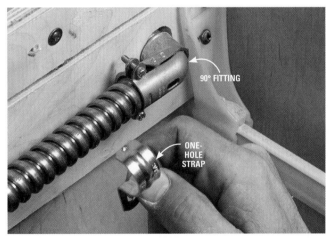

7 **SECURE THE CONDUIT. Hold the conduit in place with** straps. Place straps near the 90-degree fittings and one more in the middle if the conduit travels more than halfway across the length of the cabinet.

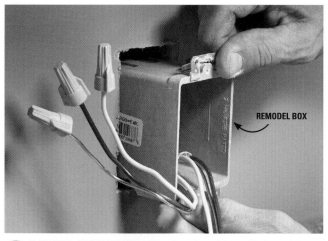

8 INSTALL NEW BOXES. Cut the sheathing off the cable before pulling the wires through the remodel boxes. Slide the boxes into the holes and fasten them to the drywall.

REMODEL BOX

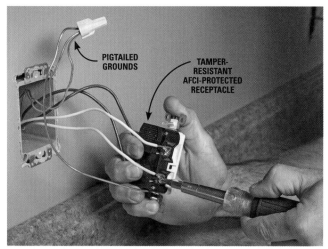

PIGTAILED GROUNDS

TAMPER-RESISTANT AFCI-PROTECTED RECEPTACLE

9 WIRE THE RECEPTACLES. Install a tamper-resistant AFCI receptacle at the source outlet as shown in **Figure A**. The outlets downstream can be standard tamper-resistant receptacles.

INSTALL THE NEW BOXES

It's easier to remove the cable sheathing before installing the new "old work" boxes, but make sure to leave enough on the cable so about an inch of sheathing pokes into the box. Once the sheathing is removed, pull the wires into the box, slide it into place and secure it **(Photo 8)**.

There are several kinds of "old work" boxes, sometimes called remodel boxes. "Old work" boxes don't get nailed to a stud but instead are secured with wings that clamp onto the drywall as a screw is turned. The type of box we used is made from sturdy fiberglass and is available at most home centers.

In this wiring scenario, five individual 12-gauge wires are occupying the source box (all grounds count as one), so the 18-cu.-in. box shown in **Photo 8** is large enough to handle all the wires and receptacle without crowding. You may need a larger box if there are six or more wires.

WIRE THE NEW RECEPTACLES

All circuits in a kitchen require AFCI and most receptacle outlets require GFCI protection. In this example, we're working with a kitchen circuit that is supplied from a GFCI circuit breaker in the panel, which means that we need to install only a receptacle that has AFCI protection (for more details, see "Dual-Function Breakers," p. 12). One properly wired AFCI outlet will protect all the other standard receptacle outlets and wiring downstream. All newly installed receptacles need to be tamper resistant, so look for the "TR" before you buy.

All the line (incoming) and load (outgoing) wires need to be in their proper places **(Figure B)**. If you've wired receptacles before, you may have used "pigtails" to connect them. That's where the hot, neutral and ground wires run continuously with small pigtail wires pulled off and connected to each receptacle. This is a great way to ensure that if one receptacle goes bad, the rest downstream stay operational. But when wiring GFCI and AFCI receptacles, only the ground wires can be hooked up with pigtails; read the instructions and pay attention to the "LINE" and "LOAD" labels on the receptacle outlet **(Photo 9)**.

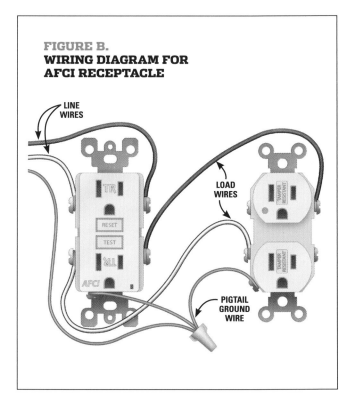

FIGURE B.
WIRING DIAGRAM FOR AFCI RECEPTACLE

LINE WIRES

LOAD WIRES

PIGTAIL GROUND WIRE

Off-the-Counter Produce Storage

This inexpensive project saves counter space, looks great and keeps fresh, healthy foods within reach.

Made with just a sheet of plywood and some hooks and baskets, this project is a breeze to build. Plus, there are plenty of opportunities to customize the design to suit your needs and style. Here's how to do it:

CUT PLYWOOD TO SIZE

Lay out your baskets on the plywood to determine the size of board that looks good. The baskets shown in this story are about 12 in. wide x 8 in. tall x 7 in. deep. We trimmed the plywood to 20 x 39 in. for a pleasing basket-to-board ratio.

WEATHER THE BOARD

While you can stain or paint the board however you like, we recommend trying this easy barn-door-style distressing technique to give the board a weathered look: First, use an angle grinder with a knot cup wheel to create texture. Add random welts and wormholes with a hammer and awl. Next, apply a light

stain, removing the excess with a rag, and then apply streaks of a dark stain, again removing the excess with a rag. Finally, apply a gray stain unevenly, removing the excess with a rag, and allow the board to dry completely.

ADD HOOKS FOR BASKETS

Lay out the baskets on the finished plywood board and mark the placement of each hook. Be sure to check the measurements from the sides, top and bottom of the board to make sure you get the baskets centered. Then screw in the hooks.

MOUNT THE BOARD TO A WALL

Since this piece will be holding heavy fruits and vegetables, be sure to use a DIY or store-bought cleat to mount the board to the wall. Then hang the baskets on the hooks and fill them with your fresh produce.

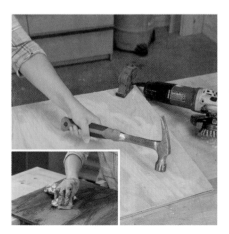

DIY Granite Countertops

Get the beauty and durability of granite for half the cost.

Gorgeous and tough, granite makes a great countertop material. Unfortunately, greatness has its price: Granite slab countertops are notoriously expensive. But you can get granite countertops without breaking the bank by using granite tile instead of professionally installed slabs. Budget-conscious builders and homeowners have done this for decades—and now there are even granite tiles designed especially for countertops.

This article will show you how to install these special tiles. Since a countertop sits just a couple of feet below eye level, minor mistakes are easy to see. We'll show you how to set your tiles flat, even and perfectly aligned.

MONEY, TIME AND TOOLS

The materials bill for our countertop and backsplash was less than $50 per sq. ft., including everything from screws and backer board to the tiles themselves. The number of inside and outside corners has a big impact on the total cost: Corners cost us about $40 each. Standard bullnose tiles cost $20 and field tiles just $10 each.

This is a two-weekend project for a typical kitchen. You'll spend about half that time tearing out your old countertop and creating a solid base for the tile. A countertop requires a bit more skill and precision than a wall or floor, so we don't recommend this as a first-time tile project. In addition to standard tile tools, you'll need to rent a tile saw for a day (you can't cut the tiles with a manual cutter). Aside from the tiles, all the tools and materials you'll need are readily available at home centers. Tiles are available at tile stores or online (search for "modular granite countertop").

ORDER THE TILE

A few weeks before you tear off your old countertops, pull out a pencil and pad, and calculate the number and types of tiles needed. Measure, then sketch your countertop, including the sink, on graph paper. Label the tiles (bullnose, field, corners) to assess what's needed where.

When you arrive at a final count, you're almost ready to place your order. Because many tiles are color-matched before

FIGURE A.
GRANITE TILE COUNTERTOP

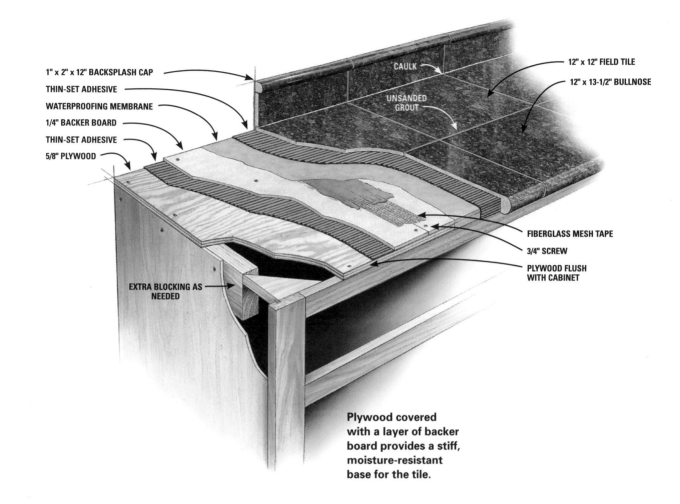

1" x 2" x 12" BACKSPLASH CAP
THIN-SET ADHESIVE
WATERPROOFING MEMBRANE
1/4" BACKER BOARD
THIN-SET ADHESIVE
5/8" PLYWOOD

CAULK
UNSANDED GROUT

12" x 12" FIELD TILE
12" x 13-1/2" BULLNOSE

FIBERGLASS MESH TAPE
3/4" SCREW
PLYWOOD FLUSH WITH CABINET

EXTRA BLOCKING AS NEEDED

Plywood covered with a layer of backer board provides a stiff, moisture-resistant base for the tile.

shipping, order a few extra to allow for cutting mistakes. Three extra field tiles and two extra bullnose tiles are a safe allowance for a simple job, but for a complex project, you might want extra insurance.

BUILD A SOLID BASE

According to the manufacturer of our tiles, they can be installed directly onto an existing laminate countertop if the laminate is attached to a 3/4-in.-thick plywood substrate. Since the vast majority of countertops have a particleboard core, chances are you'll have to tear out your countertop and start from scratch. For step-by-step instructions on how to remove your old countertop and build a base for the tile, go to familyhandyman.com and search for "granite tile countertop." For construction details, see **Figure A**. Seal the backer board with a waterproofing membrane **(Photo 1)** for extra insurance. This coating prevents moisture from passing through the backer board and causing the plywood to swell or delaminate.

WATERPROOFING MEMBRANE

PLASTIC SHEETING

1 Protect the tile base against water damage with a coat of waterproofing membrane.

Granite Tile Made Just for Countertops

The tiles we used have a thick, rounded "bullnose." These special tiles eliminate the need to cut and install thin strips of tile to cover the edges (for this and other finishing techniques, search for "granite tile countertop" at familyhandyman.com). Some manufacturers offer outside corners, premitered inside corners, standard bullnose tiles and special backsplash pieces. The field tiles are just like standard granite floor tiles.

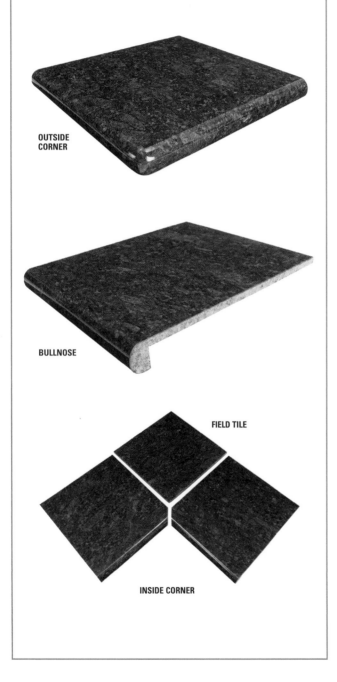

OUTSIDE CORNER

BULLNOSE

FIELD TILE

INSIDE CORNER

TILE SAW

MASKING TAPE

2 Set bullnose tiles on scraps of plywood to cut them. Granite is difficult to mark clearly, so stick on some masking tape and mark the tape.

HONING STONE

3 Rub cut edges with a honing stone to bevel the edges slightly. Rub in a circular motion to avoid wearing a groove in the stone.

4 Number the tiles and sketch a layout map after the dry run. Remove the tiles and use the map to put each tile back in the correct order later.

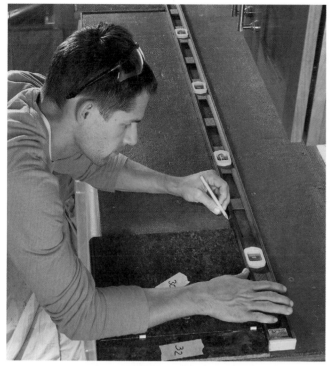

5 Draw a baseline from the inside corner tiles to the end tiles. Use this line as a guide as you set the front row of tiles.

MAKE A DRY RUN FIRST

Once the base is in place, you're set to start laying tile. But first do a dry run. Dry-fitting gives you time to experiment with the arrangement of the tiles so that the natural color and grain variations flow from one tile to the next. A dry run also lets you cut the tiles all at once and minimizes the total rental fee for the tile saw.

The manufacturer we used recommends setting tiles tightly together and filling the shallow V-shaped bevels between them with grout. But we left 1/8-in. gaps between tiles using tile spacers. That gave us a little room for error in cutting and placing tiles and allowed the tiles to conform to our L-shaped countertop, which wasn't perfectly square.

Start the dry run from an inside corner and work outward so that the two mitered inside corner tiles fit together perfectly. Continue working out from the corner, laying a few bullnose tiles and filling in the back with field tiles.

Cutting bullnose tiles with a wet saw isn't any more difficult than cutting regular tiles, except that you'll need to stack a few plywood scraps under the tile so that you can cut the bullnose edge first **(Photo 2)**. To avoid chipping or cracking the tile, guide it slowly and steadily past the blade. It's OK if a wall-facing cut is a little rough, but for visible cuts, smooth the sawn edge and create a slight bevel along the top edge with a honing stone **(Photo 3)**.

After laying out all the tiles, label them and make a simple layout map **(Photo 4)** so you can set each tile right where it belongs later. Finally, remove the middle tiles and use the remaining end and corner pieces to draw guidelines **(Photo 5)**.

SET THE TILES

It's time to mix the thin-set. To prevent the tiles from sinking, aim for a peanut-butter-thick mix. When combed out with a 3/8-in. notched trowel, the thin-set should hold sharp ridges without slumping.

Lay the tiles from the inside corner out **(Photo 6)**, just as you did during the dry run. Instead of fussing over each tile, lay two or three tiles at once, then treat them as a unit. Once you've positioned the tiles, use a straightedge to make sure they're set flat **(Photo 7)**. At the beginning, you'll need to place a dry-laid tester tile on top of a 1/8-in.-thick spacer (such as a layer or two of cardboard). As you proceed, rest the level on the first tiles you've laid to help gauge the rest. After checking the height, nudge the straightedge against the bullnose edges to be sure the front edge stays straight and lines up with your guideline.

Be careful when adjusting tiles. Granite is tough stuff, but it's surprisingly easy to crack. To slide freshly set tiles, use your utility knife. Stab the point of the blade into the backer

6 Work in small sections, spreading just enough thin-set to set eight tiles. That gives you plenty of time to set and adjust tiles before the thin-set becomes too stiff.

TESTER

SPACER

7 Lay tiles perfectly flat using a straightedge. Set a "tester" tile on a spacer to account for the thickness of the thin-set. Run the straightedge from the tester to the tile you're setting to check for flatness.

OLD CREDIT CARD

8 Plow out thin-set that oozes up between tiles before it hardens. An old credit card fits into the narrow gaps and won't scratch the tile.

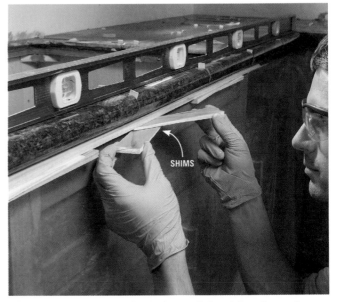

SHIMS

9 Shim the narrow tiles in front of the sink to keep them from tipping forward. Align the tops and fronts of these tiles using a straightedge.

board, then lever the side of the blade against the bottom edge of the tile. If a tile sinks lower than its neighbors, lift it straight up with a suction cup (see "A Tile Setter's Lifesaver"), scrape off the old thin-set, trowel on a fresh layer, then reset. Trying to tap down a high tile almost always causes a crack. Instead, try gently pressing and wiggling so the excess thin-set can squeeze out an open end. If that doesn't work, lift the tile and scrape away the excess thin-set. Clean any thin-set that oozes out between the tiles as you go, before it has a chance to harden (**Photo 8**).

Thin-set sets quickly, but to be safe, give the counter a few hours (preferably overnight) to harden before starting the backsplash (**Photo 10**). Make sure your new backsplash isn't higher than your outlets before mixing any mortar. To prevent sliders, give your freshly tiled backsplash a day to cure before removing the spacers and packing the grout.

GROUT, SEAL AND CAULK

Once the granite's in place, this job is like any other tiling project. Use a float to pack grout into most of the lines, but note that you'll probably need to use your finger to work the grout into curves, such as the bullnose front edge and the backsplash cap. Sponge off the excess when the grout begins to harden. Wait until the grout is fully dry before buffing off the remaining haze with a clean cotton towel. You can now reinstall the sink, stove and other appliances.

Some foods and cleaners can stain or even etch granite and grout, so apply a stone sealer (**Photo 11**). Finally, lay a thin bead of caulk along the joint where the counter meets the backsplash.

A Tile Setter's Lifesaver

A suction cup tool (about $12) is typically used for handling glass. But it's also great for tricky tile situations. On this project, you set the front tiles first and then insert field tiles between them and the wall. The suction cup lets you set these tiles perfectly. Without it, you'd have to drop the tiles into place, risking chipped edges.

Better yet, a suction cup saves the day when you notice a sunken tile that's already surrounded by other tiles. The ability to lift a tile straight up saves you the hassle of removing and resetting several neighboring tiles just to get at one sinker.

10 "Back butter" the backsplash and cap pieces to minimize the mess on the wall. Support backsplash tiles with spacers to leave a 1/8-in. gap for caulk.

11 Seal the tiles with a penetrating stone sealer after the grout has dried. A foam paint roller applies the sealer quickly and evenly.

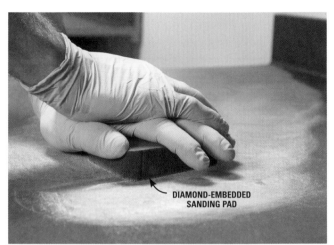

1 ROUGH UP THE SURFACE. Degloss the countertop with the diamond-embedded sanding pad in the kit so the base coat will stick to the countertop. You'll know it's deglossed when there are tiny scratches everywhere.

Countertop Renewal

Give your kitchen an instant face-lift.

Rust-Oleum's Countertop Transformations coating system (about $230 at Home Depot for 50 sq. ft. of countertop) is a simple way to transform worn or damaged laminate countertops into a new countertop surface. The product is available in four colors ranging from light to very dark (the shade shown in this story is Charcoal).

The big pluses of this system are multifold: It's not smelly or difficult, you don't have to remove your countertops(!), the instructions are clear, and the kit comes with everything you need (except basic painting tools) as well as a detailed DVD. The product can be applied to any laminate or hardwood countertop in reasonable condition. Burns and scratches are fine, but fill deep dents and chips before starting.

After using this product, we can report that it's surprisingly easy to apply. In terms of durability, the manufacturer compares it to laminate. We can't speak to its long-term durability, but when we tried to scratch the newly resurfaced countertop with car keys, it was surprisingly tough—no marks at all. And you can reapply the system to renew the surface later if you want.

SAND AND CLEAN

The first step is to completely degloss the laminate surface using the sanding tools included in the kit **(Photo 1)**. You can save on sanding time by using an orbital sander with 60- or 80-grit sandpaper on the flat areas (but vacuuming up the dust will add cleaning time). Use a light touch so you don't sand through any areas or create uneven surfaces. Vacuum up the dust and wipe all surfaces with a damp cloth until they're completely dust-free. Use painter's tape and plastic to mask off base cabinets, the sink, appliances, the walls above the backsplash and the floor. Cover the sink drains, too.

APPLY THE BASE COAT

This step is time-sensitive, so before you apply the base coat, have the decorative chips in the dispenser and ready to go. Once you've applied the base coat, you'll have a 20-minute window to apply the decorative chips before it dries. If you have a long countertop or several countertop areas, get a helper and work as a team **(Photo 2)**. Complete one section (including the chip application) before moving on to the next.

Apply the base coat thickly using a brush on the backsplash and a microfiber roller (not included in the kit) on the flat surface and front edge. You really need to lay it on thickly and evenly, and maintain a wet edge on the entire surface for the best result. The kit includes a wetting agent you can spray on to keep the base coat moist and ready for the decorative chips.

APPLY THE DECORATIVE CHIPS

Moving quickly, use the dispenser to broadcast the decorative chips so they completely cover the counter's backsplash, flat area and front edges. Don't skimp. The kit comes with a ton of chips, so use more than you need to cover every bit of the base coat. We recommend getting down on your knees and zinging the chips hard by hand against the front edge for the best coverage **(Photo 3)**. Inspect for any uncovered base coat, apply more chips and let it dry undisturbed for 12 to 24 hours.

2 APPLY THE BASE COAT. This coat is the background color and a sticky bed for the chips. One person brushes it on the backsplash; the other rolls on the rest. Work fast; you have 20 minutes to complete this and the next step.

3 HEAP ON THE CHIPS. The multicolored chips hide brush marks and give the countertop a textured, speckled appearance. Move quickly to cover every bit of base coat before it dries.

4 SAND THE CHIPS SMOOTH. Sand hard on the flat surfaces but lightly along the front edge and backsplash to avoid sanding completely through the chips and base coat. The goal is a smooth, lightly textured surface.

5 APPLY THE CLEAR TOPCOAT. Vacuum up every speck of sanding dust. Then brush a thick, even layer of topcoat on the backsplash and roll out the rest. Reroll a final pass in one direction, and let it dry undisturbed for 48 hours.

SAND AND SMOOTH

After the base coat is dry, vacuum up the loose chips. Then use the chip scraper to knock down the rough chip edges. Use a light touch so you don't gouge the surface. Vacuum again.

Sand the rough chip surfaces smooth to prepare them for the topcoat. The kit includes a sample of how smooth the countertop should be. The challenge is to sand it smooth without sanding through the chips. Use the sanding block and a lighter touch on the backsplash and front edges since these areas are likely to have fewer chips on the surface (**Photo 4**). For extra smoothness, make a very light pass with 120-grit sandpaper. Sanding will appear to lighten the chip surface, but the topcoat will darken it again. Vacuum and wipe it clean with a damp cloth until all the sanding dust has been removed.

APPLY THE TOPCOAT

The clear topcoat is a two-part formula that you mix and then apply to the countertop. Once you've mixed the formula, you must use it within four hours.

Just as you did with the base coat, use a paintbrush to apply a thick layer of topcoat to the backsplash and the back few inches of the countertop. Use a 6-in. high-density roller (not included) to roll a thick, even layer of the topcoat onto the flat counter area and the front edge (**Photo 5**). Once every surface is covered, go back and roll a final pass of the topcoat in one direction to avoid lap and brush marks. Let it dry to the touch (four to six hours), and then remove the tape and plastic. The countertop will be ready for light use in 48 hours and completely cured within a week.

Wallpaper Backsplash

Covering just a small area brings big style to your kitchen for less.

Wallpaper as a durable kitchen backsplash? You bet. When considering a design for this project, be sure to look for a "splash-proof" vinyl wallpaper (ours cost about $50 per roll). This will resist moisture and humidity and stand up well to scrubbing.

TOUGH PAPER IS EASY TO HANG

We're not going to show you everything you need to know to hang wallpaper here (for that, visit familyhandyman.com and search for "hanging wallpaper"). Instead, we're going to show you techniques that are unique to hanging vinyl.

The great news is that vinyl wallpaper goes up easier than other wallpapers because it's not as flimsy. Most vinyl wallpapers require a premixed vinyl paste (read the manufacturer's instructions). We used a heavy-duty clay-based paste available at any wallpaper store. Before starting, make sure your wall is primed with a primer/sealer for vinyl wallpapers (also available at wallpaper stores).

Set a plumb line with a level to start your first sheet. On small pieces, you can use a paintbrush to apply the paste to the back of the wallpaper. "Book" each piece for five minutes before hanging it (see our website for more on this technique). **Photos 1-3** offer our tips for finishing the job.

1 CUT OUT WINDOWS WITH SCISSORS. Make relief cuts with sharp scissors until the paper lies flat against the wall. Then use a razor to make the final cuts by following the contours of the molding.

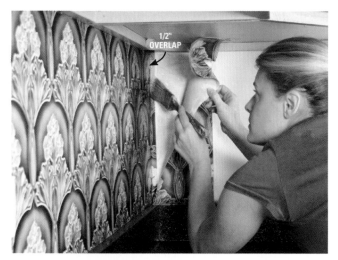

2 GLUE CORNERS TIGHT. Vinyl won't stick to itself. To keep corner seams secure, overlap the corner by 1/2 in. and brush the overlapped section with vinyl-to-vinyl adhesive before pressing the next piece into place.

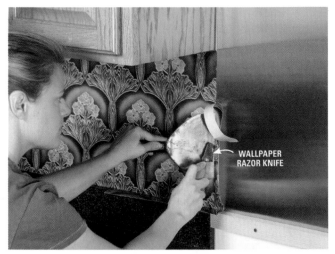

3 A SHARP BLADE IS CRITICAL FOR TRIMMING. Vinyl wallpaper dulls razor blades quickly, so each blade is good for only one or two cuts. Wallpaper razor knives give you more control than utility knives.

Better Bagel Slicer

Make your morning breakfast routine easier!

This bagel slicer is as easy to build as it is to use. Making it requires only a few simple tools, two dowels and a scrap of hardwood. When your stomach growls, drop the bagel in the cage, squeeze the dowel tops so the side dowels bend and pinch the bagel, then slice away. The slicer keeps your fingers out of harm's way (and the crumbs and knife blade off your counter).

Dowel diameters vary slightly. To ensure you get a good fit, drill a sample hole with your 3/16-in. brad point bit and take that scrap with you to test-fit the 3/16-in. dowels you buy.

Use mineral oil (available at drug stores) to finish your bagel slicer. It's nontoxic dry or wet. (If you decide to use a different finish, be sure it's nontoxic when dry.)

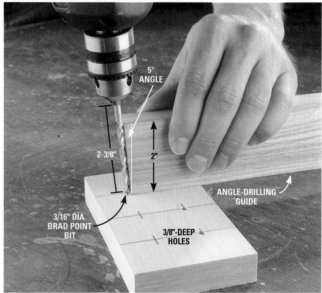

1 PREPARE THE BASE. Drill the angled holes in the base. Guide the bit against the end of a 2-in.-wide piece of scrap wood with a 5-degree angle cut on the end. Set the bit in the chuck at a depth so that when the chuck hits the guide block, the hole is 3/8 in. deep.

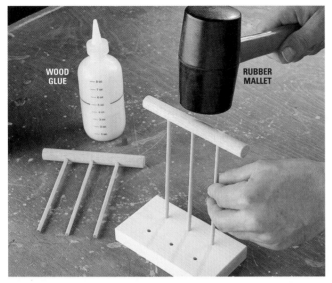

2 ASSEMBLE THE SIDES. Tap the preassembled dowel sides into the base using a rubber mallet. Start by inserting one of the end dowels, then work your way down to the other end. Glue all joints.

BUILD THE BAGEL SLICER

Cut the dowels and hardwood base to the dimensions in the Cutting List.

Lay out the holes in the base **(Figure A)**. Make a drill guide by cutting a 5-degree angle on the end of a piece of scrap wood, and then use it to guide your bit as you drill **(Photo 1)**. Use a 2-in.-wide guide and let the bit protrude 2-3/8 in. beyond the chuck. With this setup, when the chuck meets the top of the guide, you'll get uniform 3/8-in.-deep holes.

Lay out the holes in the handles. Hold each in a vise or clamp while drilling the holes. Wrap a piece of masking tape 3/8 in. from the tip of your bit to act as a depth guide.

Glue and tap the uprights into the handles. Be careful not to damage the ends of the uprights that fit into the base. Then glue and tap the uprights into the base **(Photo 2)**.

Let the glue dry, ease all the sharp edges with sandpaper and then apply a coat of mineral oil for the finish **(Photo 3)**. Let the finish dry overnight, and you're ready for breakfast.

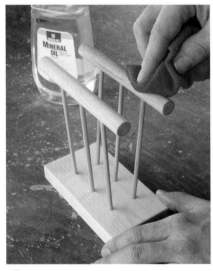

3 FINISH. Wipe on a coat of mineral oil to finish the wood.

Materials List

ITEM	QTY.
3/4" x 3" x 5-1/2" birch	1
5/8" dia. x 12" hardwood dowel	1
3/16" dia. x 36" hardwood dowel	1
Small bottle of mineral oil	1

Cutting List

KEY	PART	QTY.
A	3/4" x 3" x 5-1/2" birch (base)	1
B	5/8" dia. x 5-1/2" hardwood dowel (handles)	2
C	3/16" dia. x 5-1/2" hardwood dowel (uprights)	6

FIGURE A.

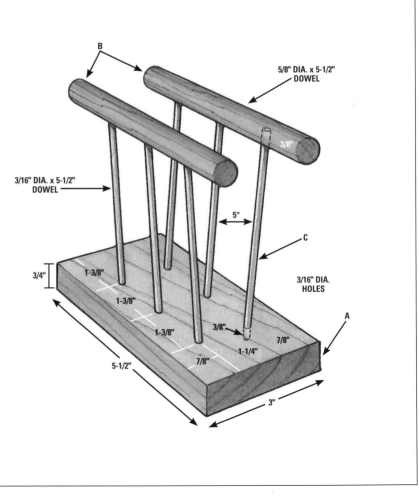

Cabinet Refacing

Get the look of new cabinets in one weekend for a third of the cost.

Cabinet refacing is a quick and easy way to change the look of your kitchen without the mess and expense of a complete remodel. You simply cover the cabinet face frame with self-sticking wood veneer and the end panels with 1/4-in. plywood. Then replace the old doors and drawer fronts with new ones. Refacing costs about one-third what new cabinets would cost, plus you can leave the countertop in place for even greater savings. And by doing the work yourself, you'll also save at least $1,000 in labor for a small kitchen, and a lot more if your kitchen is large.

Refacing does require attention to detail and some experience working with tools, but you don't have to be a master carpenter. If you can measure and cut accurately, you shouldn't have any trouble.

SPECIAL TOOLS FOR WORKING WITH VENEER

We used a Virutex laminate slitter (about $150) to cut strips of veneer (**Photo 3**). It's the perfect tool for this project, but if you don't want to spend the money, you can rent a laminate slitter. A table saw also works (see p. 33).

You'll need a veneer scraper tool (**Photo 6**) to apply adequate pressure for a good bond. The handy tool is worth the small investment; you can get a veneer scraper like the one shown for about $15 at amazon.com.

For cutting veneer strips to length, some pros use a paper cutter modified slightly for more accurate cuts. We found that even an inexpensive paper cutter works great for cutting veneer.

HOW TO ORDER NEW DOORS AND DRAWERS

There are three standard types of cabinet doors: overlay, inset and 3/8-in. lip (**Figure B**). Regardless of what type of doors you currently have on your cabinets, in most cases you can replace them with overlay doors that use modern, fully adjustable cup hinges. And that's the situation we're showing here.

To size the doors, you'll need to decide how much of the door you want to extend past the face frame opening. This is called the overlay distance and is determined by the hinges you install. A 1/2-in. overlay is the most common option. Depending on the hinge, you can choose a different overlay if you like. For example, 1-1/4-in. overlay doors hide more of the face frame for a more contemporary look. But the extra door width can cause problems. You have to measure

Three Simple Steps to Transform Your Kitchen Cabinets

Refacing your cabinets is a quick and easy way to give your kitchen a new look with minimum mess and inconvenience. In a nutshell, here's what you'll do:

Remove the doors and drawers and cover the front edges of the cabinets with peel-and-stick wood veneer.

Hang the new doors with easy-to-adjust, easy-to-install cup hinges.

Attach new drawer fronts to your existing drawers. Finish up by replacing moldings and installing new hardware.

carefully at inside corners and between doors to make sure there's enough room. And remember, the new drawer fronts will be the same width, so check at inside corners to make sure there's clearance for the drawers to open without handle conflicts. Also, there's usually not enough space to add the extra 1-1/4 in. to the top and bottom of both doors and drawer fronts, so you may have to customize these overlay distances.

For our kitchen, we ordered doors that overlay the cabinet 1-1/4 in. on the sides and bottom, but reduced the top overlay to 3/4 in. Then we reduced the top and bottom overlay of the drawers to 3/4 in. to avoid conflict with a built-in breadboard. If you decide to order an overlay greater than 1/2 in., you can check the fit by applying tape to the face frame to represent the outside edges of the doors and drawers. This allows you to visualize the doors installed and will alert you to any problems.

The most critical part of the cabinet refacing job is measuring for and ordering the new doors and drawers. Start by making a sketch of each wall of cabinets showing the doors and drawers. Then measure the openings and write down the measurements—width first, then height (**Figure A**). Double the overlay distance and add this to the opening size to get the size of the door or drawer. For example, if the opening is 18 x 20 in., the door size with a 1/2-in. overlay would be 19 x 21 in. If you want a pair of doors to cover one opening, add two times the overlay to the opening size as usual. Then subtract 1/4 in. for clearance and divide this number by two to get the size of each door. Calculate drawer front sizes the same way: Add two times the overlay distance to the opening size to arrive at the drawer front size.

Inside corner cabinets with or without rotating shelves can be a little trickier. We've found that you can replace most existing corner cabinet doors with a scissors-hinged door—that is, a pair of doors hinged together and hung from one pair of hinges (see "Corner Doors Need Special Hinges," p. 31). Ask your cabinet door supplier for help figuring the size of corner cabinet doors.

Double-check all your measurements and calculations before you place the order.

WHERE TO GET YOUR MATERIALS

In addition to new drawer and door fronts, a typical cabinet refacing job includes covering the faces of the cabinet frames with veneer and the end panels with 1/4-in. plywood to match. While it's optional, most cabinet refacing projects also include a new cove molding at the top of the cabinets and a thin layer of matching plywood to cover the cabinet toe-kick.

Contractors often order doors, drawer fronts, veneer, plywood and moldings prefinished from the manufacturer, but some such suppliers sell only to professionals. You can search online for "cabinet-refacing supplies" to find

1 PREPARE THE CABINETS. After removing the doors and drawer fronts, clean all the face frame and end panel surfaces with denatured alcohol. Then scuff the surfaces with a sanding sponge. Finally, clean again with alcohol.

MEDIUM-GRIT SANDING SPONGE

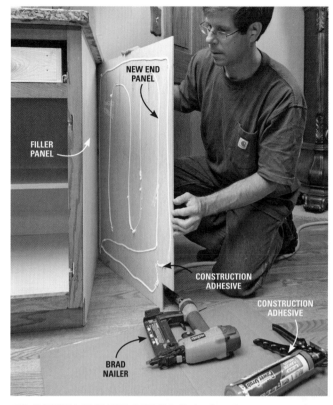

NEW END PANEL

FILLER PANEL

CONSTRUCTION ADHESIVE

CONSTRUCTION ADHESIVE

BRAD NAILER

2 INSTALL THE END PANELS. If the face frame protrudes past the side of the cabinet, add a filler panel to bring them flush. Then cut the end panels to fit, and attach them with construction adhesive and brads.

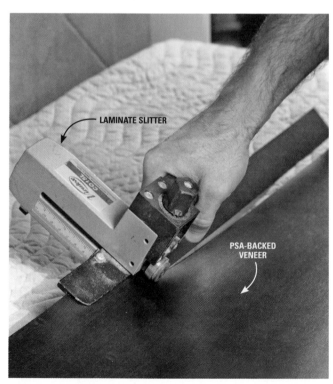

LAMINATE SLITTER

PSA-BACKED VENEER

3 CUT VENEER INTO STRIPS. Measure the width of the stiles and rails, and cut strips of veneer to fit. This photo shows a laminate slitter, but you can also use a table saw (see p. 33).

4 CUT THE VENEER TO LENGTH. A paper cutter is the perfect tool for this task. Measure the length of the stile and mark the strip of veneer. Line up the mark with the paper cutter blade and cut the strip to length.

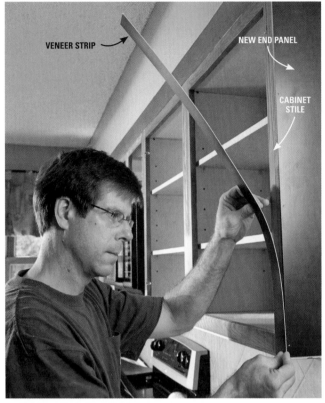

VENEER STRIP

NEW END PANEL

CABINET STILE

5 **APPLY THE VENEER. Carefully align the veneer and press it lightly to the surface of the face frame. If you don't press too hard, you can still realign it.**

VENEER TOOL

6 **PRESS THE VENEER. Pull the veneer tool along the veneer to smooth and adhere it. Press down firmly to ensure a good bond.**

FIGURE A.
MEASURING A CABINET

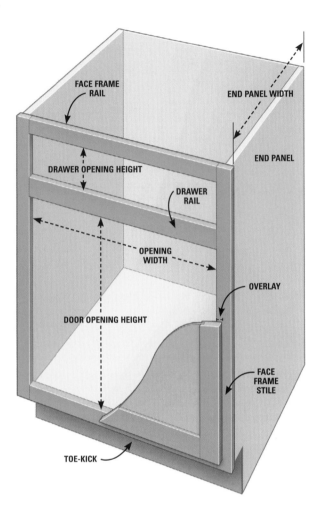

FACE FRAME RAIL

END PANEL WIDTH

END PANEL

DRAWER OPENING HEIGHT

DRAWER RAIL

OPENING WIDTH

OVERLAY

DOOR OPENING HEIGHT

FACE FRAME STILE

TOE-KICK

companies that will provide all the parts prefinished, or you can buy unfinished parts and finish them yourself. A couple of sources for unfinished doors are distinctivedoordesigns.com and rawdoors.net. At rockler.com, you'll find doors and 2 x 8-ft. sheets of veneer with pressure-sensitive adhesive (PSA) on the back. Ask at your local lumberyard for 1/4-in. hardwood plywood and moldings.

Measure and make a list of the veneer strips you'll need to cover the face frames. From this list, figure out how many 24 x 96-in. sheets of PSA-backed veneer sheets you'll need. Allow extra material, though. There are a few inches on the outside edges of PSA veneer that are unusable. On average, one sheet will cover face frames for about 15 doors. Expect to spend about $90 per sheet for the veneer.

Then measure the end panels and make a list of the sizes you need. You can order the plywood cut to rough size from some online suppliers, or figure out how many 4 x 8-ft. sheets of 1/4-in. plywood to buy from the lumberyard. The face frames on most modern cabinets overhang the end panel slightly. Rather than cut off this overhang, which is messy

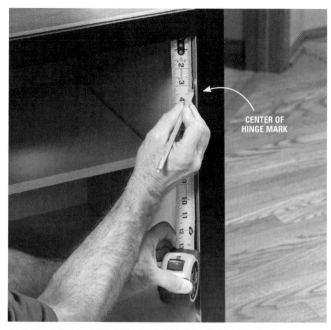

CENTER OF HINGE MARK

7 MEASURE FOR THE HINGE LOCATION. Mark the center of the top hinge on the face frame stile. Calculate this distance by measuring from the top of your new door to the center of the hinge and subtracting the overlay.

and time-consuming, you can create a flush surface by gluing a filler panel to the end first **(Photo 2)**. Most cabinets have either a 1/8-in. or a 1/4-in. overhang, so check yours and buy the appropriate thickness of plywood or hardboard to fill the space. Finally, make a list of the moldings you'll need, including the toe-kick cover.

You'll also need denatured alcohol, rags, a medium-grit sanding sponge, construction adhesive (such as Loctite Power Grab), 3/4-in. brad nails, and a stain pen and colored putty to match the new stain color.

PREPARE THE CABINETS

Since the sanding involved creates a little dust, we recommend emptying the cabinets before you start. Next, remove the doors by unscrewing the hinges from the face frames. Also remove or modify the drawer fronts. There are two types of drawers. On most new cabinets, the drawer fronts are separate pieces and can be taken off by removing the screws from inside the drawers. But some drawer fronts are attached to the drawer sides. If you have this type of drawer, you'll have to take the drawer out and remove the overhanging parts of the front by sawing them off. Then you'll screw through the old drawer fronts to attach the new ones.

Test the fit by placing the modified drawer back into the cabinet and pushing it in to make sure there's enough clearance behind the drawer for the new front to sit flush with the surface of the face frame. If the drawer protrudes, you'll have to order or build new drawers. In addition to removing doors and drawer fronts, pry off any moldings you plan to replace.

ADJUSTABLE CUP HINGE

8 HANG THE DOOR. Line up the center of the hinge with your mark and drill a pilot hole. Then drive a screw through the top hinge plate into the stile. Attach the bottom hinge the same way.

Corner Doors Need Special Hinges

Talk to your door supplier if you need corner doors like these. They require special hinges. If your doors have a 1-1/4-in. overlay like these, you may have to cut 3/4-in.-deep notches in the face frame stile to mount the hinges.

NEW DOOR

SCISSORS HINGE

To ensure that the pressure-sensitive adhesive on the veneer and the construction adhesive for the end panels bond well, the face frames and end panels must be clean and scuffed up slightly. Start by cleaning the face frames and end panels with a rag dampened in denatured alcohol. Then scuff all the surfaces with a medium-grit sanding sponge

(Photo 1). Don't use a power sander or sand to bare wood. The PSA-backed veneer won't stick well to bare wood. Finally, clean the surfaces again with denatured alcohol to remove the dust.

Don't bother to fill small screw holes or other small imperfections at this stage. The veneer is thick enough to span them without a problem. You can use a two-part hardening-type wood filler to fill large dents and chips. You might encounter a face frame stile at the end of cabinets that's rounded or beveled. If so, fill the bevel or round-over with the two-part wood filler after installing the new end panels but before applying the face frame veneer.

COVER THE FACE FRAMES AND END PANELS

With the cabinets prepped and cleaned, it's time to start making the transformation. The first step is to install the end panels. If a face frame overhangs the existing end panel, add a filler to create a flush surface. We attached plywood with construction adhesive and used a few 3/4-in. brads to hold it in place. Next, measure and cut an end panel to size so its front edge is flush with the surface of the face frame. Hold the end panel in place and mark the notch for the toe-kick. Cut out the notch. Then install the panel with construction adhesive and a few brads **(Photo 2)**. Cover all the end panels before starting on the face frame veneer.

There are two methods for applying veneer to a face frame. You can cut and install oversize strips and trim them in place with a sharp razor knife. But we prefer to cut the strips to the exact width and length needed before applying them. You can do this easily with a special tool called a laminate slitter. The tool is intended to cut strips of plastic laminate, but it works great for veneer, too. To use it, you set the depth and width of the cut. Then simply slide the tool along the edge of the sheet to create a perfect-width strip. As we show on p. 33, you can also use a table saw to cut strips of veneer.

Measure the widths of the stiles and rails, and cut strips from the sheet of PSA-backed veneer **(Photo 3)**. Then measure the height of the end stiles and cut strips to length with a paper cutter **(Photo 4)**. Start by applying veneer to the outermost stiles in a run of cabinets **(Photo 5)**. Smooth and bond the veneer by pressing it with the veneer applicator **(Photo 6)**. Next, measure the distance between the stiles and cut strips of veneer to cover the long horizontal rails. Check the fit before you pull off the paper backing. Then apply these strips and press them down. Cover the remaining stiles, and on the lower cabinets finish by covering the drawer rails.

If you have any veneer that overhangs the face frame slightly, carefully sand it flush. Finally, use a matching stain

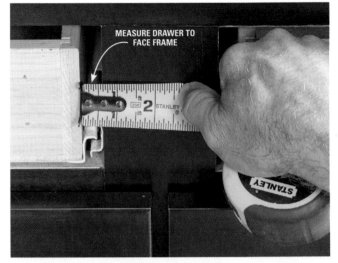

9 **MEASURE FOR THE DRAWER FRONT PLACEMENT.** Measure the distance from the drawer side to the face frame stile. Also measure from the drawer bottom to the face frame drawer rail. Add the overlay distance to these measurements to arrive at the dimensions you'll mark on the back of the drawer front **(Photo 10)**.

pen to touch up the unstained edges of the veneer and any other imperfections.

HANG THE DOORS AND INSTALL THE DRAWER FRONTS

Start the door installation by mounting the cup hinges in the doors. Simply line up a hinge and press it into the large round recess. Then tighten the supplied screws to anchor the hinge. Prepare for hanging the doors by marking the center of the top hinge on the face frame stile **(Photo 7)**. You don't need to mark for the lower hinge. Hang the door from the top hinge **(Photo 8)**. Then drill the pilot hole for the lower hinge screw and drive the screw to finish the job.

Photos 9-11 show how to attach the drawer fronts to the drawer boxes. The key is to measure the distance from the drawer box to the face frame and add the overlay distance. Then transfer these measurements to the back of the drawer front, align the drawer and attach it with four screws. To make the drawer front adjustable, drill oversize screw holes through the drawer and put washers under the screw heads. With this method, you can loosen the screws and move the drawer front slightly to align it perfectly.

When you're done with the door and drawer installation, be sure to adjust the hinges to align the doors with each other. Now you're ready to install your new cabinet door and drawer hardware. For great tips on installing door hardware, go to familyhandyman.com and search for "cabinet hardware."

Finish the project by installing cove molding along the top of the wall cabinets and covering the toe-kick with a thin strip of plywood finished to match the rest of the wood.

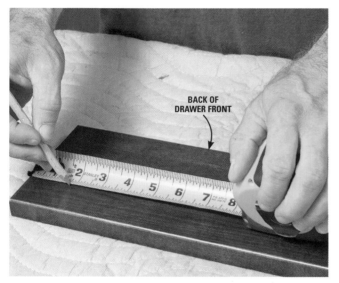

BACK OF
DRAWER FRONT

10 MARK THE DRAWER LOCATION. Use the dimensions you calculated (**Photo 9**) to mark the back of the drawer front.

11 ATTACH THE DRAWER FRONT. Align the drawer box with the marks and drive screws through the drawer into the drawer front. Double-check the screw length to make sure the screws won't go through the face of the new drawer front.

Another Way to Cut Veneer

The slitter shown on p. 29 isn't the only tool you can use to cut veneer—you can use your table saw. For the best results, build a simple veneer-ripping jig. Cut a 3-in. strip from a 24 x 24-in. piece of particleboard or plywood, and glue it to the edge of the remaining piece. Add 3/4 in. to the width of the veneer you wish to cut, and set the fence. Then send the jig through the saw, stopping about halfway through. Clamp the jig to the table saw fence and you're ready to cut veneer strips. The jig keeps the thin veneer from sliding under the fence, and the narrow slot left by the saw blade supports the veneer to help prevent splintering.

FIGURE B.
CABINET DOOR TYPES

If you have inset or lip doors, you can convert them to overlay doors during your refacing project just by using the correct overlay cup hinge.

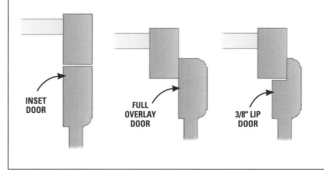

INSET
DOOR

FULL
OVERLAY
DOOR

3/8" LIP
DOOR

TONGUE

GROOVE

TONGUE & GROOVE
JOINT

Spa Bath on a Budget

Create a stylish space that's perfect for relaxing & recharging.

Outdated bathrooms can stick out like a sore thumb in an otherwise modern home, but sometimes it's difficult to know what to tackle first. Plus, the high prices of some bathroom renovations can stop homeowners cold in their tracks. But rest assured: You don't have to break the bank—or go to a fancy, expensive resort—to get the full spa treatment. If you've been looking to update a tired bathroom and give it the feel of a luxury spa without spending an arm and a leg, consider giving your space a stylish update by installing a modern freestanding tub. Setting it on a raised deck gives the feeling of stepping into a cozy yet sophisticated new space.

After removing our old tub, we considered tiling the walls. But we ultimately decided to add marblelike wall panels; they gave us a luxury look in a fraction of the time it would have taken to tile and grout. Read on to learn just what it takes to recreate these results for yourself.

What's on These Walls?

We installed Wetwall, a wood/plastic composite (similar to composite decking) topped with a high-pressure laminate surface. About 1/2 in. thick, Wetwall is waterproof and durable. It's available in a wide array of panel sizes–including custom sizes–and patterns. It can be applied to many existing surfaces, including tile. It's easy to work with and requires no special tools—just a sharp, fine-tooth saw blade for smooth cuts. Tongue-and-groove edge joints make seams virtually disappear.

Moving a Tub Drain

Relocating a bathtub to the center of the room entails moving the tub drain. Unless you're confident in your plumbing skills, call a pro for this. You'll need to cut into your flooring to access the old drain and position the new one. Since you're covering the whole area with the tub deck, you don't need to worry about patching it all afterward. Just make sure there's enough space below the new location to accommodate the drop of the P-trap. This will be easiest if you have an unfinished basement underneath. Your plumber can also connect the new drain to the old line.

FLOOR JOISTS

Build the Tub Deck

1. BUILD THE DECK FRAMING

Build the floor deck using 2x4s, 16 in. on center, as if you were building a stud wall. We wanted the tub deck to end up about 1/4 in. lower than the curb of our shower pan, so we calculated the thickness of the flooring, moisture barrier and subfloor to figure out how high the deck framing needed to be. In this case, we trimmed the 2x4s to 3-1/4 in. wide.

2. INSTALL THE SUBFLOOR

Fasten the subfloor to the framing, then apply a moisture barrier. The luxury vinyl tile (LVT) we used is waterproof, but for a wet location such as a bathroom or basement, you still need to install a moisture barrier at least 6 mil thick.

MOISTURE BARRIER

SUBFLOOR

3. APPLY THE FLOORING

Install the LVT flooring, starting in a corner of the room. The floating, click-together LVT installs quickly and easily—no glue, and no nails or staples.

4. TRIM THE LEDGE

Apply stair nosing to cover the edge of the deck flooring. We made our own, matching the stain to the color of the flooring. Next, apply flooring to the front face of the tub deck. Use construction adhesive here.

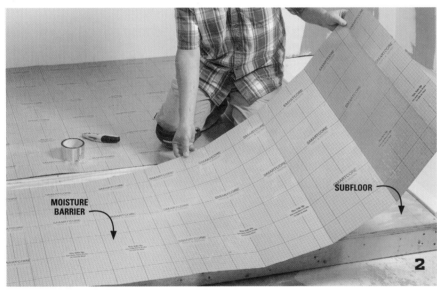

STAIR NOSING

Install the Wall Panels

1. DRY-FIT THE PANELS

Test-fit the panels and cut as needed. If you need to trim a panel, trim the edge that abuts a wall, not where two panels meet. The best way to trim large panels like this is to use a track saw or a circular saw with a cutting guide.

2. APPLY WALL ADHESIVE

Clean the back of each panel using denatured alcohol and allow it to dry thoroughly. Apply adhesive to the back of the first panel. The manufacturer recommends a 1/4-in. bead every 10 to 12 in. Clean and dry the walls before applying Wetwall panels.

3. INSTALL THE PANELS

Press the first back wall panel into place. Apply a bead of color-matched seam sealer to the tongue on the panel, then apply adhesive to the back of the next panel and install it. The joints are tight; get a helper. Tile-setting suction cups are also a big help.

PANEL ADHESIVE

SUCTION CUP

SEAM SEALER

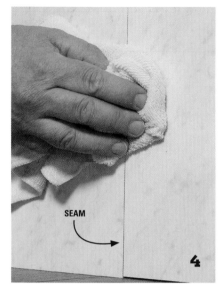

SEAM

FIXTURE HOLE

4

5

4. CLEAN THE SEAM

After pressing the panels together, wipe off any excess seam sealer with denatured alcohol. If the adhesive isn't holding the panels securely in place, you may need to use bracing boards to hold up the panels.

5. CUT HOLES FOR FIXTURES

Measure and lay out the shower's fixture holes on the appropriate panel. To cut the holes, use a jigsaw with a fine-tooth blade or a hole saw, as your fixtures dictate.

6. INSTALL SIDE PANELS

Apply the side panels as you did the back panels, trimming as needed and using adhesive on the backs and seam sealer on the tongue-and-groove joints.

7. CAULK JOINTS

Apply a bead of seam sealer to the corners where the wall panels meet. Wetwall has color-matched sealer for all of its products. For outside corners, you can order Wetwall with a bullnose edge. We chose to trim our outside corners around the shower with 1-in. aluminum angle applied with construction adhesive.

1/8" GAP

6

COLOR-MATCHED SEAM SEALER

7

No-Demo Bathroom

Add a bathroom in your basement without busting up the concrete floor.

The addition of a full bathroom, including a shower, sink and toilet, can be a huge improvement to any home, particularly if you have only one bathroom and a growing family. It can also be a huge, expensive job. Upflow bathroom systems simplify the plumbing of a basement bathroom, putting this valuable home improvement job within reach of a DIYer.

These systems include a macerator/pump that can be tucked into a wall directly behind a rear-discharge toilet. All the fixture drains flow to the macerator/pump, which grinds solids and then pumps waste upward, instead of relying on gravity, to connect to your main drain line. Shower and sink drains do use gravity to reach the pump, and those are easy installations.

What Is a Macerating Toilet?

Think of it as similar to a garbage disposal in your sink. In a macerating toilet, waste is channeled to the macerator/pump, which reduces solids to be easily pumped through a 3/4-in. discharge pipe. Our system, the SaniAccess 3 from Saniflo, includes a rear-discharge toilet and a macerator/pump with fittings. You'll supply the rest of the standard plumbing pipes and fittings.

MACERATOR/
PUMP

System Advantages

The biggest advantage of an upflow system is not having to break up a concrete floor to run drains. But there are other advantages too: First, the discharge line is much smaller than a standard drain line, so you can fit it into places where a standard drain might not work. Second, you can install a bathroom anywhere—you don't need to be concerned with how the toilet's drain aligns with existing drain lines in your home.

1

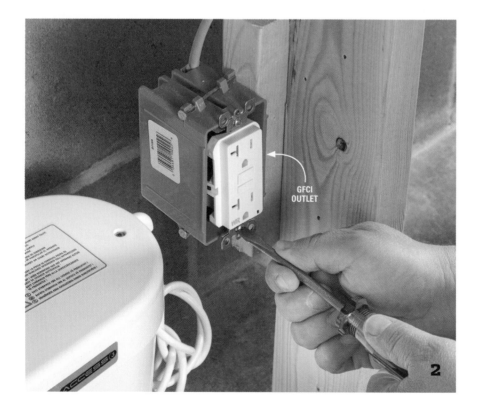

GFCI
OUTLET

2

1. PLACE THE MACERATOR/PUMP

Set the macerator/pump in place behind the wall framing. The unit needs to be on the same level as the toilet. Install the rubber feet and secure the pump to the floor. If you're in a cold climate, allow space between the pump and the wall for insulation. Insulation in front of the pump will help dampen the minimal noise from the macerator/pump.

2. INSTALL A GFCI OUTLET

The macerator/pump needs its own GFCI outlet. Install the outlet inside the wall framing, near the pump. The outlet needs to be within 12 in. of an access panel and facing the room. Be sure to check local codes before installing this outlet.

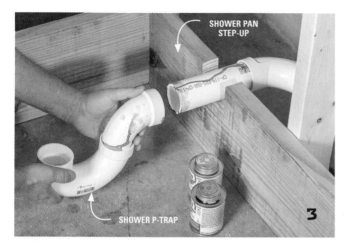

SHOWER PAN STEP-UP

SHOWER P-TRAP

3

DRAIN FROM SHOWER AND SINK

4

3. BUILD THE SHOWER PAN STEP-UP

With your shower plumbing in hand, calculate the height of the platform, including the P-trap as well as a 1/4-in. drop per foot of horizontal run to the pump. The minimum height is 6 in., and that's usually enough depending on your P-trap and the distance to the pump. You may need to add an extra step, depending on the finished height. To lower the platform height, you can chip out some concrete for the P-trap. If your basement has low ceilings, you may need to consider a tub instead of a shower.

4. CONNECT THE SHOWER AND SINK DRAINS

Hook up the shower drain and run the pipe into the wall. Use an elbow to turn the pipe toward the pump. In our bathroom, the sink is between the shower and the toilet, so we tied in the sink drain on the way to the pump. The pump has a drain entrance on both sides, so you can configure your bathroom however you like. In our case, we used a provided plug to cap the entrance on the other side of the pump.

5. INSTALL THE VENTS

Along the drain line, you'll install a vent for each fixture. Connect these vents and tie them into the vent system on your existing plumbing. Mechanical vents won't work with this system; only a free air vent can be used.

LINE TO EXISTING VENT

PUMP VENT

SINK VENT

SHOWER VENT

SHOWER/SINK DRAIN

5

DISCHARGE LINE

VENT LINE

6

6. CONNECT THE DISCHARGE TO THE PUMP

Slip the flexible discharge tube onto its port on the pump and secure it with a hose clamp. At the end of the tube, you can install a shutoff ball valve. If you ever need to remove the pump, that valve will prevent backflow. After the first hard 90-degree turn from the pump, any turns in the discharge pipe need to be sweeping—no more hard 90s. Use a sweep elbow or two 45-degree elbows instead.

7. CONNECT THE DISCHARGE TO THE MAIN SEWER LINE

The discharge line can run horizontally at first, but for no more than 18 in. before it turns vertically. After the first vertical turn, the pipe can run horizontally again but not make another vertical or diagonal turn. The total run from the pump to the main sewage line must be a minimum of 3 ft. The easiest place to tie into the main drain is at a cleanout using a reducer fitting. If that's not an option, you can install a Y-fitting (not a T-fitting) on any horizontal run, but the discharge must enter the pipe from the top or side. No other lines can feed into the discharge from the pump.

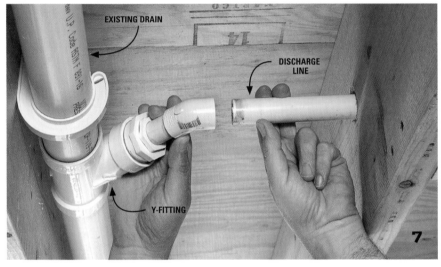

EXISTING DRAIN

DISCHARGE LINE

Y-FITTING

7

Discharge Options

If you have a cleanout in a convenient spot, you can connect the discharge there. Just remove the plug and install a reducer to connect the 3/4-in. discharge pipe. If your drains are steel pipe, you'll need to cut out a section and install a Y-fitting using mission clamps. You can't use the type that just have hose clamps though, only the fully banded type.

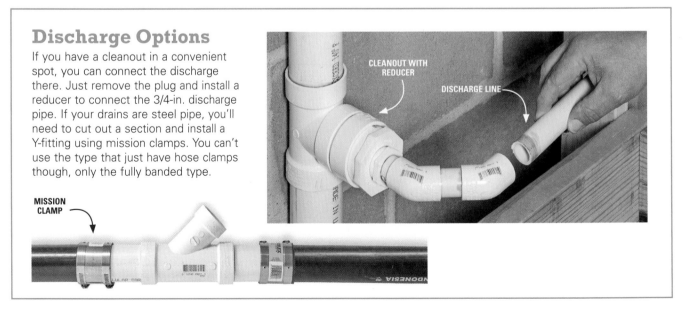

CLEANOUT WITH REDUCER

DISCHARGE LINE

MISSION CLAMP

TOILET DISCHARGE EXTENSION

8

8. CONNECT THE TOILET

Set the toilet into position, then connect the flexible boot to the toilet's discharge port. Next, connect the boot on the other end to the pump. Make sure the connection boot faces the right direction. Zip ties keep the boot in place, as this is a drain, not a pressurized supply line.

9. INSTALL THE TOILET

Mark holes on the floor through the holes on the toilet's base. Slide the toilet out of the way, then drill the holes for the supplied concrete anchors using a correct size masonry bit. Slide the toilet back into position, and then install the lag screw anchors. Use shims under the toilet as needed to keep it from rocking. Be careful not to overtighten the bolts; you can crack the toilet.

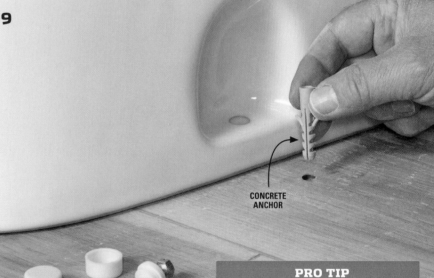

9

CONCRETE ANCHOR

PRO TIP

To make the cut, first saw all the way around the pipe just enough to remove the mark. Keep sawing a little deeper each time around until you're through the pipe.

PRO TIP

Making a straight cut on a large-diameter pipe starts with an accurate line. Wrap a piece of cardboard with one straight edge around the pipe and mark your line with a Sharpie.

CARDBOARD

CHAPTER **TWO**

GARAGE & SHED

13 Easy Auto Repairs

Save a truckload of money by doing it yourself.

If you've ever had to take your car to a mechanic (and who hasn't?), you know that costs can easily spiral out of control, especially when you're not sure what's causing the problem. Here are some common (and not so common) issues, along with the affordable steps you can take to solve or prevent them. The goal is to save you money and, if need be, help you hold a more informed conversation with your mechanic.

1. AC BLOWS WARM AIR

If you turn on your car's AC only to find hot air blowing out, try to recharge the system yourself before you take your car to the shop. Modern cars use R-134 refrigerant, which is sold at all auto parts stores. Most brands offer refrigerant with a sealant added to help keep the system healthy. Buying a can with a gauge is worth the extra cost because it's critical to monitor the pressure in the system while you add refrigerant, and you can keep the gauge for next time. A large can with a gauge costs about $35. For complete instructions, go to familyhandyman.com and search for "charging AC."

2. LIGHTBULB BURNOUT

Headlamps and lightbulbs are expensive, and it can be very frustrating when they keep blowing. This is often caused by handling the bulbs with bare hands. When you touch a headlight bulb, the oils on your skin transfer to the glass. This can cause hot spots, resulting in a blown bulb.

A loose ground, a shorted wire or even a small water leak can also cause bulbs to blow. If you find that you're still blowing bulbs even after doing everything right, a faulty voltage regulator may be the culprit. Time for a visit to your mechanic.

3. STINKY AIR CONDITIONING

Does it smell a little musty when you turn on the air conditioning? You might simply need a new cabin air filter. Changing this filter is easy; it's often located under the dashboard near the glove box or in the glove box itself. The dealership is always more than happy to do it for you, but you'll pay a lot for the convenience. Expect to pay about $20 for cabin air filters.

4. WHEEL VIBRATION AT HIGHER SPEEDS

It might not be perceptible at low speeds, but if your car starts to shake and vibrate at higher speeds, it's probably because a wheel is out of balance. This can be caused by a little snowpack during winter months or even dried mud in the summer. Use a brush or ice scraper to knock out any snow that might have packed itself, or just go to a self-serve car wash and spray out your wheels. It's a simple fix that you'll want to do right away.

5. WORN-DOWN TIRE TREAD

Tread depth is an important safety concern in wet or winter weather, but proper tread depth also contributes to shorter stopping distance, better gas mileage and a smoother ride. You don't have to take your car in to determine when you need new tires. Just pick up a tire tread gauge (around $4) at an auto store. If your tread measures 4/32 in. or less, it's time for new tires.

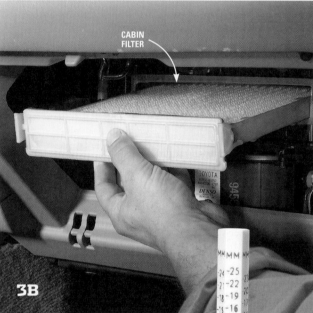

ERROR CODES

SCANNER

6

6. THE CHECK ENGINE LIGHT JUST CAME ON

The check engine light, or CEL, can indicate a wide range of problems. Fortunately, all vehicles produced after 1996 can reveal which problem when you plug in an OBD2 diagnostic scanner. We splurged on an $80 scanner that connects to a phone via Bluetooth, but you can find basic scanners for about $25. Once it's plugged into your vehicle, it will display the error codes that are causing your CEL to shine. You'll need to do an internet search to find out what the codes mean, but now you'll know if it's simply a loose gas cap or a more serious problem inside the engine. This tool can also clear the old codes from your vehicle.

7. SOFT BRAKES

Soft brakes can mean a couple of things. One cause is low brake fluid, and that's an easy fix. If it seems that you're topping off brake fluid regularly, it's time to inspect the master cylinder, calipers and brake lines for fluid leaks. Another common cause of a soft brake pedal is the age of the fluid. It's recommended that you flush your brake fluid every 24,000 miles.

8. BATTERY WON'T KEEP A CHARGE

A car's battery is charged by the alternator, but a few things might interfere with the process. Corroded terminals are the most common cause of poor battery function, and that's an easy fix. Start by pulling off the negative battery terminal. Then remove the positive terminal and clean it thoroughly with a wire brush. If a terminal needs to be replaced, get one at any auto parts store (about $7).

Also inspect the ground cable that runs from the negative battery terminal to the chassis or frame; it can get loose or corroded over time. If needed, clean that connection too. If the battery still won't take a charge, take the car in to test the battery and the alternator.

9. SLUGGISH ACCELERATION

Does it feel as if your vehicle has been working harder to reach highway speeds? Oftentimes, that simply means the car is overdue for an oil change and a new air filter. The smaller engines of today's cars are more susceptible to sluggish acceleration than the V-8 in your old Firebird, and conventional motor oil will also contribute to this problem as the oil ages. If you haven't already, switch to synthetic motor oil; it maintains its viscosity over its lifetime and will last longer too.

7

8

REPLACEMENT TERMINALS

9

10. DRIPPING A LITTLE FLUID

For as many things that can leak in our cars, there are pour-in solutions that claim to fix them. Here's a surprise: Some actually work! Bar's Leaks Radiator Stop Leak can extend the life of your radiator and delay the cost of replacing it. Lucas makes an additive for your power steering pump to stop minor leaks, and the transmission sealer from Blue Devil can help the transmission shift more smoothly.

However, we don't recommend using products like these on major leaks from rear main seals or head gaskets. They're great temporary fixes for small leaks, but using them as a cure-all without further repair is a bad idea.

11. STICKING HOOD LATCH

A broken hood latch cable is a nightmare. You'll definitely have to take your vehicle in to get it fixed, but the problem can be avoided with a little maintenance. Use an aerosol white lithium grease from B'laster, which you can get at any auto parts store for about $7.

12. DRAGGING POWER WINDOWS

When our windows get dirty, we simply wash them, but we often overlook the channels they slide in. Spraying a little silicone lubricant in the channels will help those windows slide nice and easy. Do this once a year and your windows will slide smoothly.

13. BLOWER FAN WORKS ONLY ON HIGH

Fan speed is controlled by a resistor cluster, and when it starts to go bad, the fan won't work at lower speeds. The hardest part of this job is actually finding the resistor cluster in your vehicle, but a quick search online will help. Once you locate it, disconnect the electrical harness and remove the two bolts. Replace the old cluster with the new one and reassemble.

10

11

12

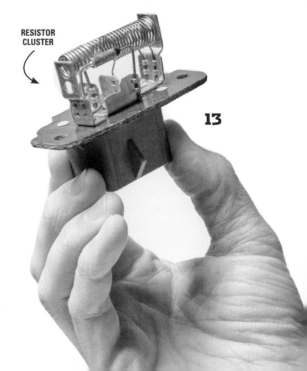

RESISTOR CLUSTER

13

Snow Blower Smarts

Follow these simple tips to avoid serious headaches (and expenses).

Running a snow blower seems like a skill you could master in two minutes. But we wondered: If it's really that simple, why are there 6,000 blower-related injuries in the United States every year? And why do repair shops get overwhelmed after a big storm?

To get answers, we consulted experts at all the major manufacturers—as well as several people who fix blowers professionally. It turns out that operator error is the No. 1 cause of clogs and breakdowns, and improper clearing of clogs is the most common cause of injuries. The experts shared some great tips on how to avoid these issues. So even if you're an experienced snow blower operator, read on.

GET YOUR PROPERTY READY FOR SNOW

Before the snow flies, take a few minutes to inspect your property. Remove any stray rocks, dog tie-out cables, extension cords, holiday light cords, garden hoses and other small obstacles. Then stake out any paths that run near gardens so you don't accidentally suck up rocks and garden edging. Mark your walk and driveway perimeters by pounding in driveway markers. If the ground is frozen, you can just drill holes using a masonry bit and your battery-powered drill.

DON'T WAIT FOR IT TO STOP

If you're in for a huge snowfall, start clearing the snow before it reaches 6 in. Sure, you'll spend more time snow-blowing, but your machine won't have to work as hard and will throw the snow farther. That'll reduce the height of the snowbanks flanking your driveway.

COOL OFF, THEN GAS UP

If your snow blower runs out of gas halfway through a tough job, you'll be tempted to refill it right away. But think about this: The engine is hot and the gas tank sits right on top of that hot engine. Even worse, you're standing right over the machine holding a gallon of gas. If you spill gas on the engine or overfill the tank, you could instantly turn your snow-blowing adventure into a dangerous and painful burn-unit experience. Even if you manage to escape injury, you could still wind up with a freshly toasted snow blower.

Snow blower fires happen often enough that the manufacturers strongly recommend you let the engine cool for at least 10 minutes before refilling. Take that opportunity to grab a hot drink and warm up your fingers and toes. Then, once your personal tank is refilled, refill your snow blower and carry on.

HALF WIDTH

TAKE SMALLER BITES TO PREVENT CLOGS

When you get blasted with wet, heavy snow and you're in a hurry, it's tempting to crank up the speed and plow right through it. However, that's the single best way to clog your machine and wear out (or break) the drive belts. And when you consider how long it takes to constantly stop and unclog the chute, ramming at full speed doesn't actually save you any time.

Worse yet, improperly clearing a clogged chute is dangerous and the most common cause of snow blower–related injuries. Instead of making a full-width pass through the snow, manufacturers recommend taking smaller bites about one-third to one-half the width of the machine. It's faster than slogging through a full path of heavy snow, it's easier on the machine and it allows the machine to throw the snow farther.

ADD STABILIZER TO FRESH FUEL

Follow the stabilizer dosing recommendations on the bottle label. Add the stabilizer to the gas can right at the gas station so it'll mix up on the way home.
Or, add a premeasured packet to the gas can before filling it with gas.

SWITCH TO SYNTHETIC OIL FOR EASIER STARTING

Small engines typically have to reach at least 400 rpm before they'll fire up. But traditional motor oil thickens when cold, making it much harder to reach that 400-rpm threshold. Synthetic oil allows the engine to spin faster when you yank the cord, so it starts with fewer pulls.

START WITH FRESH FUEL

Stale gas is the No. 1 cause of hard starting. So don't use what's left in the lawn mower can. It's better to dump that summer blend into your car's tank, then refill the can with a winter blend, which is more volatile and provides better starting.

THROW IT FAR

Avoid throwing snow only partway off the driveway and then throwing it a second time. That just creates a heavier load for the blower. There are four ways to get the maximum throw: Take smaller bites of snow (see p. 51), run the blower at full rpm but at a slower ground speed, adjust the chute diverter to its full raised position and blow with the wind.

DON'T SWALLOW THE NEWSPAPER

A frozen newspaper is the leading cause of snow blower jams. It can break the machine's shear pins or belts and damage expensive auger and impeller components. A fresh layer of snow over newspapers makes them hard to see, and they're easy to forget. So protect your machine by scouting the area before you hit one. If you do suck up a newspaper, shut down the engine and remove the bundle with a broom or shovel handle—never with your hands. If you can't remove the paper, take your machine to a pro, who will charge a whole lot less than even the cheapest emergency room surgeon.

Preseason Maintenance

Get your snow blower ready for action by installing a new spark plug, changing the oil and checking the condition of the belts. Replace the belts if you see cracks, fraying or glazing, or if you notice that chunks are missing.

Next, sand any rusted areas and repaint. Once the paint cures, apply a high-quality polymeric car wax (such as Meguiar's Ultimate Liquid Wax, about $20 from any auto parts store) to all painted surfaces. The wax will shed the snow and water and protect the paint. Also wax the inside of the chute to help prevent clogs.

Then consult your owner's manual to find the lubrication points and the recommended lube. If the type of lube isn't listed, here's some general guidance: Use motor oil on metal linkage joints, gears and cables, but use dry PTFE lube on plastic parts (knobs, gears and chute). Spray the auger, second-stage impeller and chute with silicone spray to prevent snow from sticking.

■ PREVENT MAJOR AUGER DAMAGE

The drive shaft applies torque to the shear pin, which then applies it to the auger. However, if the auger rusts to the drive shaft, they'll become one and the shear pin will never break. If that happens, the auger clog can cause major damage to the machine. Lubricate the drive shaft to prevent it from rusting to the auger.

LUBE THE DRIVE SHAFT. Remove shear pins and lubricate the drive shaft with lubricating oil.

SPIN THE AUGER. Spin the auger to spread the oil along the length of the shaft. Reinstall shear pins.

LUBRICATE ALL METAL
LINKAGE JOINTS WITH
MOTOR OIL

LUBRICATE THE
CHUTE CABLE,
GEARS AND
KNOBS WITH THE
PROPER LUBE

CHECK THE
CONDITION OF
THE BELTS

WAX THE
INSIDE OF THE
CHUTE WITH A
PREMIUM
POLYMERIC
CAR WAX

LUBRICATE
THE AXLE
WITH MARINE
GREASE

COAT THE
SECOND-STAGE
IMPELLER WITH
SILICONE SPRAY

NEW
SHEAR
PINS

PIN
PUNCH

REPLACEMENT
BELTS

■ BUY PARTS BEFORE YOU NEED THEM

Belts and shear pins always seem to break in the middle of a blizzard. If you break a shear pin and try to improvise using the wrong shear pin— or, worse yet, an ordinary bolt—you risk major damage that can easily cost you $200. So buy replacement parts at the start of the season—a set of belts and a few extra shear pins will cost you only about $25. Be sure to have the right size wrenches and sockets, and the correct size pin punch to drive out the broken pin. Then assemble a parts and tool kit.

Fix a "No-Start" Small Engine

A little know-how can save you the hassle and expense of hauling your lawn mower, pressure washer or other machine to the service center.

When a small engine just won't start, the usual suspects are bad gasoline, a corroded or plugged carburetor, or a bad ignition coil. Typical professional repairs for these common issues start at about $100. But there's no need to enlist the expensive services of a pro. You can fix any of these problems yourself easily, cheaply and quickly, and if you do the work yourself and order the replacement parts online, you can usually save enough to justify replacing parts even if you're not sure they're bad. (Psep1.biz is one source of discount small-engine parts.) In this article, we'll cover a few basic tests, explain how to order parts, and show you how to replace a carburetor, an ignition coil and a recoil starter. You can replace any defective parts in just a few hours with basic hand tools.

CHECK THE BASICS FIRST

If your machine has a shutoff valve, first make sure it's in the On position. Then make sure the engine has fresh gas. If the gas is more than 30 days old, replace it with fresh, stabilized gas. Next, check the air filter to confirm it's not clogged.

If the tank has fresh gas and you've primed the carburetor and set the choke but it still won't start, it's time to remove the spark plug. If the spark plug is wet with gas, it proves the engine is getting fuel. Dry off the plug with compressed air, and examine it for signs of carbon buildup or oil deposits. Check the gap to make sure it's within specs. If you have any doubts about the plug's condition, replace it—they're cheap.

If the plug is dry, it's a sign of a fuel problem and most likely a messed-up carburetor. Shoot a substitute fuel

(WD-40 or B'laster Small Engine Tune-Up) into the carburetor throat and then try starting the engine (**Photo 1**). If it won't start or fire with spray fuel, you probably have an ignition system problem—most likely a bad ignition coil. But if it starts and dies, that proves the ignition is working and the problem is fuel starvation.

Check the fuel filter first by disconnecting the fuel line from the filter to the carb. Gas should run out. If it doesn't, replace the filter. If gas flows freely through the filter, then the problem is inside the carburetor.

Testing an ignition coil is a bit trickier. To do it right, you need a small-engine spark tester. Holding the spark plug boot close to the engine to check for spark isn't a reliable test because a bad coil can produce a spark in open air but fail when the cylinder is under compression. If you own several small engines, it may pay to buy a tester. (One choice is the Briggs & Stratton No. 19368; $16 at briggsandstratton.com.) To learn how to use it, go to familyhandyman.com and search for "ignition coil." However, since a new coil doesn't cost much more than a tester (about $25), replacing the coil without testing may be the way to go.

FIND THE RIGHT PARTS

Lawn and garden tool manufacturers often use several different engine brands for a certain model, so you can't buy parts based on the model number of the mower or snow blower. Instead, you need the engine model, serial number and date of manufacture to find the parts. The Toro lawn mower featured in this story, for example, was built with a Tecumseh engine, while a different Toro mower may be built with a Briggs & Stratton engine. We found the Tecumseh engine information on a label (**Photo 2**). But other brands may stamp the numbers into the engine block, valve cover or engine shield.

Once you have the engine information, locate a parts list and

1 **GIVE IT A BLAST OF "FUEL."** Remove the air filter and shoot a one-second burst of an aerosol petroleum-based lubricant (not starting fluid, silicone or Teflon spray) directly into the carburetor throat. Try starting. If the engine starts and then dies, that confirms you've got a fuel problem.

2 **SHOOT THE MODEL AND SERIAL NUMBERS.** Take a digital photo of the engine model, serial numbers and date of manufacture, as well as any other engine data on the label. You'll need that info to order parts.

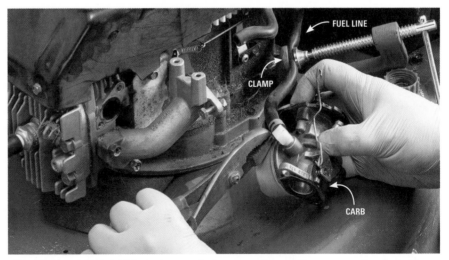

3 **REPLACE THE CARB.** Tighten a C-clamp on the gas line or turn the shutoff valve to Off. Then remove the fuel line and two carburetor hold-down bolts. Rotate the carburetor to disconnect the throttle linkage. Reverse the procedure to install the new carburetor.

an exploded diagram by entering the brand and model number into a search engine. Find the engine manufacturer's part number and enter that into a search engine to find the lowest price or nearest seller.

CARB REBUILD VS. NEW CARB

These days we don't recommend rebuilding a carburetor. First, a brand-new carburetor from a discount online seller usually costs less than a rebuild kit and a bucket of carburetor soaking solution. Plus, rebuilding a carburetor is time-consuming and doesn't always work, especially if the internal parts are corroded.

Once you have the new carburetor in hand, remove the old one and swap in the new unit (**Photo 3**). After you reinstall the fuel line and prime the engine, it should start right up.

REPLACE AN IGNITION COIL

If you've determined that you have a weak spark or no spark, go ahead and buy and install a new coil. Start by removing the plastic engine cover and setting it aside. Then lift off the gas tank and remove any engine shields to access the ignition coil. Remove the old coil (**Photo 4**). Then install the new coil and set the air gap (**Photo 5**).

REPLACE A RECOIL STARTER

If the starter rope is broken, you can buy a recoil rebuild kit for about $15. The kit contains a new rope, dogs and dog springs. Setting the proper spring tension can be tricky, and if you get it wrong, you'll break the spring and have to replace the entire unit. Frankly, we recommend skipping the rebuild and just replacing the entire recoil assembly (**Photo 6**). It's much faster, and the complete assembly (about $40) includes a new housing and spring (set to the proper tension).

4 REMOVE THE OLD COIL. Remove the two coil retaining screws. The instant they're loose, the coil will snap against the magnet on the top of the crankshaft. Grab the coil and yank it off the magnet.

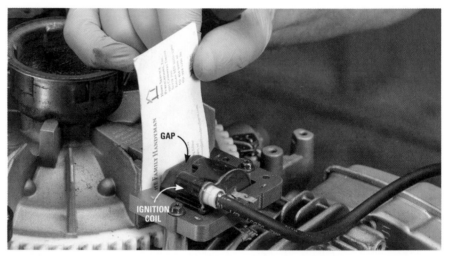

5 INSTALL THE NEW COIL. Place the coil and snug the retaining screws. Align the crankshaft magnet to the center of the coil. Use a business card to set the air gap—move the coil in and out until you feel some drag on the card. Tighten the coil screws and check the gap. If it's correct, reinstall the engine shield and cover.

6 REPLACE THE RECOIL STARTER ASSEMBLY. Remove the engine cover retaining screws and lift the cover off the engine. Next, remove the recoil assembly hex-head screws. Then lift off the old unit and drop in the new one. Reverse the procedure to reinstall.

When Power Pays

These rental tools are well worth the investment.

Doing things yourself is supposed to save money. So starting a job by spending money on rental equipment may seem like a step in the wrong direction. But before you bypass your local rental center, consider how much time and strain you can save with the right tools. You may find that spending $50 to avoid 10 hours of backbreaking labor is a bargain. The right equipment also lets you tackle jobs that you would otherwise have to pay a pro to do. And some of the tools we tried are just plain fun to work with.

We rented the most popular outdoor power equipment and put it through its paces so we could give you tips based on actual experience. Overall, each machine did its particular job as advertised. Here are our favorites:

BOOM LIFT

A boom lift can take you to new heights to trim trees, paint an exterior, or apply siding and soffit material. Even if you can climb ladders with ease, this machine will still save you tons of time. Plus, it's much safer than working on a ladder. If you rent it for a week, expect to pay about $1000. Make sure the rental fee includes a safety harness, or rent a harness separately.

A typical boom can hoist you 37 ft. into the air and pivot 360 degrees. Picking the right parking place is critical for safety and ease of operation. You'll need firm level ground, 20 ft. of clear overhead space to raise the bucket and 5 ft. of clear space around the sides for the outriggers. Since you'll be towing it into position with your truck (it's too heavy to move by hand), plan your route to minimize lawn damage. Then unhitch the boom from your truck and drop the outriggers. Protect grass or asphalt by placing large scraps of wood under the outriggers. Hook up your safety harness, hop into the bucket and take a few minutes to familiarize yourself with the boom's operating controls. There are fast and slow icons on the controls. You'll want to use the slow buttons until you get used to operating the machine. The battery-powered boom will run for about eight hours before needing a recharge.

POSTHOLE DIGGER

Digging postholes for a fence or footing holes for a deck is usually the most time-consuming, backbreaking part of the project. The solution is a power posthole digger—but not just any model. "Two-man" diggers supported by hand are hard to handle. They toss you and your partner around, especially in hard soil. A one-person trailer-mounted model (shown above left) is much easier to use. Just move it into position, start it up and tip the auger into the soil. The weight of the machine keeps it drilling straight down with minimal guidance from you. But you'll need extra muscle to move it to the next hole, especially if you're on a hill. Use your lawn tractor or truck if you're working solo. Or, remove the auger to lighten the load and move it by hand. It takes longer to move the unit than it takes to drill the holes. If you're drilling on a flat surface, plan on eight holes per hour. On hills, always block the wheels before drilling.

POWER TRENCHER

Digging a trench for cable or gas lines means hours or days of hard manual labor. But a power trencher can do all that digging for you in a fraction of the time. The trencher pictured at left can dig down 24 in. (other models can dig to 36 in.) and is self-propelled, so you don't have to pull it. Steering it around curves will still be a workout, however. Also be aware that rocky soil and tree roots can jam the trencher and cause the tires to dig ruts in the grass, so don't try to power your way through a jam. Instead, shut down the unit, clear the jam and then restart. On hills, start at the top and work your way down. However, before you start ripping up your yard, call 811 to get all the utility lines clearly marked (go to call811.com for more information). Be sure to call at least a few days before you begin work on your property.

WALK-BEHIND LOADER

A typical front-end loader makes quick work of moving piles of gravel, sand and dirt. But it won't fit through most fence gates or other tight spots. Worse yet, the wheels dig into your lawn every time you make a turn. Instead, rent a walk-behind, track-style machine with a loader attachment. Unlike other loaders, this one is easy to master—you'll operate it like a veteran after only a few minutes of practice. The version pictured at right (the Toro Dingo) fits through a 35-in. opening and runs on grass-friendly rubber tracks. The bucket can move tons of material in a four-hour rental period. Follow the safety directions for the maximum bucket lift height so the unit doesn't tip over (don't ask how we learned this). The bucket is great for moving gravel or soil but not for digging. To dig holes, rent a backhoe attachment instead.

BACKPACK BLOWER

A typical electric leaf blower throws out about 70 cu. ft. of air per minute (cfm). A commercial-grade backpack unit, on the other hand, throws out an enormous 465 cfm. With all that extra power, you can clear leaves a whole lot faster, of course, but a backpack blower will also do things a smaller blower can't. It will peel wet leaves off the ground, blast out debris that's stuck in cracks and move a mountain of leaves in a single pass. And with the gas engine strapped to your back, you can do it all more comfortably than you could do it with a handheld model.

BRUSH CUTTER

If you've left the back forty unmowed for too long and Mother Nature is taking over, don't waste time—and possibly wreck your lawn mower—by mowing down the brush. Instead, rent a machine designed specifically for clearing tall weeds and saplings (up to 1-1/2 in. dia.). This self-propelled monster knocks the brush over and whacks it to bits with its machete-like blade. It moves quickly, even at its lowest speed (1.8 mph), so you can clear a large area in a few hours.

STUMP GRINDER

There's no need to pay hundreds of dollars to have a professional come to your house and grind out a stump. With a rented stump grinder, you can do it yourself in a few minutes. For a stump that's no more than 18 in. dia., rent a light-duty grinder that's mounted on a trailer. For bigger stumps, rent a heavy-duty self-propelled monster like the one shown below. Make sure you remove any rocks around the stump to avoid breaking the teeth on the grinding wheel (the rental center will charge you big bucks for broken teeth). Work the grinding wheel side to side and advance slowly over the stump. Then repeat the process, digging deeper each time. In most situations, two hours is plenty of time to pull the grinder home, chew up the stump and return the grinder.

WEED TRIMMER WITH A BRUSH BLADE

If you want to cut saplings and brush in your yard without mowing down everything else, rent a commercial-duty trimmer with a brush blade. It will slice through saplings up to 1-1/2 in. dia. The shoulder harness carries the weight of the gas motor.

Just tap the blade against the base of a sapling; don't swing the trimmer like an ax—doing so can destroy the drive shaft. And to avoid bogging down the machine, make repeated jabs rather than a single cut. If you have a large area to clear, rent the trimmer for a whole day.

PRO-GRADE CHAIN SAW

If you have only one tree to fell and cut up, it's certainly not worth investing in a $350 chain saw. And you'll be sorely disappointed (and just plain sore) if you attempt the task with a small, underpowered chain saw. Do yourself a favor and rent a pro-grade model for a few hours—it'll have more power, cut faster and tire you out far less. For chain saw safety tips, go to familyhandyman.com and search for "chain saw safety."

Get What You Pay For

You can rent most power equipment for two- or four-hour periods, or by the day. Here are some tips to help you make the most of the rental period:

■ Ask about the cost of a trailer. It's usually not included in the rental price. If you use your own trailer, make sure it's rated to handle the weight of the machine and that your truck (and hitch) can tow the load.

■ Remember that the rental period includes your drive time to and from your project. If the machine requires a trailer, also factor in time to unload the machine and reload it when the job is done. That can eat up 30 minutes or more of your rental time.

■ Ask about delivery services. Having the rental center deliver and pick up the machine may cost $85 or more. But since the rental period won't include drive time, loading or unloading, you have more time to actually use the equipment. Delivery service may save you money in the long run.

■ Make sure the rental center staffers show you how to start and use the equipment. Then try it yourself before you drive away. That way, you avoid learning and making mistakes during the rental period.

■ Be ready to use the machine the minute you get home. You can waste a lot of money letting the rental equipment sit idle while you mark posthole locations or clear rocks away from tree stumps.

Replace Worn-Out Struts

Less than two hours of work can save you $500—and even more down the road.

If you've put 80,000 or more miles on your struts, they're worn out and must be replaced (see "How to Tell if You Need New Struts"). We know they're expensive (sometimes front strut replacement can be $900 at a shop). But in the long run, driving on worn struts actually will cost you more. The unchecked bouncing will destroy your tires and quickly wear out other expensive suspension components like ball joints, control arm bushings, stabilizer bar end links and tie rod ends. And worn struts are dangerous because they increase your stopping distance by almost 10 ft. from 60 mph and cause steering instability, especially on curves at higher speeds.

Replacing struts used to be a dangerous job for a DIYer. You had to compress the spring and remove the strut while praying the spring wouldn't let go and take out an eye or a limb. Plus, removing the rusty nut at the top of the strut could turn into a nightmare if the internal hex stripped out. But these days you can buy a complete strut assembly that eliminates the strut/spring/mount disassembly process. These assemblies allow you to replace both of your front

struts yourself in less than two hours. You'll have to get an alignment done afterward (about $100), but you'll still save about $500 by doing the job yourself. You'll need rust penetrant, wrenches, a pin punch or large screwdriver, and a thin piece of plywood. You may also need to buy a few large sockets and a breaker bar. Here are the steps.

SHOP FOR STRUTS AND TOOLS

Find complete strut assemblies (Quick-Strut by Monroe, Strut-Plus by KYB and ReadyMount by Gabriel are three brands) at any auto parts store or online auto parts supplier (rockauto.com and autoanything.com are two examples). Complete strut assemblies are available for most makes and models. They cost more than just the strut but are a much better option because they allow you to do the job yourself and get all new parts **(Photo 1)**. The new spring restores factory ride height and firmness, and the new strut mount and bearing provide smoother turning and quieter operation. The strut assemblies for the 2005 Dodge Grand Caravan featured in this story cost about $194 each (the strut alone is $85).

The strut-to-steering-knuckle nuts and bolts are fairly large, so you'll need 18mm through 23mm 1/2-in.-drive deep sockets and a beefy 1/2-in.-drive breaker bar and ratchet. Some strut bolts are a single-use "torque-to-yield" (TTY) style that can't be reused. Ask the parts store clerk if yours are TTY. If so, buy new bolts and follow the proper shop manual torque procedure when installing the new struts.

To get the strut and wheel aligned close enough to drive the vehicle to a shop for a professional alignment, you'll need an angle gauge. Use a digital or mechanical angle gauge (AccuRemote Digital Electronic Magnetic Angle Gauge Level, about $34 at amazon.com, or Johnson Level & Tool 700 Magnetic Angle Locator, about $14 at amazon.com).

PREP AND MEASURE

You'll have to disconnect a few components from the strut. Replace one side at a time, and note the position and location of all nuts and bolts as you remove them. Use the other side as a reference.

Raise the vehicle and support it with jack stands. Start by soaking the strut flange nuts and bolts with rust penetrant. Then pop the hood and spray the strut-tower mounting nuts. While they're soaking, measure the camber angle **(Photo 2)** and write it down.

Next, disconnect the stabilizer bar end link **(Photo 3)**, the wheel speed sensor wiring harness and any brake lines that may be secured to the strut.

REMOVE THE OLD STRUT

Loosen the strut flange nuts and bolts and then remove them **(Photo 4)**. Next, separate the steering knuckle from the strut **(Photo 5)**. Place a thin piece of plywood under the strut flange to prevent it from damaging

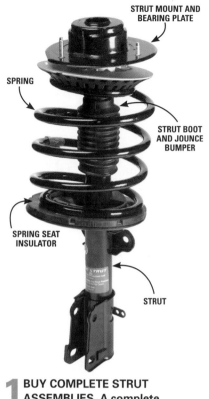

1 BUY COMPLETE STRUT ASSEMBLIES. A complete strut assembly comes assembled and includes all new parts (where applicable): strut, spring, spring seat insulator, strut boot, jounce bumper, strut mount and bearing plate.

2 MEASURE THE CAMBER ANGLE. Spin two lug nuts onto studs and tighten them to secure the rotor to the hub. Then mount the angle gauge to the top of the rotor and note the angle.

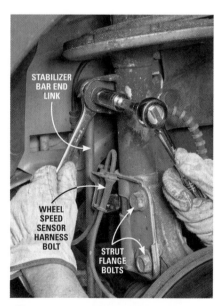

3 DISCONNECT THE END LINK. Hold the stabilizer bar end link with a wrench. Then loosen the nut with a socket and ratchet. Push the end link out of the strut hole and move it to the side. Disconnect the wheel speed sensor wiring harness and put that aside.

the CV boot once you disengage the top portion of the strut. Loosen and remove most of the strut mount nuts (**Photo 6**). Then reach into the wheel well to support the strut while you remove the last nut. Lower the strut onto the plywood and let it rest there. Remove the old strut (**Photo 7**).

INSTALL THE NEW STRUT

Installing the new strut is the reverse of the removal, but it's very tricky and sometimes impossible to get into place and hold there while you get the nuts started. So enlist the help of a friend for the actual installation. Once it's in place, torque the strut mount nuts to spec. Then push the steering knuckle into the strut flange and use a pin punch to align one hole so you can insert a bolt. Remove the punch and insert the other bolt. Snug up the nuts, but don't tighten them fully.

Reattach your angle gauge and push the knuckle in or out to come as close as possible to the original camber angle (**Photo 8**). Torque the nuts to spec and recheck the camber angle. Adjust if necessary.

Reinstall the stabilizer bar end link and wheel speed sensor wiring harness, along with any other components you removed earlier.

GET A PROFESSIONAL ALIGNMENT ASAP

The angle gauge method shown in this article is meant to get you close to the alignment you had before replacing the struts. But it's no substitute for a real alignment from a pro. Since incorrect camber can cause tire wear, get your vehicle into a shop for a full alignment. This isn't something you should postpone. When we say ASAP, we mean the next day—not weeks or months after you've replaced the struts.

4 LOOSEN AND REMOVE THE NUTS AND BOLTS. Lean in and put some muscle into loosening the strut nuts. Remove them and then loosen the bolts. Push the steering knuckle in and out to wiggle the bolts out of the holes.

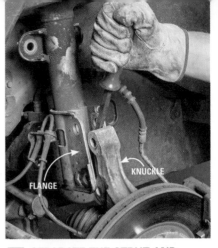

5 SEPARATE THE STRUT AND KNUCKLE. Jam a pry bar between the strut and the knuckle, and pry the knuckle toward you until it pops out of the strut flange.

6 REMOVE THE STRUT MOUNT NUTS. Use a ratcheting wrench or socket/ratchet to loosen the strut mount nuts located on the strut tower. Loosen all of them and remove all but one.

7 REMOVE THE STRUT. Grab the strut bottom and spring, and tilt the bottom out toward you. Then lower the strut until it clears the strut tower and lift it out.

8 RESET THE ANGLE. Attach the angle gauge to the rotor and push the knuckle in or out until you return to the original camber angle. Tighten the nuts.

DIY Motorcycle Detailing

The right products and techniques yield professional-quality results—and pay for themselves over time.

Getting your bike professionally detailed can cost a bundle, from $200 all the way up to $600 for a complete job with the optional protectant package. So it makes sense that you'd want to do it yourself to save the dough.

To learn the right way to detail a bike, we consulted Renny Doyle, owner of Attention to Details, a school for professional detailers. Renny walked us through his step-by-step method for detailing a motorcycle. His technique may seem like overkill, especially his recommendation for multiple rinse/dry cycles, but that's how he achieves perfection. He can detail a bike in less than four hours, but you'd better plan on a full day. While you'll need to make some upfront investments in cleaners and tools for the first round of detailing, for every round after that you'll detail like the pros and save money every time.

The products we show in this story are Renny's personal favorites, but other major brands of motorcycle cleaners will work just as well. Find these products and tools at auto parts stores and online (detailing.com is one online source).

REMOVE THE LEATHER AND START WITH A LIGHT WASH

Work in a shaded area and don't start cleaning until the engine is cool to the touch. Remove the seat and leather saddlebags, and set them aside. Then cover the battery with plastic sheeting, and seal off the exhaust pipe (or pipes) with plastic wrap and a rubber band.

Do a prerinse with plain water to remove surface dust and grit. A firefighter's-style garden hose nozzle works great because you can dial in a different spray pattern for each area of the bike. You can also use a pressure washer to rinse the bike, but dial down the pressure to its lowest setting and maintain a healthy distance from the bike to avoid damaging the softer metal and plastic parts. Use a gentle stream around wheel hubs to avoid forcing water into the bearings.

Follow the rinse with a prewash **(Photo 1)**. Use a gentle car wash soap (Meguiar's Gold Class Car Wash Shampoo and Conditioner is one choice), a microfiber wash mitt, and separate soap and rinse buckets. The prewash is just to remove the light road dirt and mud, so don't go scrubbing the really dirty and greasy areas with your mitt. Save those for the special cleaners you'll use later on. Rinse off the suds and dry the bike right away to prevent water spots. Rather than hand-wiping the entire bike, use a power blower (such as the MetroVac SK-1 Motorcycle Dryer) or compressed air, keeping the pressure under 70 psi. Wipe off any remaining water with a waffle-weave microfiber towel.

Next, clean the tires, wheels and spokes with an aluminum-safe cleaner, such as Sonax Full Effect Wheel Cleaner **(Photo 2)**.

1 **PREWASH WITH A DAMP MITT AND SUDS.** Dip the mitt into soapy water and wring out the excess. Then wipe the damp mitt over the entire bike. Avoid soaking the dash gauges, buttons and switches.

BOAR-BRISTLE BRUSH

2 **CLEAN THE WHEELS.** Spray the wheels and spokes with wheel cleaner, and let it soak for about 30 seconds. Then brush the rim and spokes with a boar-bristle brush. Rinse everything with water and dry with the blower and towel.

3 **CLEAN AND POLISH THE DASH.** Squirt a small dollop of polish onto a microfiber towel and work it into the dash using a random circular motion. Continue wiping until the haze is almost gone. Then wipe off the remaining product with a clean towel.

4 **CLEAN THE ENGINE AND DRIVETRAIN.** Spray cleaner on all engine and drivetrain components. Let it penetrate for about one minute. Brush the greasy areas with a boar-bristle brush. Rinse off the cleaner. Blow dry. Repeat if necessary.

Removing Dried Wax

The best way to remove old dried-on wax is to apply new wax and let it soften the old. But if it's still stuck in crevices, use a household steam cleaner and direct the steam right onto the dried wax. Then wipe it clean with a rag.

5 **SHINE UP THE CHROME.** Apply polish to a cotton rag and polish the chrome until the haze almost disappears. Wipe off any remaining haze with a clean section of the rag.

Move up to the dash and clean it with a gentle cleaner like Leather Therapy Wash or Meguiar's D180 Leather Cleaner and Conditioner. Then polish the dash with Meguiar's M205 Ultra Finishing Polish **(Photo 3)**. Use the same polish on the windshield.

Then clean the engine, transmission, chain or driveshaft housing with a spray cleaner, like S100 Total Cycle Cleaner, and brushes **(Photo 4)**. If the S100 product isn't strong enough to remove caked-on grease, dilute a heavy-duty degreaser 4 to 1 with water or cut a mild degreaser like Simple Green 1 to 1 with water. Apply the diluted degreaser and expect to put some elbow grease into the job. Don't ever apply full-strength degreaser to your bike.

Before you polish the chrome, switch out your microfiber towel for a smooth 100% cotton rag. You can use an old T-shirt or dish towel as long as you cut off the seams first. Seams that are stitched with synthetic thread can scratch chrome, and the seams can retain grit. Then use the Meguiar's M205 polish that you used on the dash **(Photo 5)**.

Clean the leather seat and saddlebags with Leather Therapy Wash as well as Leather Therapy Restorer and Conditioner, or with Meguiar's D180 **(Photo 6)**. These products rejuvenate and condition the leather, and they don't contain any slick additives, so you won't slide off the seat.

Next, use a new batch of soapy water to remove any remaining traces of the cleaners. Then rinse and dry the bike completely **(Photos 7 and 8)**.

Clean and treat rubber foot pegs/rests and pedals with 303 Aerospace Protectant. The product contains UV inhibitors to prevent rubber degradation and dries to a nonslip matte finish. Then seal painted areas with Sonax Polymer Net Shield **(Photo 9)**.

6 CLEAN AND PROTECT THE LEATHER. Apply the leather cleaner to a sponge and gently work it into the leather. Then wipe dry and apply the conditioner with a different sponge. Wipe with a rag and let dry.

7 DO A FULL RINSE. Rinse again with water and blast off the final rinse with a blower or compressed air. Wipe off any remaining water drops to prevent spotting.

8 BLOW IT DRY. Starting at the top, blow the water down and to the front and back. Use a compressor set to 70 psi or less, or use a power blower.

Remove Melted Rubber from Exhaust Pipes

Use household oven cleaner to remove melted boot heel residue from hot exhaust pipes. Test it first on your bike by spraying it in an inconspicuous spot on the chrome. If it doesn't discolor the chrome, run the bike until the pipe is warm. Then spray the oven cleaner directly onto the melted rubber and let it soak in for a few minutes. Wipe it off with a cotton towel.

9 APPLY PAINT SEALANT. Spray sealant onto the paint and spread sealant evenly with a wax applicator sponge, working in small sections. Buff the paint with a microfiber towel (don't let the product dry before buffing).

Avoid These Mistakes

- Never use full-strength automotive or household degreaser products. They can permanently stain aluminum and strip off paint. Also avoid dishwashing detergent and household spray cleaners.
- Never let cleaners sit on the parts for more than a few minutes, and always rinse the cleaned areas with water. Never allow cleaners, even diluted degreaser, to dry on the bike.
- Never use scrub pads or coarse wheel brushes anywhere on the bike.
- Work in the shade, and dry each component after you rinse it to avoid water spotting.
- Never use tire dressing on your bike. The silicone in such a product presents a slipping/safety hazard.

Flexible Garage Storage

Here's how to cheaply squeeze more stuff into less space!

This storage system solves two challenges: first, how to design storage space for the narrow alley between the garage side wall and the family car; and second, how to create a solid mounting surface to hold shelves and hooks that are capable of carrying hundreds of pounds of stuff.

The solution is to create a framework of horizontal wood strips and inexpensive shelf standards. It can hold almost any arrangement of shelving and hooks, at any point on the wall, and it's easy to rearrange.

PLANNING AND MATERIALS

Pull your car into the garage and measure how much space is available. Then look at what needs to be stored and figure out where it will fit. Generally, it's best to hang narrow shelves and smaller hooks lower where space is tight, then have wider shelves near the ceiling so you don't bump your head or interfere with car doors.

Planning the layout and buying materials can take a few hours, but you can do the actual installation, including ripping the plywood shelves and strips, in less than a day. Put up horizontal strips even if you have exposed studs or block walls—they'll make it much easier to install shelf standards and hooks. Apply finish, if desired, to the strips and shelves before installing them.

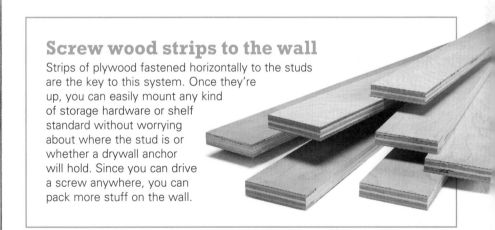

Screw wood strips to the wall

Strips of plywood fastened horizontally to the studs are the key to this system. Once they're up, you can easily mount any kind of storage hardware or shelf standard without worrying about where the stud is or whether a drywall anchor will hold. Since you can drive a screw anywhere, you can pack more stuff on the wall.

We used 3-1/2-in.-wide strips of 3/4-in. plywood because plywood is always straight and never splits—but pine 1x4s would also work. Birch plywood was our choice for the strips and shelves. You can rip 12 strips from one 4 x 8-ft. sheet, and that's enough for an average wall. If you don't have a table saw, go to familyhandyman.com and search for "circular saw" for tips on making straight cuts.

We used four sheets of plywood for our system. For shelf edging, we used 1-1/2-in.-wide strips of solid birch **(Photo 6)**. The total cost for our 20-ft.-long system was about $500, but you could cut that cost in half by skipping the fold-down workbench **(Photo 5)** and using less-expensive wood and plywood.

Install the Strips and Standards

Locate studs using a stud finder and mark them with masking tape, then draw a level line 3 ft. above the garage floor. Start at the center of the wall with a 4-ft. level and work to each side. Garage floors often slope, so don't simply measure from the floor to establish the line. Set the first strip above the level line, screwing it to every stud with two 2-1/2-in. screws **(Photo 1)**. Space the remaining strips so they line up with screw holes on the standards you use—ours were 22 in. from center to center.

Screw on the first standard with 1-5/8-in. screws **(Photo 2)**. Install the other standards, spacing them no more than 24 in. apart—less if you have lots of heavy boxes to store.

1 Screw plywood strips to studs. Cut the strips to length so the ends meet on the studs.

2 Mount the first shelf standard, then use it as a reference to locate the others. Space standards no more than 24 in. apart.

3 Lock brackets together with a wood lip to create a lumber and pipe rack. The lip keeps pipes and lumber from falling off.

Customize the System to Fit Your Needs

Attach pegboard, different widths and lengths of shelving, a workbench, a lumber and pipe rack, and any other type of storage you need **(Photos 3-5).**

Use a table saw or circular saw to rip shelving 1/2 in. wider than the depth of the shelf bracket. Use 3/4-in.-thick plywood or solid wood for the shelves—either is stronger and resists sagging better than any particleboard shelving product available.

If you want to make the shelves more rigid as well as more attractive, nail on 1x2 front edges **(Photo 6).** Use an air nailer, or predrill if hand nailing. Finally, line up the shelves and attach them to the brackets from underneath with screws 1/2 in. longer than the depth of the brackets.

4 Add a section of pegboard. Frame the edges with wood strips and fasten all four sides of the pegboard.

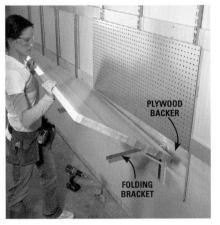

5 Mount heavy-duty folding brackets on a 3/4-in. plywood backer to create a fold-down workbench.

6 Apply a bead of wood glue to each shelf edge, then nail on edging with finish nails every 12 in.

Hooks, Hangers and Brackets for Everything and Anything

Home centers and hardware stores sell a wide variety of products for storing almost anything. You can also install wire rack shelving or special wire baskets on double-slot shelf standards. Try to mix shelf brackets and accessories from different manufacturers—but check the fit, if possible, before buying. Shelf standards, however, are not interchangeable, as slots and screw holes don't always line up.

Avoid getting locked into one garage system or brand—it's often cheaper to use a variety rather than just the special matching accessories.

Giant storage hanger—for ladders, chairs, hoses

CLOSETMAID (FOR WIRE SHELVES)

RUBBERMAID

All-purpose hang-up—for ladders, lawn chairs

Shelf brackets— available in 6-, 9-, 12-, 14-, 16-, 18-, 20- and 24-in. sizes for wood or wire shelves

Pegboard and accessories— buy as a kit or individually

Adjustable tool holder— for garden tools, brooms

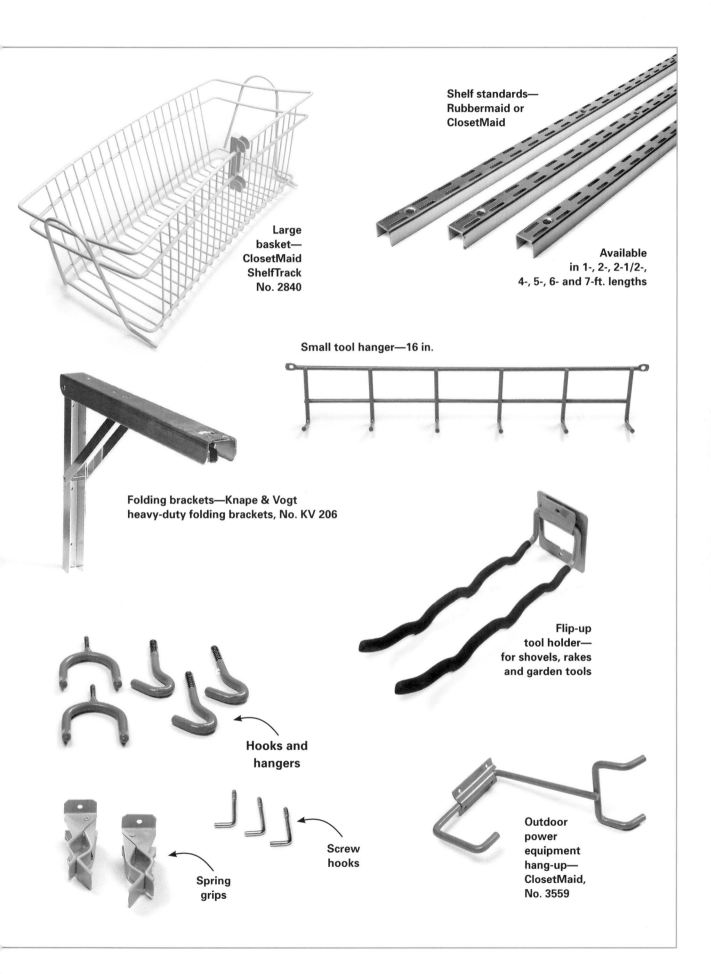

Large basket—ClosetMaid ShelfTrack No. 2840

Shelf standards—Rubbermaid or ClosetMaid

Available in 1-, 2-, 2-1/2-, 4-, 5-, 6- and 7-ft. lengths

Small tool hanger—16 in.

Folding brackets—Knape & Vogt heavy-duty folding brackets, No. KV 206

Flip-up tool holder—for shovels, rakes and garden tools

Hooks and hangers

Screw hooks

Spring grips

Outdoor power equipment hang-up—ClosetMaid, No. 3559

Utility Wardrobe

Tuck away off-season gear in this spacious cabinet you can build in a weekend.

This simple wardrobe is the perfect spot to store those heavy jackets, boots, hats and gloves until winter rolls around and it's time to store your summer things. Or you could add shelves

Materials List

ITEM	QTY.
3/4" x 4' x 8' BC-grade plywood	1
1/2" x 4' x 8' BC-grade plywood	2
1/4" x 4' x 8' BC-grade plywood	1
1x6 x 8' poplar	1
1x3 x 8' poplar	12
1x2 x 8' poplar	2
1x2 x 6' poplar	1
6' chrome closet pole	1
Closet pole brackets	2
Self-closing flush door hinges	6
Door handles	2
Threaded metal base glides	4
Magnetic catches	4
1-1/2" brad nails	1 box
1" brad nails	1 box
1-1/2" pocket screws	1 bag

to make it the permanent storage cabinet for backpacks, tents, life preservers or any other seasonal items that stack up in your garage.

In this article, we'll show you how to build this practical, sturdy cabinet out of low-cost materials. We'll also show you how to make simple, strong joints using pocket screws. The only specialty tool you'll need is a pocket screw jig. A miter saw, a table saw and an air compressor with a brad gun will make the job a lot easier, but you can get by without them. Allow about a day to build the cabinet, plus a half day for painting.

MATERIALS AND COSTS

To keep costs low (about $250, including hardware), we made the wardrobe from BC-grade plywood and knot-free 1x3s. If you want to make the cabinet even more utilitarian, you can

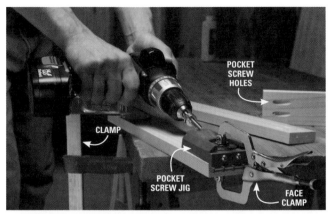

1 Cut the 1x3 rails and stiles to size for all the frames, following the Cutting List on p. 77. Drill a pair of pocket screw holes in each end of each rail.

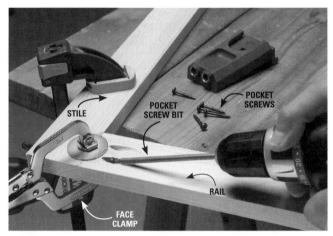

2 Spread glue on the rail ends and fasten them to the stiles with pocket screws. Clamp the boards as you fasten them to hold the board edges even.

3 Spread glue on the leading edges of the side frames and clamp them to the front frame so the top and sides are flush. Nail the frames together with 1-1/2-in. brads.

4 Cut the side panels to size. Apply glue to the inside face of the frame, set the side panels in place, clamp them, then nail them with 1-in. brads.

use lower grades of wood and cut the cost in half. However, the doors might twist a bit and not shut evenly. BC plywood has a smooth sanded face that's nice for painting. The knot-free poplar 1x3s (available from a local home center) are stable and easy to cut and join. Be sure to choose straight ones!

BUILD THE FRAME

Start by cutting the 1x3 rails and stiles for the frames (**A, B and C**) to length, following the Cutting List on p. 77. Then use a pocket screw jig and the step bit that comes with it to drill two holes at each end of each rail (**Photo 1**). You'll cover these holes with plywood later, so begin your holes on the less attractive side. We fastened the jig to the end of the rail with a face clamp.

To create solid, smooth joints, apply a bead of wood glue along the end of a rail (**B**), then butt it against the top of a stile (**A**) so the top edges are flush (**Photo 2**). With the joint overhanging your work surface, clamp the rail and stile together with a face clamp (part of the pocket screw kit) to keep them

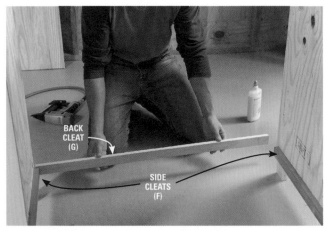

5 Cut the bottom 1x2 cleats to length. Glue and nail the side cleats first. Then glue and nail the front and back cleats.

BACK CLEAT (G)

SIDE CLEATS (F)

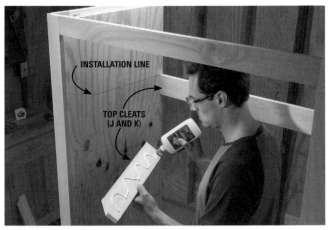

6 Cut the top cleats to length. Nail the back cleat into place. Then glue and nail the side cleats.

INSTALLATION LINE

TOP CLEATS (J AND K)

7 Lay the wardrobe face down. Spread glue and nail the back panel (E) into place with 1-in. brads spaced every 8 to 10 in.

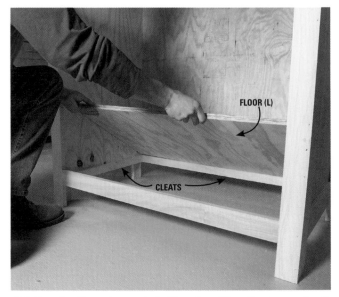

8 Cut the floor, top and shelf to size. Glue the top and nail it into place. Stand the wardrobe upright, then glue and nail the floor and shelf to the cleats.

FLOOR (L)

CLEATS

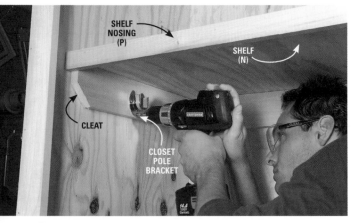

9 Position the closet pole brackets 4 in. below the shelf and 10-3/4 in. from the back cleat. Screw them into place. Measure and cut the closet pole to length.

SHELF NOSING (P)

SHELF (N)

CLEAT

CLOSET POLE BRACKET

aligned. Also clamp your stile to the work surface. The key is to make sure the edges and the faces of the two boards are flush before you drive the screws. Then, using the special pocket screw drive bit, fasten the joint with 1-1/2-in. pocket screws. If you're a pocket screw rookie, practice on scrap wood first to get the hang of it. (For more information on pocket screw joints, go to familyhandyman.com and search for "pocket screw joints.")

Assemble the two side frames, the front and the two door frames in this manner, using **Figure A** as a guide. If your end cuts are perfectly square, your frame should also be square, but check them with a framing square anyway.

With the frames built, apply glue along the edge of a side frame, clamp it to the front frame so the edges are flush

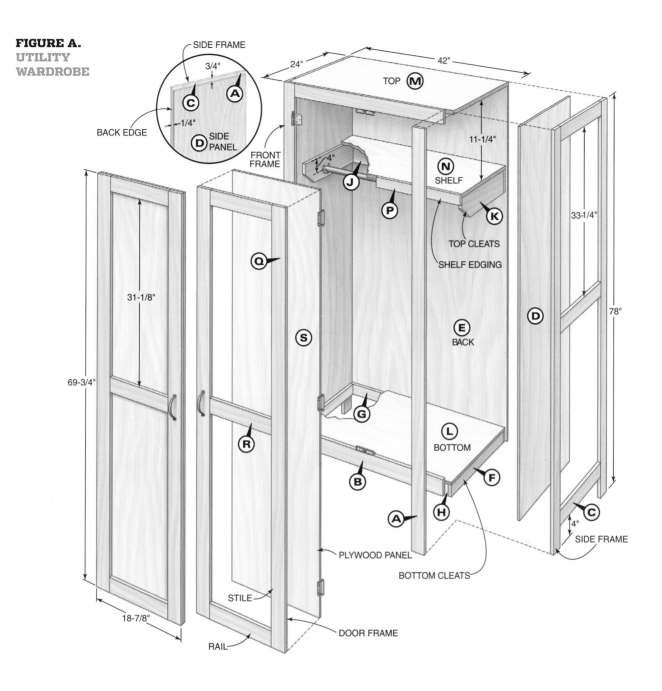

FIGURE A.
UTILITY WARDROBE

SIDE FRAME
3/4"
C
A
BACK EDGE
1/4"
D SIDE PANEL
FRONT FRAME

24"
42"
TOP M

11-1/4"
4"
J
N SHELF
P
K
TOP CLEATS
SHELF EDGING

33-1/4"
D
78"

31-1/8"
Q
S
R

E BACK

69-3/4"
G
L BOTTOM

B
A
H
PLYWOOD PANEL
BOTTOM CLEATS

F
C
4"
SIDE FRAME

18-7/8"
STILE
DOOR FRAME
RAIL

(make sure the pocket screw holes face inside), then fasten them together with 1-1/2-in. nails **(Photo 3)**. Do the same for the other side frame. Wipe away any glue that oozes out. The glue provides the primary holding power. The nails simply hold everything in place until the glue dries.

ADD THE SIDES AND BACK

We added 1/2-in. plywood to the side frames for stability. We held it 3/4 in. short of the top and 1/4 in. from the back to provide convenient grooves for inserting and nailing the top and back panels **(Figure A)**.

Cut the side and back panels **(D and E)** accurately. If they're not square, the cabinet won't be square. Building a support spacer with two 2x4s and 1/2-in. plywood simplifies

Cutting List

KEY	QTY.	SIZE	PART
A	6	3/4" x 2-1/2" x 78"	Poplar stiles
B	2	3/4" x 2-1/2" x 37"	Poplar front rails
C	6	3/4" x 2-1/2" x 18-1/4"	Poplar side rails
D	2	1/2" x 23" x 73-1/4"	Plywood side panels
E	1	1/4" x 40-1/2" x 73-1/4"	Plywood back panel
F	2	3/4" x 1-1/2" x 22-1/4"	Poplar bottom cleats (side)
G	1	3/4" x 1-1/2" x 39-1/2"	Poplar bottom cleat (back)
H	1	3/4" x 1-1/2" x 38"	Poplar bottom cleat (front)
J	1	3/4" x 5-1/2" x 39-1/2"	Poplar top cleat (back)
K	2	3/4" x 5-1/2" x 19-1/4"	Poplar top cleats (side)
L	1	3/4" x 23" x 39-1/2"	Plywood floor
M	1	3/4" x 23-1/4" x 40-1/2"	Plywood top
N	2	3/4" x 20" x 39-1/2"	Plywood shelf
P	1	3/4" x 1-1/2" x 39-1/2"	Shelf nosing
Q	4	3/4" x 2-1/2" x 69-3/4"	Poplar door stiles
R	6	3/4" x 2-1/2" x 13-7/8"	Poplar door rails
S	2	1/2" x 18-7/8" x 69-3/4"	Plywood door panels

the side panel installation (**Photo 4**). Set the spacer under the bottom rail on a side frame. Apply a generous bead of glue to the inside of a side frame, then set the side panel in place (the good side facing out), resting it on the spacer. Butt the panel against the front frame. The frame may not be exactly square, so flex the frame if necessary to align it with the panel.

Clamp the panel to the framing. Use several clamps to keep the panel tight against the rails and stiles. Nails won't close any gaps between the plywood and the framing—that's the clamps' job. Anchor the panel with 1-in. nails. Install the panel on the other side the same way.

Now cut the 1x2 bottom cleats and 1x6 top (shelf) cleats to length (see the Cutting List, p. 77). First glue and nail the 1x2 side cleats (**F**). Align them with the bottom of the plywood panels, and butt them against the front frame. Clamp them before nailing them. Also glue and install the front and back cleats (**G and H; Photo 5**).

Measure down 12 in. from the top of side panels. Install the 1x6 top back cleat (**J**) so the back is aligned with the edges of plywood side panels (toenail the cleat into the plywood). Glue and install the top side cleats (**K; Photo 6**). Drive 1-1/2-in. nails through the cleats into the stiles and drive 1-in. nails through the plywood panels into the cleats from the outside.

Now place the wardrobe face down on the floor. Apply glue along the back edges of the side panels and cleats. Install the back panel (**E**) and tack it into place with 1-in. brads (**Photo 7**).

INSTALL THE TOP, BOTTOM AND SHELF

We used 3/4-in. plywood for the floor, ceiling and shelf to add stiffness and strength. Cut the floor, top and shelf (**L, M and N**) to size. With the wardrobe still on its face, apply glue along the tops of the side and back panels. Fasten the top into place using 1-1/2-in. brads.

Then stand the wardrobe back up and install the floor (**Photo 8**). Cut the 1x2 nosing (**P**) to length. Glue and nail it along the front of the shelf, then install the shelf. The nosing will stiffen the shelf and keep it from bowing.

Mark the side cleats under the shelf 10-3/4 in. from the back cleat (the halfway point inside the wardrobe) and install closet pole brackets. Fasten the brackets into place with screws (**Photo 9**).

Cut the closet pole to length and install it. We recommend a chrome pole rather than wood, since chrome can hold a heavier load without sagging.

10 Cut the door panels to size, then glue and nail them to the door frames. All edges should be flush.

11 Lay the wardrobe on its back. Screw the hinges to the doors, then center the doors over the opening. Insert a 1/8-in. spacer between the doors.

PAINT THE WARDROBE, AND BUILD AND ATTACH THE DOORS

Follow the Cutting List to cut the door panels **(S)** to size. Apply glue to the back of a door frame, set a panel over it, aligning it with the top and sides of the frame, then tack it into place **(Photo 10)**. Do the same for the second door.

We don't show it, but it's easiest to prime and paint the wardrobe and doors at this point. We used an exterior latex paint since we planned to keep the wardrobe in a garage. For a smoother finish, lightly sand the first coat with 120-grit paper before applying the second coat. Once the paint is dry, fasten the door hinges. You have some flexibility where you place the hinges, but keep the locations the same on both doors. We installed ours 2 in. from the top and bottom, and at the middle.

3/8"
SELF-CLOSING
INSET
HINGE

Installing the doors can be tricky. You want the doors to open and close without banging together, yet you want the gap between them kept to a minimum. To do this, place the wardrobe on its back and make a tiny mark on the rails at the midpoint of the door opening. Center the doors over the opening, overhanging the sides, top and bottom by 3/8 in. Insert a shim between the doors at the top and bottom to create a 1/8-in. gap **(Photo 11)**. Use the midpoint marks to keep the doors centered.

Predrill the hinge holes on the stiles using a 3/32-in. bit. We used a special Vix bit **($10; Photo 12)**, which precisely centers the holes. Standard drill bits may shift slightly, offsetting the hole and keeping the doors from closing properly.

Stand the wardrobe upright to attach the remaining hardware. Installing metal magnetic catches at the top and bottom of the doors will hold them firmly closed and help keep them from warping.

The wardrobe is designed for function, but you can still have fun with its appearance. We gave ours three coats of "red pepper" latex paint, then spot-sanded it for a weathered, rustic look. To complete the theme, we used galvanized pipe for the closet pole instead of chrome, along with complementary hinges and door handles.

1/8" SHIM

VIX BIT

DOOR HINGE

12 Predrill holes in the front stiles, and screw on the hinges. Stand the wardrobe upright, then install the magnetic catches and door handles.

Editor's Note

Since most garages and some basement floors are not level, we installed adjustable feet. A package of four threaded metal base glides costs only a few dollars at home centers and hardware stores. Drill a 1/4-in. hole in the bottom of the stiles, stick in the inserts, then place the glides inside the inserts. When you move the wardrobe to the garage or basement, adjust the glides until level. If you live in a hot, humid climate, consider adding two 4-in. round vents to the top to allow for better air circulation.

INSERT

THREADED
METAL SLIDE

CHAPTER **THREE**

WALLS, CEILINGS, WINDOWS & MORE

Paneled Statement Wall

Transform a wall—and a room—without the expense of solid lumber or the skill of a master carpenter.

Achieving a new look for one wall or a whole room can be as easy as nailing a few boards over the drywall. We fashioned this attractive paneled wall using strips of inexpensive MDF (medium-density fiberboard). The square-edged strips are easy to join, and the smooth MDF makes a perfect surface for a flawless paint job.

With a little perseverance, you'll be done in a weekend—nail up the strips on Saturday, then sand and paint them on Sunday. You'll need a basic set of hand tools, a circular saw, a power miter saw, a sander and a finish nailer to complete the job. We show you how to rip the MDF strips with a circular saw **(Photo 2)**, but if you own (or have access to) a table saw, use that instead. Making accurate square cuts on the ends of the strips is easy with a power miter saw, but you can just use a circular saw and guide. If you don't have a finish nailer, consider renting one for a day. There's a lot of nailing to do, and it will speed up the job considerably.

TAPE A MOCK-UP TO THE WALL

Start by prying off the baseboard, and the window and door trim. Slip a wide, stiff putty knife behind the pry bar to spread out the pressure and prevent damage to the drywall. With the moldings out of the way, tape up 4-in.-wide strips of masking paper to simulate the look of the MDF strips **(Photo 1)**. If you can't find 4-in.-wide

masking paper at your local home center or paint store, cut a wider roll to 4 in. with a miter saw. Start by placing strips at the top, bottom and sides of the wall. Then run vertical strips along the windows and doors. Line up horizontal strips above doors and windows. Add a horizontal strip under windows too. Now divide the remaining spaces to create an attractive grid. When you're happy with the arrangement, make a dimensioned sketch to guide you later. Then count the number of 8-ft.-long strips you'll need to complete the project. You'll get twelve 3-7/8-in.-wide by 8-ft.-long strips from every 4 x 8-ft. sheet of MDF.

If you're going to change the wall color, patch any imperfections in the wall with spackling compound. Even if you're not changing the color, sand and paint before applying the MDF strips. You'll have to do some touch-up painting later, but at least the bulk of the work will be done. This is especially important if you're going to paint the MDF strips a different color from the wall.

4" MASKING
PAPER

1 Tape up strips of masking paper to lay out the wall pattern. Adjust the arrangement until you like the results. Take a photo as a reminder of the pattern.

CUT MDF INTO STRIPS

The 4 x 8-ft. sheets of 1/2-in. MDF you'll need for this project are available at lumberyards and home centers. If you don't have a way to haul large sheets, ask a store employee to cut the sheets into 16-in.-wide strips that you can tie to your car top. Also pick up a few tubes of paneling adhesive to attach the strips that don't align with studs **(Photo 7)**.

Cut the MDF into 3-7/8-in.-wide strips. If you don't have a table saw to cut the strips, assemble a cutting guide **(Photo 2)**. Start by cutting a 6-in.-wide strip from the edge of a sheet of MDF. Cut another strip 4 in. wide to use as a stop. Position the stop and screw it to the bottom of the guide so that you can cut 3-7/8-in.-wide strips by running the edge of the saw base against the guide. With this setup, you won't have to measure for each strip. Just reposition the guide and clamp it to the MDF sheet after each cut.

Note: The sawdust that results from cutting MDF is very fine and will cover just about everything in sight if you're not careful. Make your cuts outdoors if possible. If you can't, we recommend putting an exhaust fan in the window and using a shop vacuum to collect the dust from power tools. Make sure to wear a dust mask and safety glasses when cutting.

After ripping the strips, sand the edges to remove saw marks. Clamp a bunch of the strips together and sand all of the edges at once to speed up the job and avoid rounding over the corners **(Photo 3)**. We used a random orbital sander and 80-grit paper. After sanding, leave the clamps in place while you roll on a coat of quick-drying, stain-blocking primer such as Kilz or B-I-N **(Photo 4)**. After the primer dries, sand lightly and apply one coat of paint. Prepainting the edges will save you a lot of time on the final paint job.

What's MDF, and Why Should I Use It?

MDF (medium-density fiberboard) is a pressed wood product that offers several advantages over solid wood for a project like this. First, it's less expensive than solid wood, and the smooth surface looks great painted. Unlike strips of lumber, which can be bent or twisted, strips ripped from MDF are perfectly straight, simplifying installation. And the material is flexible enough to conform to slightly wavy walls. Finally, we preferred the look of 1/2-in.-thick strips, and it's hard to find 1/2-in. lumber.

MDF isn't perfect, though. It's heavy, and the 4 x 8-ft. sheets are hard to handle without help. Some home centers will cut the sheets into smaller pieces for you. Also, the dust from cutting and sanding is so fine that it'll drift and settle on everything in sight unless you take special precautions. Collect the dust with a vacuum or dust collection system if possible. Otherwise, try to do most of your cutting outdoors.

NAIL THE STRIPS TO THE WALL

Start by locating the studs. Look for drywall screws or baseboard nail holes as a clue to the stud locations. If you have an electronic stud finder, use it for this step. Stick pieces of masking tape to the floor to mark the stud locations. Cut MDF rails (horizontal strips) from the sheet to fit along the floor and ceiling, and nail them to the studs with 2-in. brads, joining the ends with 30-degree bevel cuts **(Photo 5)**. Next cut stiles (vertical strips) to fit between the rails at the corners and along the sides of windows and doors, and nail them to the wall **(Photos 6 and 7)**. Position the stiles 1/4 in. from the inside edge of door and window jambs to leave 1/4 in. of the jamb exposed.

Determine the positions of the remaining stiles by dividing the space evenly according to your original layout. Hook your tape measure on the left side of the farthest left stile, and then measure to the left side of the farthest right stile. Divide this measurement by the final number of spaces you want. The resulting value will be the distance from the left edge of any one stile to the left edge of the next stile. Using this measurement, mark the locations of the remaining stiles on the bottom and top rails. Then cut the remaining stiles to the appropriate length. Apply two beads of construction adhesive to the back of the strips before tacking them to the wall with 2-in. brads **(Photo 7)**. The brads will hold the strips in place as the adhesive dries.

With the top and bottom rails and all the stiles in place, it's time to fill in the rest of the rails. Start by stretching a mason's line tightly across the top of the windows or doors, making sure to leave a 1/4-in. reveal on the jamb. Make a pencil mark where the string intersects each stile **(Photo 8)**. Then cut rails to fit between the stiles, align them with the marks and nail them to the wall. If you have a window, align another set

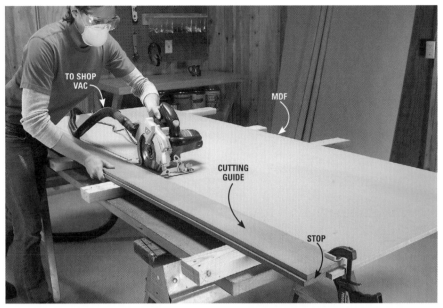

2 Cut straight, uniform strips of MDF fast using a cutting guide with a stop on the underside. If your saw has a vacuum port, use it! Cutting MDF is dusty.

3 Sand the cut edges of the strips fast by clamping several strips together. This technique will also help you avoid rounding over the corners of the strips.

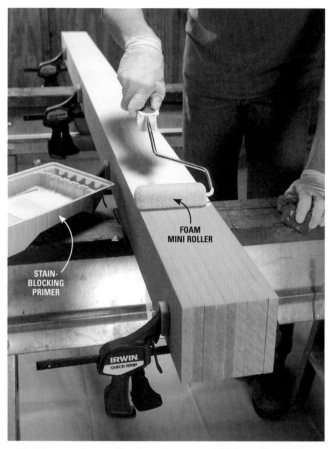

STAIN-BLOCKING PRIMER

FOAM MINI ROLLER

IRWIN QUICK-GRIP

4 Prime and prepaint the edges to avoid fussy brushwork later. Roll on a coat of primer, let it dry and sand lightly. Then roll on a coat of paint.

of rails with the bottom of the window. Then divide the remaining space and mark the rail locations on the stiles **(Photo 9)**. Complete the paneled wall by cutting rails to fit between the stiles at each mark and nailing them to the wall.

FILL AND SAND FOR A PERFECT PAINT JOB

Fill the nail holes and other imperfections with spackling compound. Let the spackling compound dry and then sand it smooth. Nail holes may require two coats of spackling. Where they intersect, sand the MDF strips flush with an orbital sander **(Photo 10)**. Caulk the cracks where the MDF meets the side walls and ceiling. When you're done filling, sanding and caulking, roll or brush a coat of stain-blocking primer onto the face of the MDF strips. Finish the job by painting the face of the MDF strips and touching up the wall paint. Once the paint dries, you'll be ready to style and enjoy your updated space.

PRO TIP
Use a 4-in.-wide foam mini roller **(Photo 4)** to apply the primer and paint. You'll get a smooth finish free of brush marks.

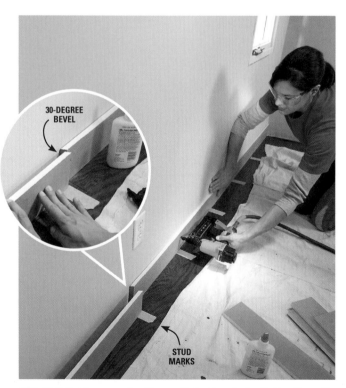

30-DEGREE BEVEL

STUD MARKS

5 Nail the base and ceiling rails to the studs. Splice the rails over the studs. Join the ends with 30-degree bevel cuts.

STILE

STILE

6 Hold the stiles in place and mark them with a utility knife rather than a pencil to create fine, precise cutting marks.

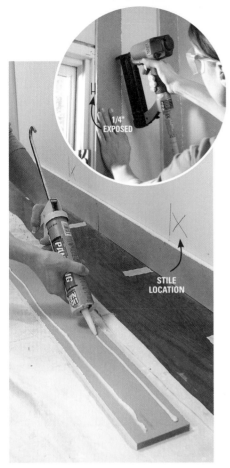

7 Fasten stiles without worrying about stud locations. Apply adhesive to the stiles and tack them to the drywall with brads. The brads hold them in place until the glue dries.

8 Mark the position of the rails above and below the windows. Use a string to align the marks with the windows.

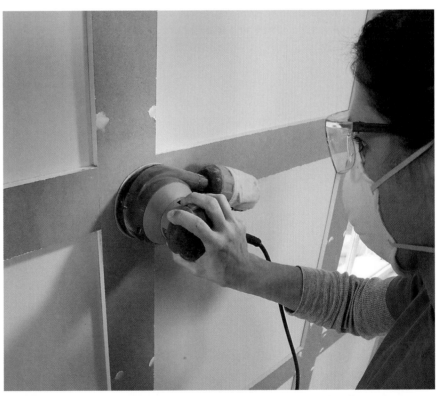

9 Divide the remaining space and mark the locations of the rails on the stiles. Cut the rails and nail them to the studs.

10 Fill nail holes with spackling compound and let it dry. Sand any uneven areas for a smooth, flush surface.

Venetian Plaster Makeover

**Give any room a wallet-pleasing face-lift with two simple projects:
Venetian plaster wall texture and urethane moldings.**

Maybe you've decided that red bedroom walls just aren't your thing or that your 2-year-old could have sponge-painted better than the previous owners. Whatever the case may be, if you're ready for a new look in your bedroom, bathroom, dining room or just about any other room in the house, we'll show you how to redo it in a weekend with two simple projects.

The first is a sophisticated decorative wall technique called Venetian plaster. Once a difficult project tackled only by pros, Venetian plaster is now easy to apply in a straightforward multistep process. With a solid-color product that comes in a can, you can add an impressively rich visual texture with highlights and shadows. It's as simple as patching and painting walls—and the supplies are inexpensive too.

The second project is an easy-to-install urethane molding that you can cut with a handsaw (no power miter box needed), then simply glue and nail to the walls. The molding is a durable product with the crisp details and shapes you'd expect from solid wood, but it's a lot easier to work with. Many sizes and profiles are available, so you can customize the room to your liking. For more information on the moldings, see p. 93.

Part One:
Venetian Plaster

GETTING STARTED

Before you start, choose a color from the brochure available at your home center (or go to the company's website if the product isn't available locally). The supplier will mix and blend the colored plaster just like ordinary paint, so it's ready to be used right out of the can. Don't be fooled when you open the can and see just a solid color. The subtle color differences Venetian plaster is known for will emerge throughout the process of applying, sanding and tooling the plaster.

Prep the room as you would for any paint job by cleaning walls and filling holes. Mask the areas you don't want painted, such as around windows, doors and baseboards. You can plaster over any paint that's sound, but if the paint is glossy or semigloss, wipe it down with a deglosser (available at paint stores).

You can create a two-color wall like ours or use the Venetian plaster product from floor to ceiling with dramatic effects. If you want two colors, paint the top first and allow it to dry so you won't drip paint on the Venetian plaster below. When figuring the proportions for a wainscot, keep in mind that it'll look best about one-third of the way up from the floor to the ceiling. You can go a bit higher up the wall, but keep from going as far as halfway—that would divide the room into a distinct top and bottom and look odd.

With the room prepped, mask off the wall just above where you'll be plastering. Measure up from the floor in several locations and mark a level line with a straightedge. Use a 2- to 3-in.-wide strip of tape so you can stroke freely and not be tempted to make smaller strokes at the top. Also, open a window in the room. Although this product has very low odor, adequate ventilation is necessary until it dries.

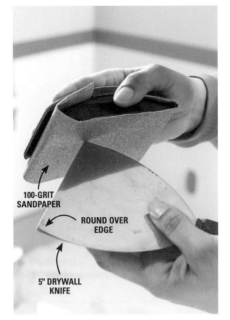

100-GRIT SANDPAPER
ROUND OVER EDGE
5" DRYWALL KNIFE

1 Round the corners of a standard 5-in. drywall knife to prevent the tool from digging in.

MASKING
DRYWALL MUD PAN

2 Transfer the Venetian plaster mix to a drywall pan so it's easier to scrape the excess off the knife. The plaster is a bit thinner than drywall compound but thicker than paint.

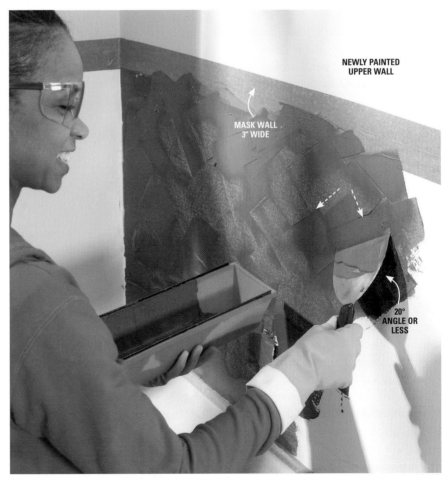

NEWLY PAINTED UPPER WALL
MASK WALL 3" WIDE
20° ANGLE OR LESS

3 Apply the colored plaster mix with your drywall knife in random strokes back and forth, holding the knife at a 15- to 20-degree angle. Avoid heavy buildup.

TROWEL IT ON

When you're at the home center, pick up a drywall mud pan like the one shown in **Photo 2** to hold the colored plaster while you're spreading it on the wall. The pan's long top edges have a sharp rim to wipe your drywall knife clean. Also buy a 5-in. flexible drywall knife to spread the product on the walls. You could use a 4-1/2 in. or a 6-in. knife instead, with slightly different effects. I found it helpful to practice on a scrap of painted drywall to get the hang of it. Your home center paint department may also have small boards available to practice on.

Before you start, sand the corners of the drywall knife to round them slightly to keep the tool from leaving sharp ridges and digging into the wall **(Photo 1)**. Start applying the plaster to the wall in a corner, and work your way along the wall as shown in **Photo 3**. Don't try to do the whole wall in one coat. You'll find it easiest to trowel an even coat on a 3- to 4-ft. section with your knife at a sharp 15- to 20-degree angle, and then go back and do random strokes with the knife, alternating left to right and right to left. You'll see the original color of the wall show through on the first coat, but this is good. If you don't see some of the wall beneath, you're putting the plaster on too thick. After each 6-ft. section, stop and examine the wall. Tool any section with heavy ridges and even it with a clean trowel before it dries **(Photo 4)**, then move along.

FILL ANY VOIDS WITH THE SECOND COAT

Wait for the first coat to dry, from two to four hours, then apply the second **(Photo 5)**. Load plaster and fill in the voids with strokes of your knife. Repeat the randomness of the first coat—the combination of the two coats will add up to a great-looking, varied texture later. Hold the drywall knife at a bit steeper angle, at least 45 degrees to the wall. Look for the spots where the first coat didn't cover and apply plaster in those areas. Again, after each 6-ft. section, go back and check your work, making sure the wall is adequately covered and the wall color behind doesn't show through. The plaster should be about 1/8 in. thick in the thicker areas and thinner elsewhere, so judge your job accordingly. Remember, the finished job will have more visual texture than actual texture.

You'll find that outside corners can build up quickly, so try to keep them as even as the rest of the wall. If the plaster is too thin, you can always go back and dab corners with a small paint brush later. When you've finished the room, let this coat dry for 24 hours before moving to the next step. The job will look a bit sloppy at this stage, so don't be disappointed. The final steps will bring the walls to life.

FINISHED FIRST COAT

4 Finish one wall section at a time. Go back after each section and remove any blotches thicker than 1/8 in. before they dry.

VOIDS IN FIRST COAT

SECOND COAT

45° ANGLE OR MORE

5 Trowel on the second coat once the first is thoroughly dry. Again using random strokes, fill in the voids where the undercoat shows, turning the knife from left to right and then from right to left.

400-GRIT
SANDPAPER

6 Sand the second coat (once it has dried 24 hours) with 400-grit sandpaper to remove heavy ridges. Each area the size shown needs about one minute of vigorous sanding. Rub down the entire surface with clean, dry cotton cloths.

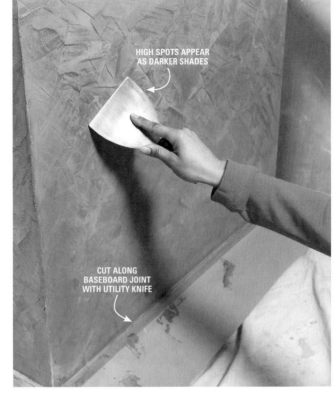

HIGH SPOTS APPEAR
AS DARKER SHADES

CUT ALONG
BASEBOARD JOINT
WITH UTILITY KNIFE

7 Pull the knife briskly over the surface in long, bold strokes to smooth the high spots, create a luster and darken areas to develop contrast and character.

SANDING AND BURNISHING CREATE VISUAL DEPTH

Sand the walls with 400-grit sandpaper clamped into a stiff rubber sanding block **(Photo 6)**—just fold a full sheet into thirds and then put it into the block. As you sand (wear a dust mask), you'll see the character in the finish develop as the foreground appears lighter and the background stays a bit darker. Keep sanding until you get a uniform appearance. Don't worry about sanding through the plaster finish because the paper is very fine. Change sandpaper as the sheets wear out or clog. You'll need about four sheets for an entire room. Wipe all the sanded areas with clean, dry cloths to remove the residue, and then vacuum the floor and sanded areas with a brush attachment.

Now it's time to burnish the surface **(Photo 7)** with your steel drywall knife. Start anywhere, holding the knife at a 30-degree angle to the wall. Pull the knife blade along the wall firmly with long, bold strokes. The direction isn't particularly important; just be sure you go over each square foot of wall several times. The high spots of the thin texture will get a bit darker and polished as you move along the wall from one end to the other. You'll start to see three distinct levels of color from the background to the foreground. Once you've finished the wall, remove the masking tape slowly **(Photo 8)** and get ready to apply your chair rail molding.

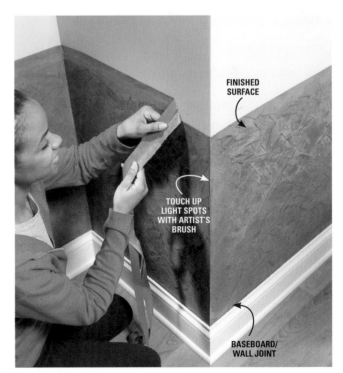

FINISHED
SURFACE

TOUCH UP
LIGHT SPOTS
WITH ARTIST'S
BRUSH

BASEBOARD/
WALL JOINT

8 Pull the painter's masking tape gently from the wall to avoid lifting the paint beneath. Using your utility knife, carefully cut the texture along the joint where the baseboard meets the wall (see Photo 7). This will allow you to easily peel back the tape.

Part Two: Urethane Chair Rail

URETHANE CHAIR RAIL AND MOLDINGS

Urethane moldings are both lightweight and easy to apply, making them a great alternative to wood molding. In this story, we used them for a chair rail and window trim.

The manufacturer recommends cutting the molding about 1/4 in. overlong for long runs (12 to 16 ft.) to help make up for seasonal wall expansion. The molding will compress slightly and snap into place. Shorter lengths to 8 ft. should be cut about 1/8 in. overlong, and anything less than 4 ft. should be cut to fit. When splicing long lengths, the company also recommends butting crosscut ends together instead of bevel-cutting moldings at mid-wall joints. The molding is applied just like wood molding, but it cuts and nails easier.

Set the molding in your miter box (screw the miter box down to your sawhorse or worktable) and, as you hold the molding firmly with your other hand, cut it on your mark with slow, steady strokes. Support long ends with additional sawhorses. Don't bother coping joints in corners; just lay the molding on its backside and cut at 45 degrees for inside and outside corners **(Photo 2)**. Nails alone won't do—use the polyurethane adhesive caulk and nails to bond the molding to the wall to make up for the low density **(Photo 3)**.

Fill nail holes with spackling compound and then wipe the surface clean with a damp rag **(Photo 4)**. This process will take two coats. Sand urethane molding as little as possible because, unlike wood, the factory finish on the urethane molding is thin. Because you'll be painting the molding, you can touch up joints with acrylic caulk and wipe the excess away with a damp rag. You can save yourself a lot of time by prepainting the molding and then touching it up after you've cut and installed it.

PRO TIP

To widen your miter box as shown in **Photo 1**, use a hammer to tap the sides free of the original base. Drill pilot holes and screw the sides to the new base. With the wider base, you'll be able to crosscut and bevel-cut the moldings. However, the other miter operations won't be possible since the precut slots will no longer line up. This won't be a problem for cutting the moldings we show here.

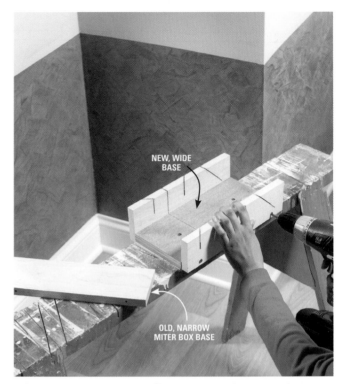

1 Hand miter boxes and fine-tooth hand saws are best for cutting urethane moldings. The moldings, however, are often wider than the miter box bed. Widen the bed by removing the screws on the side of the box and adding a wider base. See pro tip below left.

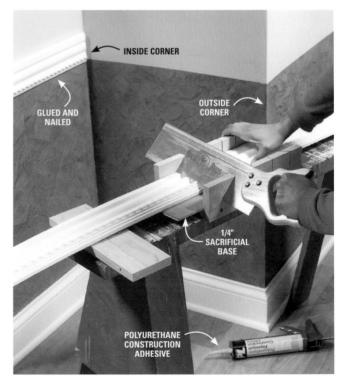

2 Measure the length, then cut the moldings with 45-degree bevel cuts in the corners. Glue backsides and joints with polyurethane molding adhesive.

Labels on image: SET NAIL HEADS, 6d FINISH NAIL, FILL VOIDS WITH ACRYLIC CAULK

3 Glue and nail the moldings to the wall. Make small reference marks along the wall with your level to make sure you keep the molding straight as you nail. Set the nails with a nail set.

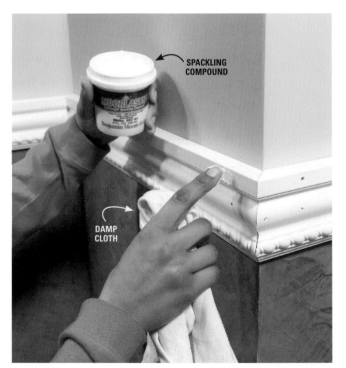

Labels on image: SPACKLING COMPOUND, DAMP CLOTH

4 Fill the nail holes with spackling compound and the joints with acrylic caulk, then wipe with a slightly damp cloth. You'll need a second application once the spackling compound and caulk are dry. Wipe smooth or lightly sand, then paint.

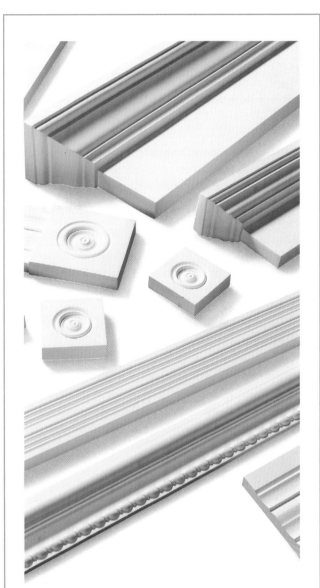

Buying Urethane Moldings

Home centers and lumberyards carry a selection of urethane moldings. They come in a wide variety of preprimed profiles and sizes for windows, doors, crown moldings and decorative panels. While they aren't cheap, they cost less than decorative wood moldings with the same profiles. To see all your options, go to the help desk. There you can order moldings to suit your taste. The moldings shown here are only a small sample.

For more information on urethane molding options, go to focalpointproducts.com or call (800) 543-0553 to find a dealer in your area. You can also check with fypon.com or call (800) 446-3040.

Weekend Wainscoting

Achieve traditional elegance with home-center materials.

For this room, we wanted a frame-and-panel wainscoting that would match the doors and traditional trim—well, we wanted it until we saw the price tag. That's when we came up with a design we could make quickly and cheaply, using stock material.

Here's the basic idea. The frame is made from 1/2-in. MDF; this thickness makes a better transition where the wainscoting meets the door or window trim. Instead of a traditional panel, the frame has rectangular openings, through which you see the wall. This gives some interesting options: another paint color (our choice), a decorative paint texture like rag-rolling, or even wallpaper. Moldings frame the openings and also form the cap along the top edge.

Wainscoting has to be fit to the length of your walls, so we can't give you complete dimensions here. You'll have to adjust the width of the openings so that they're the same all along the wall. The simplest way is to figure out how many openings fit along the wall. Then take the leftover and spread it out between them. Draw your proposed wainscoting on the wall to check your layout.

Once you have a layout that works, cut your MDF and moldings. Prime all the parts, then nail the MDF to the wall. Attach to studs if possible, or use a little construction adhesive and nail at an angle to give some grip. Attach all the moldings, fill the nail holes and then paint. That's all there is to it!

FIGURE A.
UPPER RAIL CONSTRUCTION

FIGURE B.
WAINSCOTING CONSTRUCTION

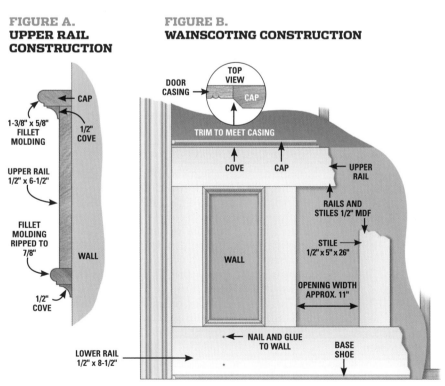

CAP

1-3/8" x 5/8" FILLET MOLDING

1/2" COVE

UPPER RAIL 1/2" x 6-1/2"

FILLET MOLDING RIPPED TO 7/8"

WALL

1/2" COVE

TOP VIEW

DOOR CASING

CAP

TRIM TO MEET CASING

COVE

CAP

UPPER RAIL

RAILS AND STILES 1/2" MDF

STILE 1/2" x 5" x 26"

WALL

OPENING WIDTH APPROX. 11"

NAIL AND GLUE TO WALL

BASE SHOE

LOWER RAIL 1/2" x 8-1/2"

You say tomato, I say tomahto; you say potato, I say potahto. Wainscoating, wainscotting, wainscoat and wainscott— let's call the whole thing off!

(With apologies to George and Ira Gershwin. And for the record, even dictionary gurus can't agree on which version is correct.)

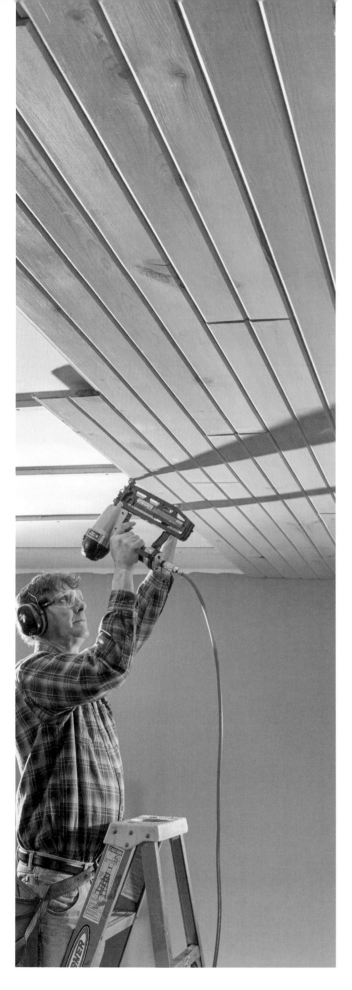

Installing T&G Boards

Our top 10 tips make the process foolproof.

Installing tongue-and-groove (aka T&G) boards is a fast, inexpensive way to panel any ceiling or wall. You can install T&G over bare framing, drywall or plaster, so it's a great cover-up for any ugly ceiling.

Most of the T&G boards you'll find at home centers and lumberyards are 1x6 or 1x8 spruce. But other wood options and sizes can be special-ordered. Some boards are rough on one face and smooth on the other. Others, like the 1x8 boards used in this story, have a groove down the middle of one face to give the impression of additional narrower boards. Most stores carry 1x4 beaded ceiling board as well. The tips here apply to any of the styles.

1. FINISH BEFORE INSTALLATION

Tongue-and-groove boards are notorious for shrinking and expanding with changes in temperature and humidity. Unfinished boards installed in humid summer conditions can be an ugly mess during the dryness of winter. As the wood dries and shrinks, unfinished stripes will appear where the tongues withdraw from the grooves. But if you apply finish before installation, the tongues will be completely finished—no unfinished stripes will appear later!

2. START WITH BATTENS ON FINISHED CEILINGS

If you're installing T&G over drywall (or plaster especially), it's a good idea to install 1x2 battens and fasten them directly to the framing with 2-1/2-in. screws. Battens will give you a much more solid nailing surface. If you try to nail through the T&G and the drywall, you can't be sure the nail will penetrate far enough to hold securely. Also, the battens will somewhat flatten out uneven ceilings. Another plus: You can run the battens either parallel or perpendicular to the ceiling framing, depending on which way you want the T&G to run.

3. PREP THE ENDS

Recut the ends of every board. You'll remove staples left over from shipping wrap, cut away any splits and get clean, square edges. One of the best tricks to get a professional-looking installation is to add a 45-degree bevel, called a chamfer. This technique is called V-grooving. The V-groove will mask small inconsistencies in butt joints. You can either apply finish to the raw wood on each chamfer before nailing up each board or touch up the entire ceiling after it's finished.

4. BLIND-NAIL THE TONGUES

Always plan your work so that the tongues point toward the direction of installation. One of the cool things about T&G is that you can use a technique called blind-nailing. If you do it properly, you won't have any nail heads showing or holes to fill. Drive the nails through the shoulders of the tongues into the framing at about a 45-degree angle. The next grooved edge will hide the nail holes. A 15- or 16-gauge brad nailer with 2-in. nails is the best choice for fastening, although an 18-gauge nailer will do the job too.

1x2 BATTEN

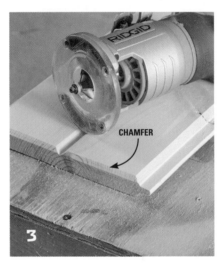

CHAMFER

5. BEAT THEM IN!

Installing T&G can be a real workout. Think about it: (1) You're usually working over your head. (2) You have to seat the tongues and grooves together, and they don't always want to marry. (3) T&G isn't always flat, so you have to force the boards together to get them seated. The best way to do that is also the fastest way: Use the side of the nailer to tap (and sometimes pound) the boards together. If you start crushing the tongue too badly to get the next board seated, grab a short chunk of waste to use as a sacrificial board. But don't beat yourself up trying to preserve a pristine tongue—it gets buried in the joint anyway.

6. STAGGER BUTT JOINTS

There's no reason to try to join butt joints directly over framing members. The butt joints can fall anywhere because the tongue-and-groove joints support one another. Plus, if you cut the boards so they fall directly over framing, you'll waste a lot of material. Instead, choose lengths so that the joints look as random as possible.

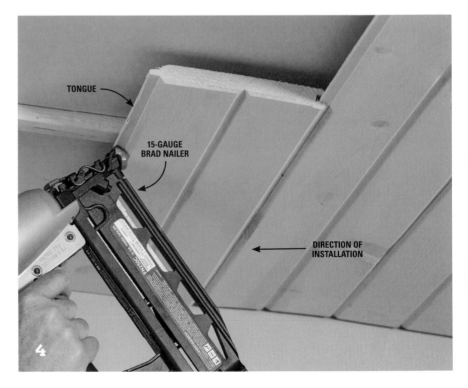

TONGUE

15-GAUGE BRAD NAILER

DIRECTION OF INSTALLATION

7. SNEAK UP ON CUTOUTS

It's really tricky to accurately mark cutouts for electrical boxes and other ceiling openings on T&G. The secret is to scribe and/or mark as much as possible in place on the ceiling rather than to try to measure everything perfectly beforehand. After you draw the opening **(Photos 7A-7C)**, make the cut with a jigsaw and test-fit the board. If it doesn't fit, you can tweak the cut. But if you really blew it, don't sweat it. Just cut out the bad spot, use the parts elsewhere and take another swing at it. You'll be wasting only a few inches of material.

A. Hold the board in place next to the box and mark the sides.

B. Mark the front and back of the box on a scrap.

C. Transfer those marks to the board and lightly draw a square. Draw the opening using another box as a pattern.

8. BREAK OFF THE GROOVE FLANGES

On any installation, you'll have times when you can't fit the groove in the previous tongue to seat the board. In fact, it's almost always the case with the very last board. But it can also happen at ceiling protrusions or even at projecting inside corners.

The only option is to eliminate the back of the groove so you can lift the board directly into place without locking the joint together. The easiest way to do this is to break off the flange with a few hammer raps. These pieces can't be blind-nailed—you'll have to face-nail them and fill a few nail heads.

9. CLOSE THE END JOINTS

Once you get a board seated, go ahead and add a nail or two. But before you permanently nail the entire piece, check the butt end to make sure it's tight against the neighboring board. If there's a gap, tap on the end with a block to close it. Then finish nailing the board.

10. CUT PROBLEM BOARDS SHORTER

Don't fight warped, twisted or bowed boards; cut them shorter. In fact, it's OK to install boards that are only a couple of feet long. They'll look great, and you won't waste any expensive wood.

Beam & Panel Ceiling

This quick, inexpensive way to transform a room is also a beautiful cover-up for damaged ceilings.

Paneling a ceiling is a great way to add character to a plain room. And if the existing ceiling is cracked or water-stained and in need of a makeover, all the better. Covering it with panels and beams is more elegant and less expensive than hiring a pro to restore a damaged ceiling to its original condition.

A paneled ceiling like this normally calls for expensive tools and lots of carpentry skill, but we designed this project to be DIY-friendly. It's made easy by a homemade circular saw ripping jig, the installation of a simple 2x4 framework

and miter-free joinery **(Figure A)**. The visible finished material over the framework is MDF. It's inexpensive, readily available at home centers, and smooth and easy to work with. However, cutting, sanding and routing MDF is extremely dusty, so do all your power tool work outside or at least in the garage with the overhead door open, and be sure to wear a dust mask.

While the ease of construction is a big plus, the real beauty of this project is the low cost of the materials—and the expensive-looking results.

WHICH CEILINGS ARE CANDIDATES?

Our system is ideal for dressing up any ceiling—whether it's damaged or perfect, textured or flat, drywall or plaster. If your ceiling is flat and in good shape, you can omit the MDF panels, then simply paint the ceiling and apply the grid work and trim right over the existing material. But keep in mind that you'll have to make the side trim strips 1/2 in. wider to account for the missing panel thicknesses.

The nine-panel pattern works for rooms up to 13 ft. wide and 33 ft. long. The use of materials is efficient and the shape of the panel will automatically be proportional to the shape of the room. A square room will have square panels; a rectangular room will have rectangular panels.

LAYING OUT THE GRID

The first step in laying out the grid work is to chalk lines around the room's perimeter, 4-1/2 in. away

FIGURE A.
CEILING CROSS SECTION

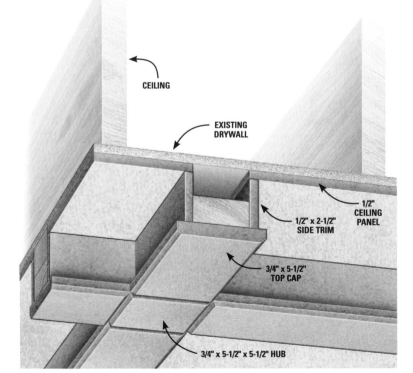

CEILING

EXISTING DRYWALL

1/2" CEILING PANEL

1/2" x 2-1/2" SIDE TRIM

3/4" x 5-1/2" TOP CAP

3/4" x 5-1/2" x 5-1/2" HUB

Three Shortcuts Make It DIY-Friendly

1. **Miter-free joints:** There is no such thing as a miter on this project. Every end joint is a straightforward square cut. Just get the length right, cut at 90 degrees on your miter saw, and all the joints will look like a million bucks.
2. **Chamfered edges:** Small 45-degree chamfers routed on the edges of the exposed trim hide all but the worst imperfections.
3. **Overhangs:** The vertical side trim overhangs the ceiling panels to hide any sloppy cuts. And the caps overhang the side trim, so small gaps there will be hidden as well.

from the walls. That will allow the full 5-1/2-in. cap to fit against the wall and match the rest of the finished trim. Then measure the length and width of the space inside. It's up to you how many panels to use and how big to make them. Most average-size rooms work well with nine panels. In other words, divide both room dimensions by three. You'll be able to have perfect square panels only if the room is square. Otherwise, you'll have rectangles, which is fine—they'll look great as long as they're all a consistent size. And you can always make the panels exactly the same size. Make them as large or as small as you wish, as long as they're under 4 ft. wide and 8 ft. long—which is as much as the sheets will allow.

Once you figure out the panel sizes, snap the grid layout on the ceiling **(Photo 1)**. To avoid some confusing math (accounting for the width of the 2x4 grid), just snap center lines to lay out the grid and then snap lines 1-3/4 in. on both sides to mark the outsides of the 2x4s. At this point it's a good idea to snap lines marking all the ceiling joists, so you'll know where to put the fasteners for the grid and ceiling panels.

ATTACH THE GRID FRAMING

Start by screwing on the uppermost layer of 2x4s oriented perpendicular to the ceiling joists **(Photo 2)** with 3-in. screws. That way you'll have great support. Toe-screw the ends through the drywall into the wall top plates. Next, screw 2x4s in the opposite direction with two screws at each intersection **(Photo 3)**. Lastly, add a second layer of short 2x4s over the 2x4s against the ceiling. That will give you a continuous flat surface for the caps and hubs **(Photo 4 and Figure A)**.

CUT AND INSTALL THE PANELS

Cut the panels 1/2 in. shorter than the grid openings to make them easy

STAINS FROM
BATHROOM
DISASTER

1 Mark out the beam pattern with chalk lines. Then make it easy on yourself by marking the joists with a different color chalk.

JOIST
DIRECTION

2 Screw 2x4s to the ceiling, perpendicular to the joist direction, with a couple of 3-in. screws into each joist.

You've Got Options

If you love a natural look, you can panel your ceiling with any type of wood and still use the techniques we show. Use painted MDF for the panels and solid natural wood for the beams, or go all out and use matching veneered plywood for the panels. To save money when you use this technique, rip plywood for the side trim pieces. That'll look fine since the plywood edges will be hidden. You can also use any type of wallpaper or covering on the panels, or on the existing ceiling drywall if it's in good shape.

WALLPAPER
OVER
DRYWALL

MDF

PAINTED
MDF

CHERRY

to slip into place. Cut them to width first and set aside the 8-ft.-long waste pieces to use for trim caps and hubs. Then cut them to length. You can just snap chalk lines and cut the panels freehand since the side trim pieces will hide imperfections. Then roll on a stain-blocking primer (KILZ and B-I-N are two brands) with a 3/8-in.-nap roller sleeve. If you're working alone, make yourself a support crutch **(Photo 4)** to hold the panels tight

3 Screw the overlapping 2x4s to the first ones at each intersection. Fill the spaces between the lower 2x4s to complete the grid work. Space screws every 16 in.

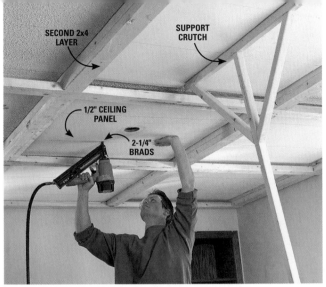

SECOND 2x4 LAYER

SUPPORT CRUTCH

1/2" CEILING PANEL

2-1/4" BRADS

4 Cut the panels to size, prime them and then nail them through the drywall into the joists.

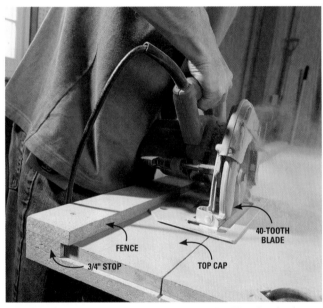

40-TOOTH BLADE

TOP CAP

FENCE

3/4" STOP

5 Rip the top cap trim using a ripping jig. The simple three-part jig gives you straight cuts and perfect widths.

TAPE UNDER TRIM

CEILING PANEL

2" BRADS

SIDE TRIM

6 Nail the side trim to the framing. Paint and mask the panels with painter's tape first to avoid fuss when you paint the trim.

against the ceiling while you nail them into each joist with 2-1/4-in. nails spaced every 8 in.

Fill the nail holes with wood filler. Sand down any excess filler and surface imperfections. Spot-prime those areas, then roll on two coats of latex paint.

MAKE A TRIM CUTTING JIG

MDF panels are heavy—90 lbs. for a 3/4-in. sheet! So even if you have a table saw, you're better off cutting side trim and caps with a ripping jig (**Photos 5 and 9**) and a circular saw.

Here's how to make jig setups (**see Figures B and C**) that will accurately cut the trim pieces you need for the ceiling:

1. Rip an 8-ft.-long, 3-in.-wide fence for a top cap ripping jig.
2. Rip one 2-1/2-in.-wide stop out of 1/2-in. material for ripping the trim strips for the side trim, and a 3/4-in.-thick stop for ripping the caps and hubs. Rip the stop and fence from the edges of new sheets, and always face the factory edges toward the saw for straight, true guide surfaces.

3. Screw each stop to the jig base with countersunk 1-1/4-in. screws spaced every 12 in., and then screw the fence to each stop wherever it needs to be to match the width you're ripping.

The key to both jig setups is the distance from the left side of your circular saw's base to the edge of the saw blade. That distance will determine fence placement.

You'll have to set up the ripping jig twice with two different fence locations and the stop that matches the thickness of the material you're cutting

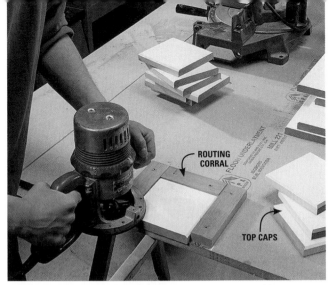

7 Cut the hubs to length, then rout the edges using a corral tacked to your workbench to safely hold the small pieces in place.

8 Center and nail the hubs at each intersection. Don't forget to prime the freshly routed edges.

9 Use the top cap ripping jig to hold the caps in place while you rout the edges. Cut them to length and nail them to the grid with 2-in. brads.

10 Patch the nail holes, lightly sand, spot-prime and then paint the grid-work trim.

FIGURE B.
TOP CAP AND HUB JIG

FIGURE C.
SIDE TRIM JIG

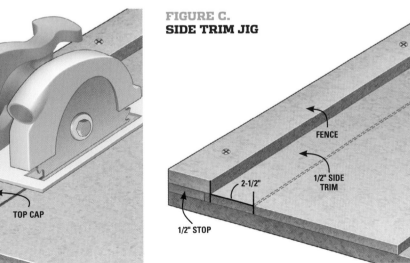
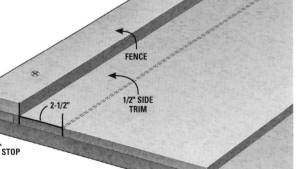

(1/2-in.-thick side trim or 3/4-in.-thick caps and hubs). The base of the jig is the same for both jig setups—a 1/2-in. or 3/4-in. sheet of any flat sheet goods. Or use one of the MDF sheets and make panels with it later. Hubs are cut from the 5-1/2-in. cap strips, so while you still have the jig set up, make sure you rip enough stock for those too.

CUT, PAINT AND INSTALL THE HUBS AND CAPS

Cut the side trim pieces to length and nail them to the grid sides **(Photo 6)**. Figure out roughly how long the caps will be, and cut and rout the hubs from the extra material. Sand off any saw blade marks on the edges of the cap stock and rout those edges **(Photos 7 and 9)**. Prime the pieces. Then nail on the hubs **(Photo 8)**. Cut each top cap to length. Chamfer the ends and nail each into place. Patch, sand, prime and paint the grid-work trim **(Photo 10)**. Then peel away the trim tape **(Photo 11)**, and you're done!

11 After you paint the trim, slice through the tape at the inside corners and peel it away.

Improve Your Lighting

Since you're covering the drywall with panels, this is a great time to add or move ceiling light fixtures. If you have a floor above, just cut channels in the drywall and drill holes through the middle of joists, or staple the cables on the sides of joists to get the cables to the new electrical boxes or recessed light canisters. If you have an attic above, you'll have to crawl up there to run the cables. Just remember that when you mount the new boxes, they should be flush with the finished MDF surface. You'll need to add 1/2-in.-deep plaster rings to existing boxes before you install the finished ceiling.

DIY Success Story

When Brian Dohrwardt added a small second-floor bathroom, he ran into a big problem. The undersized floor joists didn't allow a path for the drain lines (drilling 4-in. holes through 7-in. joists is a recipe for floor collapse!). His only option was a bad one: He had to run the pipes under the floor joists and along the ceiling of the dining room below. But those ugly, exposed pipes inspired a beautiful solution. Brian built false, hollow beams to enclose the pipes. The resulting coffered ceiling is the best feature of his home, Brian tells us.

Make Old Windows Like New

Don't replace aging casement windows—repair them!

If you're thinking about replacing your casement windows (the type that open like doors) because they're drafty, fogged up or just hard to open, consider this: You can fix most of the problems yourself for a fraction of the cost of new windows—and it won't take you more than an hour or two per window.

In this story, we'll walk through fixes for the most common casement window problems. You won't need any specialty tools, and materials are available from most window supply companies. Although your windows may look different from the ones shown here **(see Figure A)**, the techniques for removing the sash and fixing problems are similar.

REPLACE A STUBBORN CRANK OPERATOR

If the splines on the crank operator shaft are worn or broken off and the gears don't turn easily or at all, then it's time to replace the crank operator (about $17).

You don't need the make, model or serial number of the crank operator to replace it. You just need a picture. Snap a digital photo, send it in an email to a hardware supply company and the company will sell you a new one. You can also look at online catalogs to find an operator that matches yours.

To replace the operator, you'll first need to take the crank arm off the sash. Most crank arms slip out of a notch on the guide track on the sash **(Photo 1)**. Others need to be pried off with a flathead screwdriver, or a channel is unscrewed from along the bottom of the sash. If the operator also contains a split arm operator, be sure to unhook that too **(Photo 2)**.

FIGURE A.
CASEMENT WINDOW OPERATION

When you turn the handle, the operator moves the crank arm and the split arm operator. The split arm operator then opens the window sash. Casement window operators come in several styles. They may look complex, but they're easy to disconnect, remove and replace.

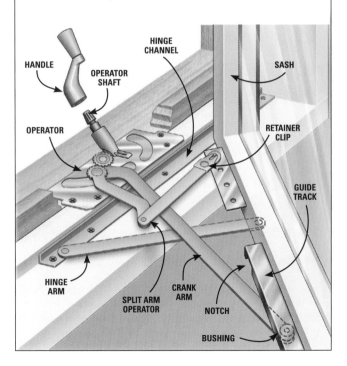

1 Open the window until the crank arm bushing is aligned with the guide track notch. Push down on the arm to pop the bushing out of the track.

2 Slide back the retainer clip on the split arm and pry the arm off the stud on the sash bracket with a screwdriver.

3 Lift off the casement cover to expose the crank operator. Remove the screws, take out the crank operator and replace it.

Slide or pry off the operator cover. If you have a removable cover, cut along the casement cover with a utility knife to slice through any paint or stain that seals it on the window jamb. Remove the trim screws along the top of the casement cover. Gently pry the cover loose **(Photo 3)**. Be careful—the cover can easily break! Unscrew the crank operator. Set the new operator in place, aligning it with the existing screw holes, and screw it to the jamb. If the cover isn't removable, crank operator screws will be accessible on the exterior of the window.

Fix a Stripped Crank Handle

If you turn your window handle and nothing happens, the gears on your handle, crank operator shaft or both are probably stripped. Take off the handle and look for signs of wear. If the teeth are worn, replace the handle (prices start at $5). If the shaft is worn, you can replace the whole operator (see "Replace a Stubborn Crank Operator," p. 105). But here's a home remedy to try first.

Start by backing out the setscrew to remove the handle (some newer handles don't have setscrews and simply pull off—if so, this fix won't work). If you have a folding handle, mark where the setscrew is on the operator shaft when the window is closed and the handle is folded up. Remove the handle and file the shaft so the setscrew can lock onto the shaft **(photo below)**. The metal is tough; it'll take about 15 minutes to get a flat side. Or use a rotary tool with a grinder bit to speed up the job. Vacuum the shavings out of the operator so they won't harm the moving parts.

Reattach the handle with a longer setscrew (less than $1 at hardware stores). But if you open and close the window a lot, this fix may not hold up in the long run.

Replace a Sagging Hinge

Over time, hinge arms that support heavy windows can start to sag, causing the sash to hit the frame in the lower corner that's opposite the hinge. First make sure the window sash is square and centered in the window opening. If it's not, see "Fix a Sticking Window" below. To eliminate drag in a window that fits squarely, replace the hinge arms at the top and the bottom of the window. You can buy the hinges at window hardware supply stores.

Remove the sash from the window. The hinge arms are located near a corner or in the middle of the window frame. Unscrew the hinge arms from the window, then install the new ones in the same locations **(photo below)**.

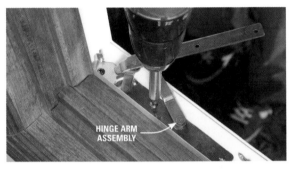

Align the new hinge arm with the screw holes and fasten it into place. If the screw holes are stripped out, fill them with toothpicks dipped in wood glue, let the glue dry, then cut the toothpicks flush.

FIX A STICKING WINDOW

If you have a window that drags against the frame when you open it, close the window and examine it from the outside. The sash should fit squarely and be centered in the frame. If it is not, you can adjust the position of the sash by slightly moving the hinge channel. (If the window is centered and square but still drags, see the next fix.)

You can move the channel at the top or the bottom of the window, depending on where the sash is dragging (but don't move both channels). Start by taking out the sash **(Photos 1 and 2)**. If the hinge arm is screwed to the sash, see **Photo 1, p. 108**.

Mark the hinge channel location on the frame, then unscrew the channel. Fill the screw holes with epoxy (for vinyl windows) or wood filler (for wood windows). Filling the holes keeps the screws from realigning with their old locations when you reinstall the channel. Scrape the filled holes smooth before the epoxy sets. Place the channel back on the jamb, about 1/8 in. over from the mark (move the channel away from the side of the sash that's dragging), drill 1/8-in. pilot holes and then reinstall the channel **(Photo 3)**.

1 Open the sash and disconnect the crank arm. Pry the split arm operator off the top and the bottom of the sash with a screwdriver (the hinge arm will easily pop off).

2 Slide the hinge shoes out of the hinge channels at the top and bottom of the window to remove the sash.

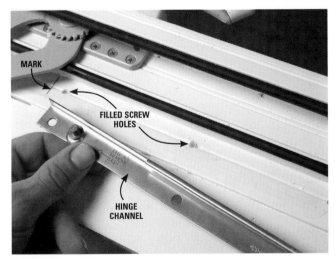

3 Set the hinge channel in place, slightly over from its former location. Drill new holes, then screw it to the jamb.

REPLACE A FOGGED SASH

If you have broken glass or fogging (condensation between the glass panes), you'll have to replace the glass or the entire sash. If the sash is in good shape (that is, not warped or cracked), you can sometimes get away with replacing just the glass. Call your window manufacturer to see whether glass replacement is an option and if a fogged window is covered under your warranty. You'll need the information that's etched into the corner of the glass and the sash dimensions.

You can contact a local glass repair specialist to have only the glass replaced. If you're looking to save a bit of money, you can order a replacement sash through the manufacturer and do the work yourself.

To replace the sash, first remove the old one. The sash here was taken off by removing the hinge screws **(Photo 1)**. For sashes that slide out, see **Photos 1 and 2, p. 107**. Remove any hardware from the damaged sash and install it on the new sash (this sash doesn't require any hardware).

Install the new sash by sliding it onto the hinge arms, then screw it to the hinges **(Photo 2)**.

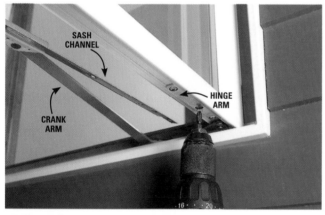

1 Take off the sash by removing the screws in the channel and the hinge arms. Then slide the sash off the hinge arms.

2 Align the sash lip with the hinge arms, then slide the sash onto the hinges. Insert screws to fasten the sash in place.

Seal a Drafty Window

Weather stripping often becomes loose, worn or distorted when the sash drags or when the strip gets sticky and attaches itself to the frame, then pulling loose when the sash is opened. Windows have weather strip on the sash, frame or both. Regardless of its location, the steps for removing and replacing it are the same. Weather stripping is available from your window manufacturer (prices start at $15). The window brand and glass manufacturer date are etched in the corner of the glass or in the aluminum spacer between the glass panes. You'll also need the height and width of your sash (take these measurements yourself).

If the weather strip is in good shape and loose in only a few places, like the corners, apply a dab of polyurethane sealant ($5 at hardware stores) to the groove and press the weather strip into place. Otherwise, replace the entire weather strip. First remove the sash and set it on a work surface so you can access all four sides. If the weather strip is one continuous piece, cut it apart at the corners with a utility knife.

Starting at a corner, pull the weather strip loose from the sash **(photo below)**. If the spline tears off and remains stuck in the groove, make a hook from stiff wire to dig it out.

Work the new weather strip into the groove, starting at a corner. You'll hear it click as the strip slides into the groove.

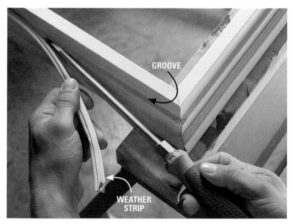

Work the old weather strip out of the groove gently to avoid tearing it and leaving the spline stuck in the groove.

Is the Window Glued Shut?

If the window is stuck shut, it's likely that the weather strip is sticking. After you muscle it open, spray silicone lubricant on a rag and wipe it on the weather stripping. Silicone lubricants from brands such as DuPont are widely available. Don't use oily lubricants; they attract dust.

Classic Trim, the Easy Way

Low cost. Low stress. High style.

You'll find a classic trim style that looks similar to this in many century-old houses. But that's where the similarity ends. Old-school carpenters carefully cut and fit mitered returns at the ends of the window aprons and crown moldings to create these classic profiles.

You could reproduce this look with wood moldings and a good bit of patience. But if you're going to paint, why not follow our lead and make your own moldings from medium-density fiberboard? MDF is easy to cut and shape, and it paints up beautifully. And even better, by cutting the parts to length first and routing the shapes around the corners, you eliminate all the fussy miters.

In this article, we'll show you how to make classic trim using three router bits. You can follow our pattern exactly or create your own using router bits you may already have. If you've never used a router, this is a great introduction to the tool. Since MDF is relatively cheap, a goof here or there won't cost much.

We'll show you how to make trim for windows and doors. Since most home centers and lumberyards stock at least one choice of primed, wide baseboard, we won't show how to make base. But if you prefer, you can use the techniques shown here to make your own baseboard too.

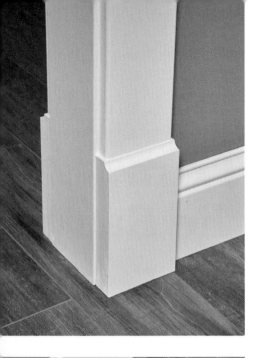

The World's Easiest Trim?

Assemble the parts, then just nail them up!

Don't let the elegant look fool you. This trim is actually easier than the standard "picture frame" trim used in most homes since the 1950s. There are no fussy miters to give you fits, just simple 90-degree butt joints. You can do most of the assembly on a workbench and then simply nail the parts to the walls. And since the trim is painted, you can hide small gaps with caulk.

OLD TRIM

1 **REMOVE THE OLD WINDOW AND DOOR TRIM. Pry off the old trim and pull out any nails remaining in the doorjambs and window jambs. If there's a** ridge of paint or finish on the face of the jambs, sand it smooth to prepare for the new trim.

TIME AND MATERIALS

For this project, you'll need 1/2-in.- and 3/4-in.-thick MDF, and some paintable 1x3 lumber for the stools. We recommend wood for the stool because, unlike MDF, it'll withstand a little moisture from window condensation. We used pine, but poplar, maple and birch would also work well. You can figure out how much material you need using your cutting list, but as a rough estimate you can cut parts for about four or five windows from one 4 x 8-ft. sheet of MDF. MDF is heavy, and full sheets are hard to handle. Ask to have the sheets cut in half lengthwise at the home center. See the Materials List on p. 114.

GETTING STARTED

After you pry off the old moldings, the first step is to measure all the openings and create a cutting list and a shopping list **(Photos 1 and 2)**. If you're careful to do the math right, it's easy to create the cutting list by simply adding to the widths of the openings.

In the Cutting List for a Window on p. 114, we show how much to add to the width inside the jamb for each part of the apron, stool and head casing assemblies. The fraction-heavy math can get time consuming. If you have several openings to trim out, consider downloading a construction calculator app on your smartphone to help.

Make a complete and accurate list of all the parts for every window and door. This will save you time by allowing you to rout the shape on all similar parts before moving to a new router bit and work surface setup.

CUT THE PARTS

Using your cutting list as a guide, rip strips of MDF on a table saw **(Photo 3)**. Cutting MDF creates tons of fine dust, so wear a mask and, if possible, move your cutting and routing operations outdoors. If you must cut indoors, put an exhaust fan in the window and connect a shop vac to your saw. Our router included a

2 **MEASURE BETWEEN THE JAMBS.** Make a list of the windows and doors that need new trim. Then measure the width between the jambs and write these measurements on your list.

3 **CUT STRIPS OF MDF.** Use the list of parts you created to calculate how many feet of each trim piece you'll need. Then cut the sheet of MDF into the correct number of strips. It's a good idea to add about 20% to your totals to allow for waste and mistakes. Use a miter saw to cut these strips to the correct lengths. Make sure to label all your parts with a corresponding window or door number.

4 **ROUT THE LONG EDGES.** Find a large, flat work surface that you can screw into. Attach a stop and a backer board to the work surface as shown above. Make sure the trim overhangs the work surface slightly to allow room for the router bit guide bearing.

MDF MOLDING

STOP

APRON

5 ROUT THE ENDS. Sandwich the trim piece between strips of MDF to hold the trim in place and provide a level surface for the router. Carefully align the ends of the trim piece and two strips of MDF, making sure the ends protrude past the work surface slightly to allow room for the router bit guide bearing. Screw the strips to the work surface. Then attach a stop behind the trim piece to hold it in place. Run the router from left to right across the trim to shape the end. Then flip the trim end-for-end and rout the shape on the opposite end.

6 ROUT THE APRONS. Rip two lengths of 2x4 to the same width as the lower window apron (3 in.) and screw them together. Toe-screw the 2x4s to the work surface and clamp the lower window apron part to the 2x4s. Now you can easily shape both ends and the long edge with the router. The 2x4s provide the support needed to hold the router level as you rout the narrow ends.

vacuum cleaner hose attachment port. If yours doesn't, you may be able to buy an attachment that fits your router.

After ripping the parts, cut them to length on a miter saw. Label the parts as you go to avoid confusion later. If your table saw leaves saw marks along the edge of the MDF strips, be sure to sand them smooth. The guide bearings on the router bits follow along the edges, and if they are bumpy or rough, the shape you rout won't be smooth either.

SHAPE THE EDGES

We used a handheld router with router bits that included a guide bearing. With this method, you move the router over the pieces to shape the edges. You could also mount your router in a router table. For information on how to build and use a router table, go to familyhandyman.com and search for "router table."

Shaping the long edges of your trim pieces with a router is straightforward. But you need a way to hold the piece steady as you shape it, and the edge

has to overhang your work surface slightly to allow room for the guide bearing. **Photo 4** shows one easy setup to achieve these two goals.

Mount your router bit in the router and set the depth. Test the depth setting on a scrap of MDF and adjust it if needed. Using the setup shown in **Photo 4**, move the router left to right. Relocate the backer board for the different width pieces and switch to a 1/2-in.-thick MDF support board for

shaping the fillet **(see Photo 7)**. Be sure to recess the screws that hold the support boards so they don't interfere with the router base.

Routing the shapes on the ends of the fillet, crown, stool and upper apron pieces is tricky because the narrow trim pieces don't provide enough support for the router. You can solve this problem by sandwiching the piece you're routing between MDF strips **(Photo 5)**. You'll have to relocate the

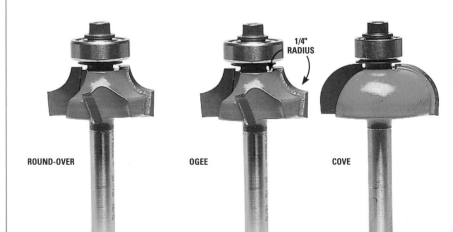

Basic router bits are the key tools for this job. Using just cove, round-over and classic ogee bits mounted in a router, you can shape the edges of inexpensive MDF to make the parts for a classic trim makeover.

1/4" RADIUS

ROUND-OVER   OGEE   COVE

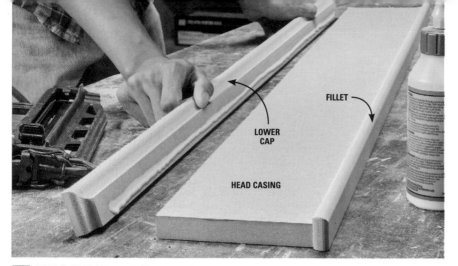

7 BUILD THE HEAD CASING ASSEMBLY. Collect the four parts for the head casing (**Figure A**) and arrange them on your work surface. Spread glue along meeting edges and pin them together with 1-1/2-in. trim nails. Before nailing them together, make sure to align the parts so the end reveals (overhangs) are even.

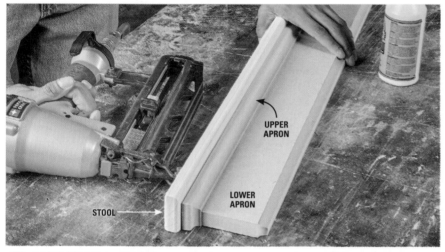

8 ASSEMBLE THE WINDOW STOOL AND APRON. Glue and nail the upper window apron to the lower window apron. Then glue and nail the stool to the apron assembly. Make sure to keep the end overhangs even.

9 NAIL ON THE STOOL AND APRON ASSEMBLY. Make pencil marks 3/16 in. inside the jamb at each corner of the window to indicate the edge of the trim and establish a 3/16-in. reveal. Also mark the center of the window and the center of the stool assembly on short pieces of masking tape. Line up the center marks and align the stool with the reveal marks. Then nail through the apron into the wall framing under the window to hold the assembly in place.

support strips and the stop for pieces of different widths and lengths.

Use a cove bit for the lower apron pieces and top cap. Switch to the classic ogee bit to shape the lower cap and upper apron. And use the round-over bit to shape the top and bottom edges of the fillet and the stool as well as the long edges of the side casings.

Photo 6 shows a method for supporting the router to cut the cove in the lower apron piece. Rip two 2x4 pieces to 3 in. and screw them together to use as the support pieces.

10 MARK THE SIDE CASING LENGTH. Cut a casing piece about an inch or two longer than needed. Rest it on the stool, and mark the top at the reveal mark. Cut the side casing to length on a miter saw and nail it into place, being careful to keep the reveal consistent from top to bottom. Mark, cut and install the casing on the opposite side using the same process.

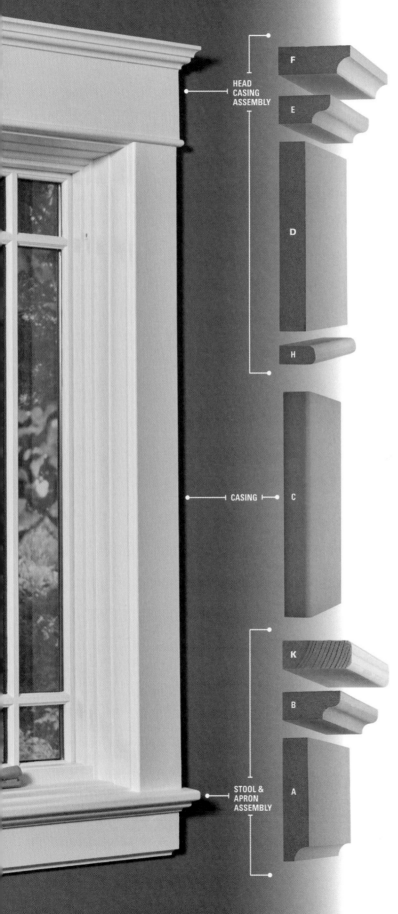

HEAD
CASING
ASSEMBLY

CASING

STOOL &
APRON
ASSEMBLY

Materials List

ITEM

3/4" MDF (calculate quantity from cutting list)
1/2" MDF (calculate quantity from cutting list)
1x3 x 3/4" paintable wood boards (rip to 2 in. for window stools)
2x4 x 8' (rip to 3 in. to support router for apron cut; **Photo 6**)
Wood glue
Spackle
100-grit sandpaper (use to sand edges before priming)
220-grit sandpaper (use to sand primer before painting)
Primer/sealer (we used B-I-N white pigmented shellac)
Paint
1-1/2" finish nails
2-1/4" finish nails

Router bits

1/4" round-over bit (we used Freud No. 34-110, $38)
3/8" cove bit (we used Freud No. 30-104, $41)
1/4"-radius ogee bit (we used Freud No. 38-154, $47)

Safety gear

Dust masks
Safety glasses
Hearing protection
Table saw push stick

Cutting List for a Window

KEY	WIDTH	ADD FOR LENGTH*	NAME
3/4" MDF			
A	3"	8-3/8"	Lower apron
B	1-1/2"	9-7/8"	Upper apron
C	4"		Casing
D	5"	8-3/8"	Head casing
E	1-1/2"	9-7/8"	Lower cap
F	2"	10-7/8"	Upper cap
G	7-1/2" x 4-1/4"		Base plinth
1/2" MDF			
H	1"	8-7/8"	Fillet
J	7-1/2" x 4-1/4"		Base plinth
1x3 PAINTABLE LUMBER			
K	2"	10-3/8"	Stool

* Add this amount to the measurement from the inside edges of the window jamb or doorjamb to calculate the length of the piece.

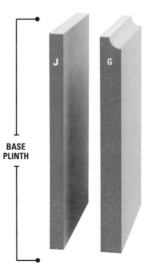

BASE
PLINTH

HEAD
CASING
ASSEMBLY

11 NAIL THE HEAD CASING ASSEMBLY INTO PLACE. Center the head casing assembly over the window, making sure the fillet overhangs the side casings evenly. Then nail through the head casing assembly into the wall framing above the window.

BASE
PLINTH

12 MAKE BASE PLINTHS FOR THE DOORS. Complete the classic look by adding plinth blocks under the side casings on doors and other openings. Make the 1-1/4-in.-thick plinths by gluing strips of 1/2-in.- and 3/4-in.-thick MDF together. Then rout a cove on the top edge. Make the plinths about 1/4 in. wider than the casing to create a small offset where the casing rests on the blocks.

ASSEMBLE THE PARTS

Photos 7 and 8 show how to build the head casing assembly and the stool and apron. Spread a layer of glue between the parts before you pin them together. For super-tight joints, clamp the pieces after gluing them together. You can remove the clamps in about 20 minutes and safely install the assemblies an hour after gluing them up.

Priming and applying the first coat of paint before you install the window and door trim will result in a neater job and save you time. Sand lightly after the primer dries, especially along the cut edges that tend to get a little fuzzy. Then apply the first coat of paint. Install the trim, then fill the nail holes and paint a second coat.

INSTALL THE NEW TRIM

You'll be surprised how easily the trim goes up. There are no miters to cut. All you have to do is cut the side casings to length. Start by marking 3/16-in. reveals at every corner. You can see the reveal marks on the inset of **Photo 10**. A combination square set to 3/16 in. works great for this. Center the stool and apron assembly and nail it on **(Photo 9)**. Then mark and cut the sides **(Photo 10)**. Finally, install the head casing **(Photo 11)**.

If the drywall around your window or door protrudes a bit past the jamb, trim it back at an angle with a utility knife, or crush it with a hammer until it's flush to the jamb. Otherwise there may be a gap between the moldings and the jamb. If you do end up with a small crack, fill it with good-quality latex caulk before brushing on the final coat of paint.

Start trimming the door or other openings by nailing on the base plinth first **(Photo 12)**. We made these plinth blocks by gluing 1/2-in. MDF to 3/4-in. MDF and then routing a cove shape on the top edge. If you have several doors to do, make a bunch of blocks by first cutting strips of 1/2-in. and 3/4-in. MDF a little wider than the height of the blocks (we made ours 7-1/2 in. tall) and gluing them together. When the glue has set, clean up both edges by running the strip through the table saw until it's the right width. Then rout the cove along one edge. Finally, cut the blocks to 4-1/4 in. wide.

Finish the door openings just as you did the windows by cutting and installing the side casings and nailing on the head assemblies. When that's done, all that's left is to install the baseboard and finish the painting. Go to familyhandyman.com and search for "baseboard" for instructions on how to install baseboard molding to complete your project.

3 Steps to a Secure Home

Fortified windows and doors will give even the wiliest burglars a run for their money.

Most crooks avoid challenges. They just want a quick, easy score. That's good news for you—it means that small, simple security upgrades are a major deterrent. If you make your home just a little harder to break into, the vast majority of burglars will bypass you and move on to easier pickings.

1. REINFORCE YOUR EXTERIOR DOORS

Burglars can open most entry doors with a few kicks or body blows. Even with a dead bolt, a blow will shatter the doorjamb and split the door itself (even steel doors). You can dramatically increase the strength of your doorjamb by installing longer strike plate screws that anchor into the stud behind the jamb **(Photo 1A)**.

The first step is to take out one of the existing screws. If it's shorter than 3 in., replace it. For even greater doorjamb security, consider installing a 6-in.-long heavy-duty strike plate (about $10). This is a much bigger job

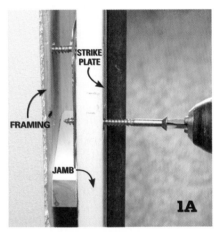

STRENGTHEN THE DOORJAMB. Remove 3/4-in. screws from strike plate. Drill pilot holes into the framing behind the jamb. Drive in 3-in. screws to anchor the strike plate to framing.

STRIKE PLATE

FRAMING

JAMB

1A

EDGE GUARD

INSTALL AN EDGE GUARD. A guard will keep the door from splitting from a sudden blow. Simply remove the dead bolt and screw on the guard.

Understand Your Foes

Most burglaries occur on weekdays between 10 a.m. and 5 p.m. The perpetrators are usually male, in their 20s, and looking for easy-to-pawn items to raise quick cash. They look for homes that appear unoccupied during the day, are dark at night and display signs of wealth (such as immaculate landscaping, expensive cars and fancy decks). They prefer homes that are secluded or shielded by fences or shrubbery. And they prefer breaking in through a ground-level side window or back door.

Most burglars don't pick locks or break glass. That takes too long, makes noise and risks personal injury. Instead, they simply kick in a door (even doors with a dead bolt) or pry open a window or sliding patio door.

In many cases, they take advantage of a homeowner's carelessness by climbing in through an open window or unlocked door (window screens and storm doors don't offer any significant protection). Burglars tend to shy away from homes with dogs and homes with an alarm system.

Once inside, burglars head right to the master bedroom, looking for gold jewelry, cash, furs and guns. Next, they scoop up prescription drugs from the bathroom and finish up with laptops, tablets and smartphones. Then they hightail it out.

Your job is to make your home less target-worthy, frustrate their attempts to break in and limit your losses if they do manage to get inside.

because you have to mortise a larger opening and drive in six 3-in. screws. If your entry door butts up to a sidelight and you can't install long screws, buy and install a 48-in.-long doorjamb reinforcement plate.

Next, prevent door splitting with a door edge guard. Measure the door thickness and dead bolt lock backset before you head to the home center. Then buy a guard (about $13) to fit around your door and dead bolt. Installing the guard takes about 15 minutes (**Photo 1B**).

2. STRENGTHEN WINDOWS

The factory latches on double-hung windows are no match for a burglar with a pry bar. But they can't get past inexpensive pin locks (about $5 each). You can install a pin in just a few minutes per window (**Photo 2**).

Pry bars work on casement or sliding windows too. But the pin lock we show here won't work with them. Find casement and sliding window locks for about $5 per window at home centers.

3. SECURE SLIDING PATIO DOORS

There are two ways a burglar can easily get past sliding patio doors: by prying the door up and off the bottom track, and by prying against the jamb and breaking the latch. To prevent latch breakage, some homeowners lay a long stick (like a broom handle) in the lower track. But a crook can easily move the stick with a coat hanger.

The best solution is to install a tension-fit drop-down security bar (aka a "charley bar") and snap latch (**Photo 3A**). They're ugly, but they work and send a strong signal to crooks that you've fortified your home. To prevent the door from being pried up, install anti-jacking screws (**Photo 3B**).

SECURE DOUBLE-HUNG WINDOWS. Add a pin lock to prevent the sash from being pried up. Drill a hole to lock the window closed and a second hole a few inches up to lock the window partly open for ventilation.

INSTALL A SECURITY BAR. Secure the pivoting end of the security bar to the door frame at mid-height, so it's easy to operate and the crooks can see it. Then install the locking latch on the sliding door. Lower the bar and extend it so it wedges against the sliding door.

INSTALL ANTI-JACKING SCREWS. Drive two 3-in.-long screws through the top track and into the header above the sliding door or window. Leave enough clearance to allow the sliding door or window to move, but not enough to allow a burglar to raise the door off the track.

Cut Your Losses If They Do Get In

- Immediately file a fraud alert with credit bureaus and contact your bank and credit card companies.
- Inspect your checkbook for missing checks—close the account if any are missing.
- Don't keep cash in your bedroom.
- Get a nice-looking jewelry box and fill it with your less expensive jewelry. Keep your valuable jewelry elsewhere.
- Keep guns locked in a safe.
- If you haven't taken steps to secure your home since the burglary, do it now! Burglars often come back about six weeks later to get the brand-new items you bought with the insurance proceeds.

How to Install a Window Insulation Kit

You can fix your drafty windows in about 15 minutes.

No one likes paying a hefty energy bill only to find that the air they've been shelling out to heat is simply slipping out the windows. Luckily, there's a simple fix that is quick, inexpensive and easy to do with just a pair of scissors and a hair dryer. Read on to learn how to install affordable window insulating film—and say goodbye to drafty rooms and needlessly high heating bills.

1. MEASURE FIRST

Before you head to the store to purchase your window insulating kit (or search for one online), measure all the drafty windows, using the height and width from the outside edge of the window trim.

Choosing the proper kit can be confusing. Most window insulating kits come with one large sheet of plastic film, out of which you'll cut two or three window coverings. The window height measurement is an important number to look for.

2. DUST AND CLEAN

Dust and wipe down everything with a dry microfiber cloth. If your window glass needs cleaning, now is a good time to do it. Next, grab some isopropyl alcohol and a clean rag to wipe down the casing where the film will adhere.

3. APPLY THE DOUBLE-SIDED TAPE

Your kit will include double-sided tape. You can stick this tape directly on the face of your window casing or along its edge.

Apply the tape to the top, bottom and two sides of the window casing. Do not pull the backing off the tape yet.

Note: Some window film products have one edge with an adhesive already applied. This is for the top of the window.

4. INSTALL THE FILM

Measure the width of the window. Add an extra 2 inches. Then cut your film accordingly.

Starting at the top left of the window, carefully peel off about 6 inches of the backing from the adhesive tape. Let an inch of film hang over the left side of the double-sided tape. Then begin sticking the film across the top of the window.

Stick the film onto the tape, working from one side of the window to the other. Keep the film tight as you go, while peeling the backing off the tape.

Once you've finished the top, move on to the left side, sticking and peeling as you go down.

Gently pull on the window film as you apply it to the tape. Repeat on the right side and then on the bottom.

5. SHRINK THE FILM

Once you've applied the film, take a hair dryer and apply high heat around the taped edges to make sure that it's completely adhered.

Shrink the rest of the film and any wrinkles with the hair dryer.

6. TRIM IT

After shrinking the film into place, cut around the perimeter of the window to trim off any excess film.

Laminate Floors

Laminate flooring is inexpensive, durable, prefinished and easy to install. We'll help you choose a style that's right for you.

TWO STYLES: ENGINEERED WOOD AND PLASTIC LAMINATE

There are two types of laminate flooring. Both come in packages of snap-together planks about 1/4 in. thick. But here's the difference: Engineered wood is made from layers of real wood glued together, with each layer perpendicular to the one below and above it for better stability. The top layer is a high-quality thin layer of hardwood coated with acrylic finish. Plastic laminate, on the other hand, is completely artificial, with a layer of melamine on the bottom, a resin-saturated fiberboard center and a wood-grain print on the top that's protected by a layer of clear hard plastic.

Engineered wood is for purists who prefer the look of natural wood. But you pay for reality. On average, it's about double the cost of plastic laminate flooring. Its thin top layer of actual hardwood makes it more susceptible to dents, scratches and staining. But unlike plastic laminate flooring, it can be rejuvenated up to three times with careful sanding and refinishing. Because of that, you can expect it to last longer than plastic laminate—if it is located away from water-prone and high-wear areas. If you're planning to sell your house in a few years, consider that buyers may appreciate and pay more for the look of real wood.

Plastic laminate is for those who want the look of wood flooring in a place that gets wet or seriously abused. The bulletproof topcoat and plastic internal components make laminate floors extremely durable. They stand up to moisture, pet claws, in-line skates and sand-infested flip-flops much better than engineered wood floors. Manufacturers have come light-years in making the wood-grain print look very realistic. Most people can't even tell it's not real wood.

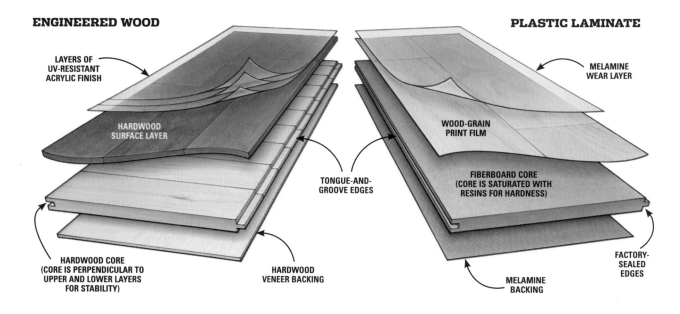

ENGINEERED WOOD

LAYERS OF UV-RESISTANT ACRYLIC FINISH

HARDWOOD SURFACE LAYER

TONGUE-AND-GROOVE EDGES

HARDWOOD CORE (CORE IS PERPENDICULAR TO UPPER AND LOWER LAYERS FOR STABILITY)

HARDWOOD VENEER BACKING

PLASTIC LAMINATE

MELAMINE WEAR LAYER

WOOD-GRAIN PRINT FILM

FIBERBOARD CORE (CORE IS SATURATED WITH RESINS FOR HARDNESS)

FACTORY-SEALED EDGES

MELAMINE BACKING

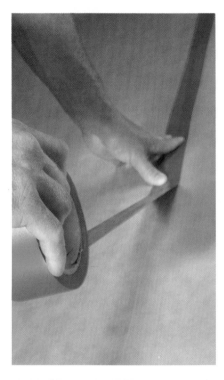

LUXURY VINYL FLOORING

Laminate floors aren't the only option for durability and ease of installation. Next time you're at the home center, take a gander at luxury vinyl (LV) flooring. There's luxury vinyl tile (LVT), which looks like ceramic tile, and luxury vinyl plank (LVP), which mimics wood (shown here). Both types are extremely resilient, about the easiest flooring in the world to install and *completely* waterproof. Since luxury vinyl is so pliable, it's a great choice over uneven subfloors. Prices start at $2 per sq. ft.

DON'T FORGET THE UNDERLAYMENT

All laminate flooring needs foam underlayment. Don't skip it. Underlayment prevents the floor from clicking on the subfloor as you walk across it and makes it feel a bit softer. It also makes the planks easier to install because it evens out small inconsistencies in the subfloor. Some underlayment has self-adhesive tape to join one row to the next. Others call for separate tape. Be careful to use whatever is required. Go ahead and buy the special laminate and wood flooring installation tool as well. You'll need it to pull together flooring ends where each row abuts a wall.

CHOOSE A FINISH BASED ON LIFESTYLE, NOT JUST LOOKS

If you lead a quiet life, choose whatever flooring style appeals to you. But if you have one of those busy households with kids, pets and lots of visitors, be a bit more careful. Flooring with a varied grain pattern, a low-gloss finish, or a distressed or hand-scraped patina will look much better and much cleaner for much longer than flooring with a glossy, monolithic grain pattern.

AVOID WIDE PLANKS UNLESS THE SUBSTRATE IS PERFECT

The directions will tell you the amount of slab or subfloor unevenness tolerated by the brand and type of flooring you buy. Over an uneven floor, wider planks will be harder to snap together, end joints won't stay flush with one another and there will be more gaps beneath the planks that you'll feel when you walk across the floor. So if your concrete or wood subfloor is quite uneven, you're better off selecting a narrower plank style and being thorough when you apply the floor leveling compound **(photo left)**.

CHAPTER **FOUR**

APPLIANCES & MAINTENANCE

Make Your Gas Grill Like New

The right paint, some new accessories and a bit of elbow grease are all it takes to get your older grill summer-ready.

If your gas grill is looking old and gray and the cart is starting to rust, you're probably thinking it's time for a new grill. Sure, it would be cool to own one of those shiny new stainless steel models—if you're willing to spend $500 or more. But if the cart, base and cover of your current grill are still sound, you can whip it into like-new shape in less than a day.

The paint and supplies are easy to find at home centers, and you can pick up new handles, knobs, emblems and a new thermometer for about $25 from a local appliance parts store or online. You'll have to wait at least 24 hours for the paint to cure, but then you can get right back to burger-flipping. Here's how to do the job.

BUY SUPPLIES

Stop at any home center and buy a bottle of heavy-duty degreaser, nitrile gloves, a respirator, a stiff-bristle scrub brush and a wire brush. Also pick up 80-grit and 120-grit sandpaper, brush-on or spray-on rust converter, primer for rusty metal and a few cans of heat-resistant paint (one choice is Krylon High Heat Max). You'll also need disposable plastic sheeting, a shop vacuum, a palm sander, a bucket and a garden hose.

CLEAN, SAND AND PRIME

Cleaning a greasy gas grill creates quite a mess. And the last thing you want is to move the grease from the grill to your driveway or garage floor. So do the project outdoors and tarp off the entire work area. Start the job by removing the burners, grates and grease cup. Use your shop vacuum to suck up all the loose crud from the bottom of the grill and any dirt and rust from the propane tank shelf. Next, remove the knobs, emblems and thermometer (if equipped). Mix up a strong solution of degreaser using the dilution ratios listed on the label. Then grab your scrub brush and gloves, and wash the entire grill **(Photo 1)**. If you have a power washer, soak the grill with degreaser, then blast off the grease and loose paint. Rinse it with water and let it dry in the sun.

Once any moisture has evaporated, mask the wheels, gas valves, warning labels, manufacturer's nameplate and any other parts that won't be painted. Then grab your respirator and palm sander, and sand the exterior **(Photo 2)**. Pretreat the worst rust spots with a rust converter product. Once that dries, prime the rusty areas and bare metal with a primer for rusty metal **(Photo 3)**. Let the primer dry.

PAINT THE GRILL AND INSTALL THE NEW PARTS

Wipe the entire grill with a tack cloth, then spray-paint the grill **(Photo 4)**. Finish up by installing the new accessories **(Photo 5)**. Remove the masking and let the paint dry for the recommended time. Then install the burners and grates, and get grilling.

1 DEGREASE THE ENTIRE GRILL. Spread degreaser inside the cover and burner area and over the entire exterior. Then scrub the entire grill with a brush. Make sure you remove grease from all the crevices.

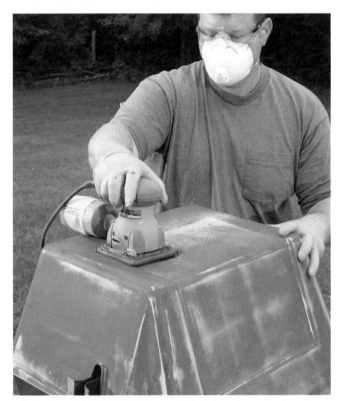

2 SAND AND USE A WIRE BRUSH. Sand corroded and pitted areas with 80-grit sandpaper. Use a wire brush in crevices to remove surface rust and chipping paint. Then switch to 120-grit sandpaper and sand the entire grill and cart.

3 SPRAY ON PRIMER. Apply rust converter, then spray primer over the converted rust and bare metal areas. Let it flash for the recommended time. Then apply a second coat.

4 APPLY THE FINISH COAT. Paint the top of the grill lid first. Then spray down each side all the way to the bottom of the cart. Paint the front of the grill last. Apply a second coat after waiting the recommended time.

5 INSTALL NEW PARTS. Attach the new cover lift handle or knobs. Snap on the new emblems. Screw in the new thermometer.

Replace a Noisy Gas Fireplace Blower

Here's your fix for a fire that's roaring a little too much.

Many gas fireplaces use a blower to drive warm air into the room. They also have a fan speed adjustment switch so you can strike a balance between blower speed and noise level. But if the fan gets loaded with dust or the motor bearings wear, the blower will make a rumbling noise at all speeds. Sometimes it's possible to quiet it by removing the blower and cleaning the fan blades (you can use a shop vacuum and an old toothbrush for this task). But if the blower still makes noise, it's time to replace it.

A professional fireplace service company charges about $400 to do the job (parts and labor), but you can replace the blower with a complete motor/fan blower assembly in about an hour

for a fraction of that cost. We'll show you how, with the input of an expert from a company that manufactures replacement blower assemblies to fit most popular gas fireplaces.

IDENTIFY THE BLOWER

Tilt out the bottom grille and shine a light inside the unit. Then snap a digital photo of the blower assembly. Locate the nameplate on the bottom of the air intake, and write down the brand and model number of your fireplace.

Then order a replacement blower from an authorized dealer or an online supplier. If your blower runs but is noisy, buy just the motor/fan assembly. However, if the motor doesn't run at all, chances are it has a bad temp sensor or speed switch. In that case, buy a complete kit. We bought just the blower for the 14-year-old Heat & Glo gas fireplace shown in this story.

REMOVE THE OLD BLOWER

Shut off the circuit breaker and use a voltage sniffer to confirm the power is off. Don't just use the wall switch. Then open the bottom grille. If it doesn't look as if you'll have enough room to remove the blower, try removing the front panel (**Photo 1**). Next, clean the area in front of the blower with a shop vacuum (**Photo 2**).

If you've ordered a complete kit, unplug the old blower and disconnect the temperature sensor mounted on the bottom of the firebox (the sensor is typically held in place with a magnet, clip or screw). Then disconnect the speed control switch and remove the old blower (**Photo 3**). Clean the air intake area again while you have access to it. Then install the new blower (**Photo 4**). Reinstall the kit's new temperature sensor and speed switch, and plug in the blower.

TEST AND ADJUST

Turn on the power and fire up the burners. Wait for the firebox to heat up enough for the blower to turn on (about 10 minutes). Then adjust the fan speed to your liking, and reinstall the front panel (if equipped) and bottom grille.

1 **REMOVE THE FRONT PANEL. Lift the front panel straight up to unhook it from the side pins. Then pull the panel straight out and set it aside.**

2 **SUCK OUT THE DUST BUNNIES. Use a shop vacuum to clean the area in front of the old blower. You'll have to vacuum again once the blower is out, but this step will keep most of the dust out of the room.**

3 **SLIDE OUT THE OLD BLOWER. Pull the blower toward the front of the fireplace. Then rotate it so it clears the grille opening. If you need more clearance, remove the rubber feet.**

4 **POSITION THE NEW BLOWER. Roll the blower through the grille area and position it with the blower outlet pointing up. Push it all the way to the back of the fireplace until it contacts the back wall. Then pull it forward 1/4 in. to prevent vibration noise.**

Replace a Sprinkler Head

This common repair is a DIY job from start to finish.

It's pretty easy to damage a sprinkler head with your mower if the head sits too high. And we're convinced that snowplow operators intentionally shear off sprinkler heads along the curb just for the entertainment value.

No matter how your sprinkler head got damaged or quit working, there's no need to call the irrigation company to do the repairs. All you need is a new head, an assortment of different-length poly cutoff riser fittings and parts to build a homemade flushing tool. You can get all the parts for around $15 at any home center. You'll also need a garden spade, poly sheeting, a wet/dry shop vacuum and a saw. Here's how to attack the job.

HOW TO BUY REPLACEMENT SPRINKLER HEADS

A replacement sprinkler head doesn't have to be the same brand as the broken head. But it does have to be the same type: pop-up (stationary, rotor or gear-driven) or impact. And the new head must also match the inches-per-hour (iph) or gallons-per-

minute (gpm) delivery rate of the old head. Plus, the spray pattern and throwing distance must also match. If you install the wrong head, it can over- or underwater that section of your lawn or garden and possibly cause other heads in that same zone to underperform. You'll need all the specs from the broken head before you buy a replacement.

Locate that information on the nozzle, the top of the head (if it's still there) or on the label stuck to the body of the head (see "Remove the Broken Head" at right). If you can't find the specifications, at least find the brand and part number. Then look up the specs on the manufacturer's website. If you strike out on the specs and part number, take the old head to an irrigation service company and ask for a matching replacement head.

Buy a replacement head at a home center or online (sprinklerwarehouse .com is one source). The replacement head will most likely come with an assortment of snap-in nozzles, so you can adapt the head's delivery rate, spray pattern and throw rate to fit your needs.

REMOVE THE BROKEN HEAD

Lay down plastic sheeting next to the broken sprinkler head. Then use a garden spade to cut an 8-in. circle around the old head. Pry out the sod and set it aside. Then dig down and around the old head, placing the dirt on the poly sheet **(Photo 1)**. When you reach the water line, unscrew the broken head.

If the head is located at the low spot of a watering zone, chances are the hole will fill with water and mud will get into the water line. Suck the mud out with your shop vacuum. (The water line will get flushed later.)

SET THE NEW HEAD HEIGHT

If the old riser fitting came out with the old head, remove it and screw it onto the new head. Then test-fit the new head by screwing it into the water line. The top of the head should be flush with the ground, not sticking up into the grass. If it's not the right height, grab a new poly cutoff riser (about $1 each at home centers) with multiple threaded sections and cut it to the correct length **(Photo 2)**. It may take a few tries (and a few risers) to get the height just right. Once you get the proper height, remove the head and flush the line using the steps shown here.

BUILD A FLUSHING TOOL AND FLUSH THE WATER LINE

No matter how careful you are, dirt is going to fall into the water line fitting. If you can't remove all the dirt with your shop vacuum, you'll have to flush the line. To do so, first build a flushing tool with 3/4-in. PVC pipe and the fittings (about $5 in parts at home centers) shown in **Figure A**. Then flush the water line **(Photo 3)**. Finish by sucking the water out of the flushing tool **(Photo 4)**.

INSTALL THE HEAD AND BACKFILL

Screw the new head into the flushed water line and begin backfilling the hole **(Photo 5)**. Align the head so it sits straight in the hole as you tamp the dirt with your hand. Finish the job by replacing the grass. Water immediately to reestablish the grass roots.

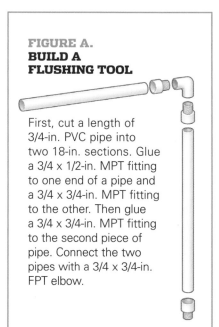

FIGURE A.
BUILD A FLUSHING TOOL

First, cut a length of 3/4-in. PVC pipe into two 18-in. sections. Glue a 3/4 x 1/2-in. MPT fitting to one end of a pipe and a 3/4 x 3/4-in. MPT fitting to the other. Then glue a 3/4 x 3/4-in. MPT fitting to the second piece of pipe. Connect the two pipes with a 3/4 x 3/4-in. FPT elbow.

1 SCOOP OUT THE DIRT. Slice a garden spade straight down the sides of the hole to give you room to maneuver. Then lift the dirt up, out and onto the poly sheeting.

2 CUT THE RISER TO LENGTH. Slice through the multiple-thread poly cutoff riser using a metal-cutting blade for a smooth cut. Deburr the cut edge with a knife. Then install the riser on the head, screw the head into the water line and check the height.

3 FLUSH THE LINE. Screw the flushing tool into the water line and aim it into the street or away from your work area. Turn on the water for that zone and let it run for about 30 seconds.

4 VACUUM OUT THE REMAINING WATER. Slide the vacuum hose nozzle over the vertical pipe and suck out all the remaining water.

5 INSTALL THE HEAD AND BACKFILL. Screw the riser fitting onto the sprinkler head, then screw the head into the water line. Backfill with dirt and sod.

How a Toilet Works

Learn the basics so you can fix it yourself and avoid pricey service calls to the plumber.

Possibly the most used yet most taken for granted household fixture, the toilet is a marvel of engineering simplicity. Even typical modern toilets employ just a couple of basic mechanical components. The rest of the flush relies on the natural forces of gravity and siphoning action.

But sooner or later, every toilet develops problems such as weak flushing, clogs or constant running. When that happens, most homeowners just live with the problem or pay a plumber a lot for a simple fix. You don't have to do either. If you know how a toilet works, you can diagnose and solve problems yourself, often in just a few minutes. So let's lift the lid to see the magic that happens inside this underappreciated fixture.

1 **FLUSH HANDLE LIFTS THE FLAPPER. When** the flush handle is pressed, it lifts the flapper, setting in motion about 10 seconds of flushing genius.

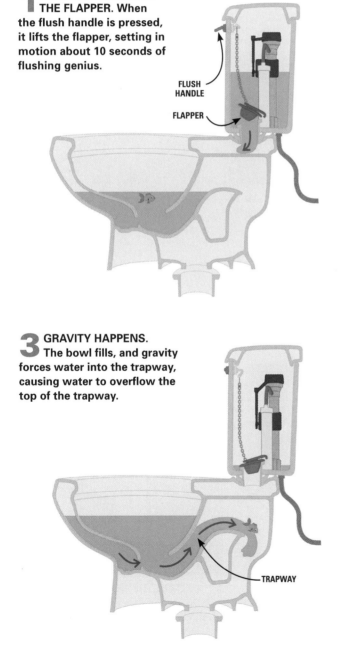

FLUSH HANDLE

FLAPPER

2 **WATER RUSHES TO THE BOWL. The lifted flapper** releases tank water into the bowl via rim jets and the larger siphon jet. The float drops as the tank empties, opening the fill valve, and the flapper drops back onto its seat.

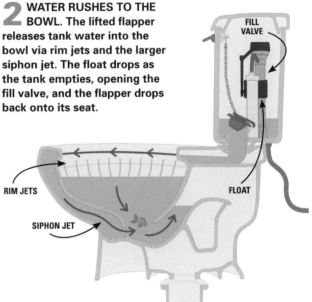

FILL VALVE

RIM JETS

FLOAT

SIPHON JET

3 **GRAVITY HAPPENS.** The bowl fills, and gravity forces water into the trapway, causing water to overflow the top of the trapway.

TRAPWAY

4 **WATER AND WASTE ARE SIPHONED OUT. Water rushing** over the top of the trapway creates suction, evacuating the waste and water from the bowl. As the water is pulled from the bowl, air enters the trapway, ending the siphon effect and also the flush.

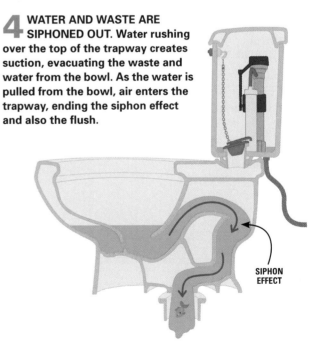

SIPHON EFFECT

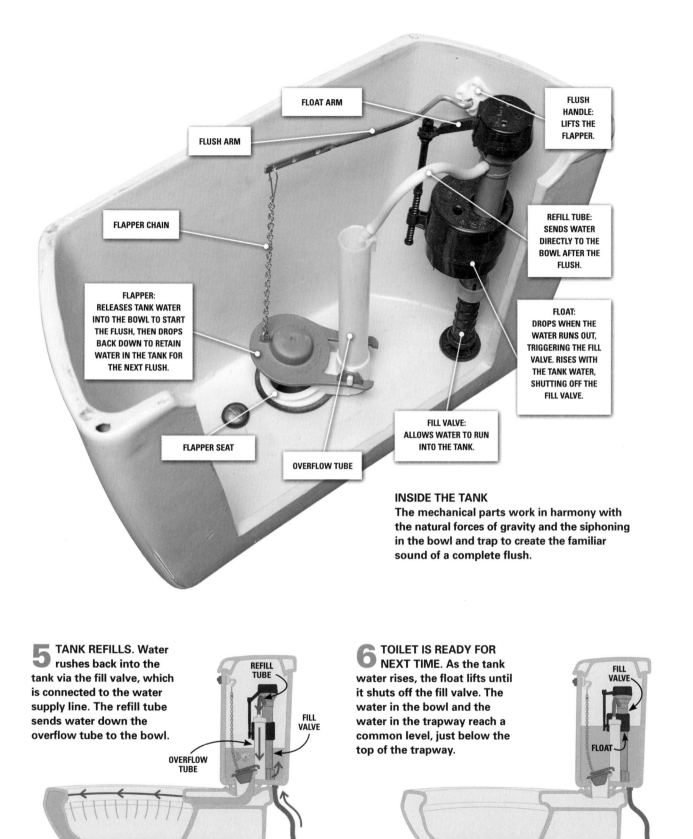

FLOAT ARM

FLUSH ARM

FLUSH HANDLE: LIFTS THE FLAPPER.

FLAPPER CHAIN

REFILL TUBE: SENDS WATER DIRECTLY TO THE BOWL AFTER THE FLUSH.

FLAPPER: RELEASES TANK WATER INTO THE BOWL TO START THE FLUSH, THEN DROPS BACK DOWN TO RETAIN WATER IN THE TANK FOR THE NEXT FLUSH.

FLOAT: DROPS WHEN THE WATER RUNS OUT, TRIGGERING THE FILL VALVE. RISES WITH THE TANK WATER, SHUTTING OFF THE FILL VALVE.

FILL VALVE: ALLOWS WATER TO RUN INTO THE TANK.

FLAPPER SEAT

OVERFLOW TUBE

INSIDE THE TANK
The mechanical parts work in harmony with the natural forces of gravity and the siphoning in the bowl and trap to create the familiar sound of a complete flush.

5 **TANK REFILLS.** Water rushes back into the tank via the fill valve, which is connected to the water supply line. The refill tube sends water down the overflow tube to the bowl.

REFILL TUBE

FILL VALVE

OVERFLOW TUBE

WATER SUPPLY LINE

6 **TOILET IS READY FOR NEXT TIME.** As the tank water rises, the float lifts until it shuts off the fill valve. The water in the bowl and the water in the trapway reach a common level, just below the top of the trapway.

FILL VALVE

FLOAT

TRAPWAY

Replace a Water Heater

Doing it yourself saves a bundle—and can prevent destructive flooding.

If your water heater is no longer doing its job, a simple fix may be all it needs. For repair help, go to familyhandyman.com and search for "water heater." On the other hand, a water heater's life expectancy is only about 10 to 14 years, so replacement may be your best move. And if you notice leaks coming from under the tank, replacement is your *only* move. Rusty puddles mean that the tank is rusting out. Someday—maybe next year, maybe tomorrow—that trickling leak will turn into an instant flood. Don't gamble. Replace the water heater as soon as you can.

If you have some basic plumbing experience, you can replace a water heater yourself and save $200 to $400 in plumber's fees.

In this article we'll show you how to replace a conventional natural gas water heater, and the procedure is the same for a propane heater. If you choose a "power-vented" gas model, all the water and gas connections are the same as we show but the venting steps are different. For these steps, go to familyhandyman.com and search for "power-vented water heater." Replacing an electric water heater is a little easier. All the water connections are the same and you don't have to deal with gas piping or venting. For details on situations different from the one we show here (such as electric models, plastic water lines or copper gas lines), go to familyhandyman.com and search for "replace water heater."

TIME, MATERIALS AND MONEY

If you have lots of plumbing experience, you might be able to complete this project in half a day. But we recommend you start in the morning so you have plenty of time to get the job done and don't have to leave your family without hot water overnight. You'll need a helper to carry the old unit out and the new one in. Check with your trash hauler or recycling center to find out how to dispose of the old heater.

The cost of a new water heater will vary depending on its size, efficiency and warranty, but you can expect to pay anywhere from $250 to $600 and up. The materials you'll need for the installation will depend on your situation and local codes.

Even if you've worked with plumbing and gas lines in the past, play it safe and contact your local department of inspections. Get a permit (if required), and go over your installation plans with an inspector.

TURN OFF THE GAS AND WATER

To get started, turn off the gas at the valve near the water heater (**Photo 1**).

If the isolation valve above your water heater is a gate valve (**Photo 3**), we recommend you replace it with a ball valve (**Photo 4**). Be sure to choose a full-port valve. Gate valves often leak or won't close tightly. To replace the valve, you'll have to shut off the water at the main valve (usually near the meter). That means your whole house will be without water until you install the new valve. If you already have a ball valve or if you choose to leave the old gate valve in place, you can simply shut off the valve. That way the rest of the house will have cold water while you work (toilets will still function!).

With the water and gas off, drain the water heater. Attach a garden hose to the drain valve at the bottom of the tank, route it to a floor drain and open the drain valve. To allow air into the hot water lines and speed up the draining process, go to the highest faucet in the house and turn on the hot side only (on single-handle faucets, push the lever all the way to the left).

DISCONNECT THE GAS, VENT AND WATER LINES

Disconnect the gas line at the union (**Photo 2**). Then disassemble the threaded tee and drip leg, and remove the nipple from the water heater gas control valve. Don't throw away these parts—you'll need them later. If your gas line is copper or a flexible supply line, just unscrew the nut.

To disassemble the vent piping, remove the sheet metal screws. Wear gloves; the ends of the metal piping are sharp. You can reuse the vent pipes if they're in good shape. But if you find even slight holes, cracks or corrosion, toss them into the trash. New pipe is inexpensive, and leaks can allow deadly carbon monoxide to build up in your home.

1 Shut off the gas by turning the handle a quarter turn. In the "off" position, the handle is perpendicular to the pipe.

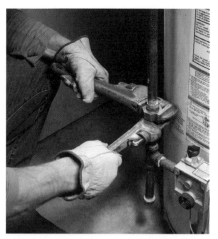

2 Disconnect the gas at the union fitting. Place the larger wrench on the nut and hold the union's collar with another wrench. Start with the wrenches a quarter turn apart.

GATE VALVE

3 Cut the cold water line above the old gate valve to make room for a new ball valve. Cut the hot water line at the same height.

Next, cut the copper water lines with a tubing cutter (**Photo 3**). If you have copper corrugated water lines, simply disconnect the nuts at the water heater. If you have galvanized steel pipes, disconnect the unions just as we did with the gas union shown in **Photo 2**. Also unscrew the blow tube from the temperature and pressure (T&P) valve. You may be able to reuse it on the new water heater.

At this point, the old heater should have drained enough so it can be moved off to the side (with a helper). If the heater isn't draining fast enough, sediment may be clogging the valve.

NEW VALVE

STUB

THREADED FITTING

NIPPLE

4 Reconnect the water. Install new valves first so you can turn on the water to the rest of the house. Then install nipples, followed by threaded fittings and stubs of pipe. Hold the final section in place to mark the length.

SLIP COUPLER

ANTI-GRAVITY DEVICE

COLD

5 Make the final connections with slip couplers. Be sure the coupler doesn't slide down as you heat it.

Allow it to drain as long as possible, and then move the heater outside so you can remove the drain valve from the tank.

RECONNECT THE WATER

Set the drain pan into place with the opening facing the floor drain. Get someone to help you lift and set the heater in the pan. If you're replacing the isolation valve, solder on the new ball valve next.

Screw dielectric nipples into the new water heater to reduce corrosion and increase water heater life. Some water heaters come with dielectric nipples already installed (buy a set if yours doesn't have them). Be sure to coat the threads with pipe thread sealant or wrap them with Teflon tape. Next, solder female threaded copper pipe fittings to short lengths of copper tubing; set them aside to cool. Tighten the cooled fittings onto the nipples. Then add short sections of pipe below the valves **(Photo 4)** and make the final connections with slip couplers **(Photo 5)**. You must use slip couplers—standard stopped couplers won't work. For tips on soldering copper pipe, go to familyhandyman.com and search for "solder."

Thread a blow tube onto the T&P valve. If the old blow tube is too short, you can use 3/4-in. galvanized steel pipe or copper pipe (along with a male threaded fitting). If you use galvanized pipe, cut off the threads on the bottom to prevent someone from capping off the blow tube if the T&P valve leaks.

INSTALL THE NEW VENT

Snap the new draft hood onto the water heater and secure it with sheet metal screws. Check the installation manual for the recommended diameter vent pipe for your new heater. If the recommended vent pipe diameter is larger than the vent hood opening, don't install a reducer. Measure a straight section of new galvanized vent pipe to rise as high as possible before you install the adjustable elbow (the higher the rise, the better the draft). On any horizontal sections of vent, make sure the pipe slopes down toward the water heater 1/4 in. per foot of pipe. Bend out small sections of the pipe and attach it directly to the vent hood with screws **(Photo 6)**. Then continue installing new vent pipe sections and connect to the flue. Most plumbing codes require a minimum of three screws for each vent pipe joint. For tips on cutting metal venting, go to familyhandyman.com and search for "sheet metal."

HOOK UP THE GAS

Apply gas-rated pipe thread sealant or tape (don't use standard white Teflon tape) to the gas nipple and thread it into the new gas control valve. Tighten the nipple using two pipe wrenches **(Photo 7)**. Assemble the tee and drip leg using the same two-wrench technique.

If the old section of pipe below the union no longer fits, you'll need to measure for a new nipple **(Photo 8)**. Make sure you assemble and tighten the gas union before you measure the length for the intermediate nipple. Add 3/4 to 1 in. to this measurement and buy a new nipple. When the gas connections are complete, turn on the gas and check for leaks **(Photo 9)**. You can buy leak detector in a convenient spray bottle ($3) or mix your own solution (one part dish detergent, two parts water).

Open the water valves and an upstairs faucet, and fill the tank. Leave the faucet open until water flows out. Then shut it off and check the new water connections for leaks. Open the gas valve and light the pilot light following the manufacturer's instructions. You're in for a pleasant (and convenient) surprise with your new water heater—manufacturers have done away with the old match-lit pilot system. Instead of igniting the

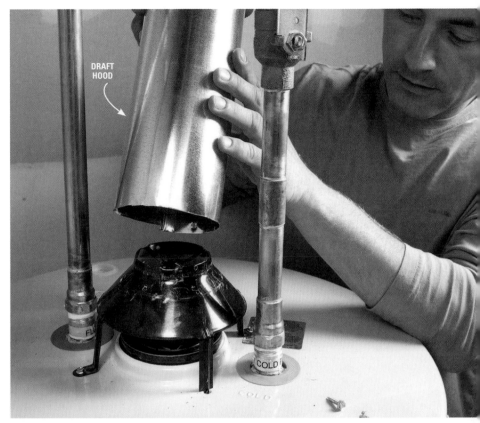

6 Connect the vent pipe to the hood with sheet metal screws. Never use a reducer, even if the hood's opening is smaller than the vent pipe.

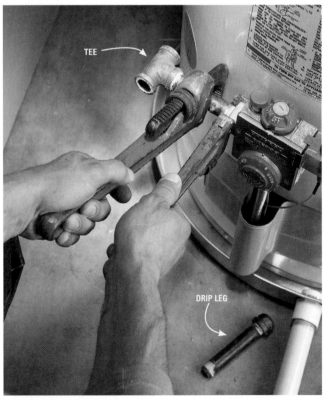

7 Reconnect the gas. Hold back the control valve to avoid damaging it. Then screw the drip leg into the tee.

8 Measure between the union and the tee, and add 1 in. to determine the correct nipple length.

pilot with a match or lighter, you just push a button.

When the burner fires up, test for backdrafting, which can allow deadly carbon monoxide into your home. Close all doors and windows, and turn on kitchen and bath exhaust fans. When the burner has been running for at least one minute, move an incense stick around the draft hood. The smoke should be drawn up into the vent. If not, the exhaust may be entering your home. Turn off the gas and call in a professional plumber.

Finally, set the thermostat to a safe temperature. (For help, go to familyhandyman.com and search for "water heater temperature.") In about two hours, you'll have enough hot water for a well-deserved long shower.

Old Gas Valves Can Leak

The grease-pack valves found in older homes tend to leak as they age. Even if your local code doesn't require replacement, we recommend you install a ball-type gas valve ($12) instead. Replacement isn't difficult; you just unscrew the old valve and screw on the new one. But you will have to turn off the main gas valve and later relight pilot lights. If you don't know how to handle these tasks, call in a professional plumber and expect to pay $80 to $150.

9 Test for leaks by brushing soapy water onto every connection. If you see bubbles, tighten or reconnect the joint.

You'll find lots of accessories for your new water heater at the home center. Some are required by local codes; others are just good ideas. Plumbing codes vary, so check with your local inspector.

1. Gas shutoff valve

All codes require a gas valve near the water heater. If you have a grease-pack valve, see "Old Gas Valves Can Leak" at left.

2. Earthquake straps

These straps prevent a water heater from tipping over and are required in earthquake-prone areas.

3. Flexible gas line

A flexible gas line can withstand movement and is usually required in earthquake-prone areas. It is easier to connect than steel pipe but is not allowed everywhere, so check with your inspector.

4. Drip leg

Any dust or grit in the gas line falls into this short section of pipe before it can reach the water heater's control valve. The required length of the drip leg varies.

5. Isolation valve

All codes require a valve on the cold water line. Though not required by codes, a second valve on the hot line makes future water heater replacement easier.

6. Flexible water lines

These flexible lines withstand movement and are required in earthquake-prone zones. But you may want to use them just because they're easy to install.

7. Overflow pan

Most plumbing codes require a pan and drain pipe in locations where a leak can cause damage. But installing a drain pan is a good idea for any location.

8. Expansion tank

Some codes require an expansion tank to absorb the pressure created when heated water expands.

9. Blow tube

The T&P valve releases pressure, and a blow tube directs the scalding hot water toward the floor. The required distance between the blow tube and floor is usually 18 in. or less.

Air Conditioner Repairs

Keeping cool is priceless, but you don't need to overpay for fixes you could make yourself.

When a central AC unit fails during a heat spell, you may have to wait days for a technician to show up. If you're lucky, you'll have to pay only about $300 for the repair. But if you're comfortable working around electricity and willing to spend about $50 on parts, you can probably fix your AC in about two hours and save a couple hundred dollars on parts markup and labor.

We talked to Ross Johnson, an HVAC technician at Superior Heating, Air Conditioning & Electrical in Anoka, MN, to get his best do-it-yourself AC repair and maintenance tips. These will help you with the most common low cooling and no cooling problems. You'll need an inexpensive multimeter, a voltage sniffer, an assortment of screwdrivers and a socket set. Here's how to start.

BUY PARTS

The contactor (relay) and start/run capacitor(s) (see "Anatomy of a Central Air Conditioner," p. 141) fail most often. Luckily, they are inexpensive, so it's a safe bet to buy and install those parts right away, especially if your AC unit is more than five years old. The condenser fan motor can also fail, but it runs about $135—hold off buying that unless you're sure that's the culprit.

To buy replacement parts, find the nameplate on the condensing unit (not your furnace). Jot down the make, model and serial number (or take a photo). Get the parts at an appliance store, furnace dealer or online (arnoldservice .com is one source).

START WITH THE EASY FIXES

If you're getting little or no cold air, check these three things first. Make sure all the registers in the house are wide open. Then be sure the furnace filter is clean. Next, go outside and clean off the condenser coils **(Photo 2)**. If several registers were closed or the filter was clogged, the reduced airflow could have caused the evaporator coil to ice up and stop cooling your home. If you've changed the filter and opened all the registers

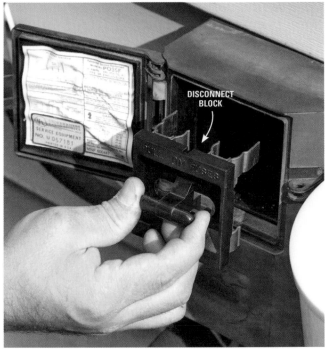

1 SHUT OFF THE POWER. Open the electrical box next to the condensing unit and pull the disconnect block straight out. Check inside the box with a voltage sniffer to make sure the power is really off.

CRUD BUILDUP UNDER THE LID

2 **CLEAN THE CONDENSER COILS.** Aim your garden nozzle upward into the top of the condenser coil to remove the buildup under the lid. Work all the way around the coil. Then aim the nozzle down and flush the debris down the coil fins. Adjust the nozzle to a gentler stream and shoot water directly into the coils to flush out any remaining debris.

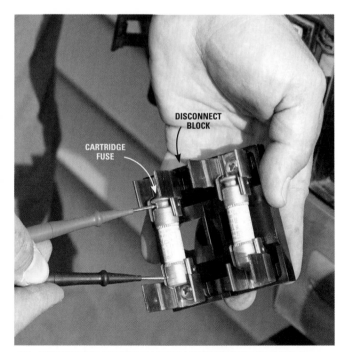

DISCONNECT BLOCK

CARTRIDGE FUSE

3 **CHECK THE FUSES IN THE DISCONNECT BLOCK.** Set your multimeter to the lowest ohms scale, and touch the red and black leads to opposite ends of each fuse. If you get a numerical reading, the fuse is good. But a zero, a minus symbol or an infinity symbol (∞) indicates a blown fuse.

Be Patient at Startup

AC units and thermostats have built-in delay features when they're shut down and then repowered. The delay can be as long as 10 minutes. And if you've subscribed to an energy-saving device from your local power utility, the unit can take even longer to reset. If you've installed the parts shown and reinstalled the disconnect block, repowered the circuit breaker, turned on the switch at the furnace, moved the thermostat to AC mode and lowered the temperature below the indoor temperature but the unit doesn't fire up after 30 minutes, it's time to call a pro.

yet you're still not getting airflow at the registers, deice the A-coil. Move the thermostat mode switch from "Cooling" to "Off," and move the fan switch from "Auto" to "On." Let the blower run for at least 30 minutes or until there's good airflow at the registers. Then turn the AC back on to test it. If it works for the next 12 hours, you've solved the problem.

If the condenser coils are clogged, the compressor can overheat and shut down. You'll experience intermittent periods of minimal cooling, followed by no cooling. Even if you're sure the condenser coils are clean, clean them again. Turn off the power. Flip the AC and furnace circuit breakers in your main electrical panel to the "Off" position. Next, turn off the power switch right at the furnace or air handler. Then yank the disconnect block **(Photo 1)** and clean the condenser coils **(Photo 2)**.

If the AC still doesn't work properly after you've cleaned the condenser coils, installed a new filter and opened all the supply vents, proceed with the following repairs.

TEST THE FUSES

Many disconnect blocks contain two cartridge fuses. Check them before you proceed with repairs **(Photo 3)**. A blown fuse is a sign of a failing part inside the condensing unit, so don't just replace the fuse and think you've solved the problem. Instead, replace the parts we show here. Then install new fuses and fire up the unit. If it blows again, call a pro.

INSPECT THE INSIDE OF THE ACCESS PANEL

Follow the electrical conduit from the house—that's where you'll find the access panel. With the power off, remove and store the access-panel retaining screws and remove the panel. Before you replace any parts, check for rodents' nests or evidence of chewing on wires and electrical connectors.

If you find broken wires or chewed insulation and can safely handle electrical repairs, discharge the capacitor first **(Photo 4)**. Then repair the wires and clean out the nest. Otherwise, call a pro.

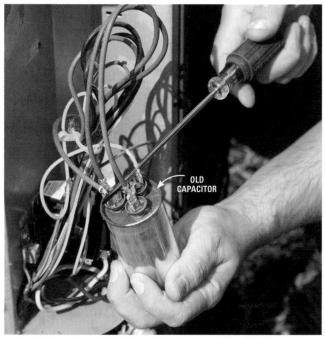

4 DISCHARGING A DUAL START/RUN CAPACITOR. Remove the capacitor from the retaining bracket. Then touch an insulated screwdriver between the HERM (or H) terminal and the COMMON (or C) terminal. Do the same between the FAN (or F) terminal and the C terminal. On single-mode capacitors, just make a short between the two terminals.

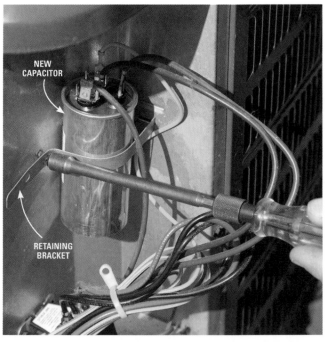

5 INSTALL THE NEW CAPACITOR. Slide the new capacitor into the retaining bracket and tighten the bracket screw. Secure the wires with a zip tie.

6 SWAP OUT THE CONTACTOR. Yank each connector off the old contactor and move it to the same location on the new part. Tighten the connectors where needed. Then secure the new contactor in the condensing unit.

7 REPLACE THE FAN MOTOR. Mark the blade to show which side is up. Loosen the fan blade setscrew and carefully pull it off the motor shaft. Then swap in the new motor. Route the motor wires through the old conduit and secure them with zip ties where necessary. Don't skip the zip ties or the blade could cut the wires.

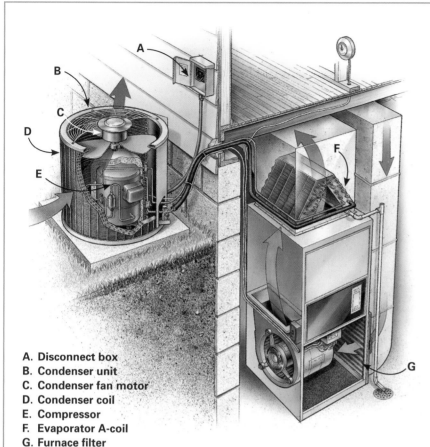

Anatomy of a Central Air Conditioner

Central AC systems consist of two major components: a condensing unit that sits outside your house and the evaporator coil (often referred to as an A-coil) that sits in the plenum of your furnace or air handler. The refrigerant in the A-coil picks up the heat from your home and moves it to the outdoor condensing unit. The condensing unit fan blows outside air through the condensing coil to remove the heat. The condensing unit houses the three parts replaceable by a DIYer: the contactor, the start/run capacitor(s) and the condenser fan motor. The condensing unit also houses the compressor, but only a pro can replace that. The A-coil has no parts that can be serviced by a DIYer.

A. Disconnect box
B. Condenser unit
C. Condenser fan motor
D. Condenser coil
E. Compressor
F. Evaporator A-coil
G. Furnace filter

REPLACE THE START/RUN CAPACITOR(S)

All AC units have at least one capacitor. The capacitor stores electricity and then releases it during compressor and condenser fan startup to give both motors an extra jolt of power. It also smooths out voltage fluctuations to protect the compressor and condenser fan motor from damage.

Capacitors can degrade slowly, providing less startup power over time. Or they can fail in an instant. Gradual capacitor failure can go unnoticed for a long time. This stresses the compressor and condenser fan motor windings, resulting in their early failure. Since capacitors are cheap (less than $25 each), it pays to proactively replace yours about every five years.

Replacing a capacitor is easy. Just take a photo of the wires before disconnecting anything (you may need a reference later on). Then discharge the stored energy in the old capacitor (**Photo 4**). Use needle-nose pliers to pluck one wire at a time from the old capacitor and snap it onto the corresponding tab of the new capacitor. The female crimp connectors should snap tightly onto the capacitor tabs. Wiggle each connector to see if it's tight. If it's not, remove the connector and bend its rounded edges so it makes a tighter fit on the tab. When you've swapped all the wires, secure the new capacitor (**Photo 5**).

REPLACE THE CONTACTOR

A contactor is a $25 mechanical relay that uses low-voltage power from the thermostat to switch 220-volt high-amperage current to the compressor and condenser fan. AC contactors can wear out and are at the top of the list of common AC failures. Even if your contactor is working, it pays to replace it every five years or so. Unscrew the old contactor before removing the wires. Then move the wires to the new unit (**Photo 6**).

TEST YOUR REPAIRS

Reinstall the access panel and disconnect block. Turn on the circuit breaker and furnace switch. Then set the thermostat to a lower temperature and wait for the AC to start (see "Be Patient at Startup," p. 139). The compressor should run and the condenser fan should spin. If the compressor starts but the fan doesn't, the fan motor is most likely shot. Shut off the power and remove the screws around the condenser cover. Lift the cover, and remove the fan blade and motor (**Photo 7**). Replace the motor, reinstall the blade and secure the cover. Then repower the unit and see if the fan starts. If it doesn't, you've given it your best shot—it's now time to call a pro.

Prevent Household Disasters

These 11 simple, low-cost tips could save you thousands.

1. TURN OFF THE WATER SUPPLY BEFORE GOING ON VACATION

Water damage from undetected plumbing leaks will quickly ruin floors and walls, leading to repair bills in the thousands. This is especially true if you're away on vacation. Yes, such a leak is unlikely, but insurance companies report hundreds of these incidents every year. Look for the main valve near the water meter and turn it clockwise to close it. If it's stuck, leaks or doesn't turn on again, hire a plumber to replace it. The ice maker in your refrigerator may freeze up while you're gone, so shut it off as well or thaw it with a hair dryer when you return.

2. ONCE A YEAR, INSPECT YOUR FOUNDATION FOR TERMITE TUNNELS

Pull out your flashlight and walk around your home, examining the foundation both inside and out to inspect for termite tunnels. Much of the damage termites do is invisible, inside walls and floors. Take the time to look for telltale sawdust and tunnels, because termites can do major damage before you even know they're there. If you spot signs of termites, call in a professional exterminator.

3. USE METAL TUBING RATHER THAN PLASTIC FOR ICE MAKER SUPPLY LINES

If you've had mice in your home, use a copper (type L) or braided stainless steel line rather than a plastic supply line for the ice maker in your refrigerator. Mice like to hang out behind refrigerators and occasionally chew holes in plastic lines. This damage can easily lead to a leak that can ruin floors and ceilings before you detect it. Plastic tubes also can harden over time and crack. Find metal ice maker lines at home centers and wherever appliances are sold.

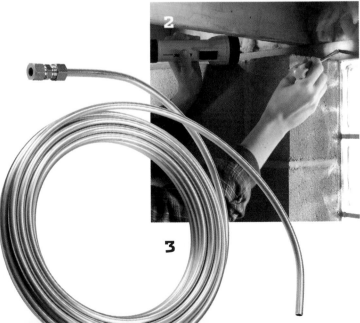

MAIN WATER SHUTOFF

1

2

3

4. TRIM TREES AROUND THE HOUSE SO DEAD BRANCHES WON'T CRASH DOWN ON THE ROOF

Insurance companies get a flood of tree-related claims after major storms. You can't prevent all of these incidents, but many you can if you trim overhanging branches and dying trees just waiting to fall. Tree trimming is a dangerous project. Call in a tree service to trim all tall trees around your home every few years. Don't procrastinate. Spending a few hundred dollars now could save you several thousands in roof and rain damage later.

4

5. MONITOR FOUNDATION OR WALL CRACKS, AND CHECK THEM MONTHLY TO DETECT MOVEMENT

Hairline cracks in a concrete foundation are normal, but cracks that continue to widen spell trouble. They'll eventually cause shifting and cracking in the walls above, tilt floors, and rack doors and windows so they won't open and close. The movement is glacially slow. To help you spot it, measure and record each gap size. Check them every few months. If the cracks widen, call in a foundation specialist to assess the foundation. Solutions can cost hundreds of dollars, but the cost of ignoring the problem is greater. A major foundation fix can cost thousands.

5

6. TEST YOUR SUMP PUMP BEFORE THE BEGINNING OF THE RAINY SEASON

The most common time for a sump pump to fail is during the first heavy rainfall after months of not being used. The submerged or partially submerged portions of cast-iron pumps may rust and seize. And they'll burn out when they switch on. Don't get caught with your pump down and the water rising. After a long dry (unused) spell, take a few moments to pour a bucket or two of water into the sump to make sure the pump kicks on.

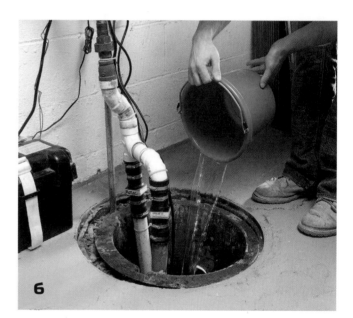

6

7. PUT SPLASH PANS UNDER WASHERS AND WATER HEATERS TO CATCH LEAKS

In the past, water heaters and clothes washers always sat on concrete floors near drains, where spills and leaks wouldn't hurt anything. Now they often sit on framed wood floors, sometimes on the second floor, where spills, overflows, broken hoses or slow drips can cause stains, rot and other expensive water damage. For about $20, you can buy special pans at home centers and appliance dealers that catch slow leaks and mild overflows. Some have drain holes where you can connect a tube that leads to a floor drain. They won't stop burst water lines or massive overflows, but they're cheap insurance against water damage caused by minor spills and leaks.

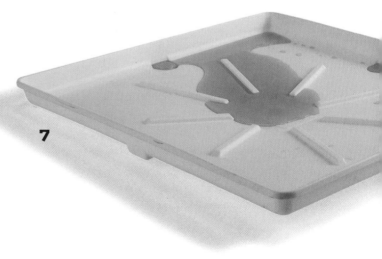

7

8. BUY NO-BURST HOSES FOR YOUR CLOTHES WASHER

If your current hoses are more than five years old, replace them with no-burst hoses. The supply hoses to your clothes washer are always under pressure, just like the supply pipes in your water system. However, eventually the rubber will harden, crack and leak. If undetected, the leak can cause extensive water damage. An inexpensive solution is to buy no-burst hoses. These high-quality hoses are less likely to leak and they'll keep any leak from becoming a torrent. You can often find them for about $20 a pair at home centers, hardware and appliance stores, or online.

9. ADD 6-FT.-LONG DOWNSPOUT EXTENSIONS

A 1-in. rainfall drops about 650 gallons of water on an average roof. And your downspouts concentrate all that water in only a few spots. If dumped too close to the house, the water will undermine your foundation, causing it to leak, shift or crack. That's a very expensive fix. Downspout extensions will prevent most major problems, including wet basements, cracked foundation walls, and termite and carpenter ant infestations.

10. STRAP YOUR WATER HEATER IF YOU LIVE IN AN EARTHQUAKE-PRONE REGION

Earth tremors can tip water heaters and break the gas lines that lead to them, causing either water damage or, worse, an explosion and fire. Water heater straps can prevent this disaster. (They're required in California and other regions.) In earthquake-prone regions, you can find them at home centers and hardware stores for less than $20. Otherwise, order them online.

11. INSTALL SURGE PROTECTORS TO PROTECT MICROPROCESSORS AND PREVENT DATA LOSS

Computer chips are sensitive and highly vulnerable to momentary power surges, especially powerful ones induced by lightning. Losing a $1,000 computer is bad enough, but losing photos, music and other irreplaceable stuff on your hard drive is often much worse. Insulate your valuable microprocessors from this danger by plugging them into a surge protector. A better surge protector ($40 and up) will have the following ratings printed somewhere on the box: Meets UL 1449 or IEEE 587; clamps at 330 volts or lower; can absorb at least 100 joules of energy or more; and handles telephone lines and video cables as well.

8

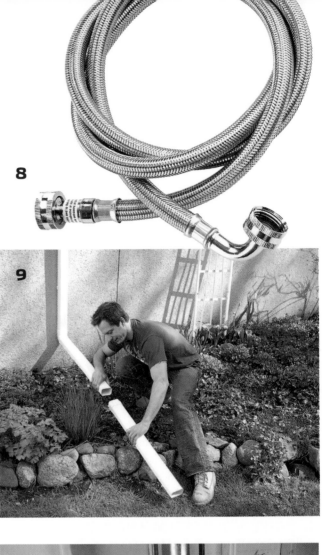

9

10

WATER HEATER STRAP

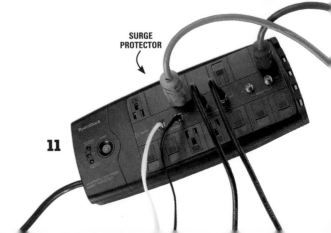

SURGE PROTECTOR

11

What Is Radon?

Radon is an invisible, odorless radioactive gas that seeps out of the soil and into the atmosphere. It's almost everywhere. In fact, you're probably breathing in tiny traces of it right now. But when it's trapped inside a home and reaches high levels, radon can cause lung cancer. Your house can have high levels of radon even if your house is new and your neighbor's house doesn't have any. The highest levels are normally found in basements, but it's possible for radon to reach other parts of your house too.

PVC PIPE

SHALLOW PIT

DIY Radon Reduction

You can save $1,000 in a weekend! Here's what you need to know before you begin.

If you've tested for radon and found you've got a problem, your next question is probably "Can I fix it myself?" This story will help you answer that question. And if you decide to go for it, we've got some great tips from professional installers to help you get it done.

In most cases, pros charge about $1,500 to install a radon mitigation system, but you can do it yourself for only about $500 in materials. So if you're fairly handy and have some carpentry, plumbing and electrical skills, you can install your own system in a weekend and save yourself a thousand bucks!

SEAL HOLES AND CRACKS FIRST

If the radon levels in your home are only slightly elevated, try sealing holes and cracks in concrete walls and floors and then test again. In most cases, sealing doesn't solve the problem. But you'll have to seal before you install a mitigation system anyway, so it's worth a try. Sealing is usually simple; caulk small openings and fill larger gaps with expanding foam or hydraulic cement.

Test for Radon

It's important to fix the radon problem in your house if a test shows a concentration of 4 picocuries per liter (pCi/L) or higher. You can buy a test kit at a home center or online for less than $20—which includes a lab fee—and perform the test yourself. Just let the tester sit in your house for a few days and then mail it to a lab for analysis. Electronic radon monitors that check continuously for radon are available online for about $130 and don't require a lab.

Planning Your System: 7 Questions to Answer

More than most projects, a radon mitigation system requires detailed planning. The planning process will also help you decide whether you're willing and able to tackle the job yourself. Here are seven questions you must answer before you charge ahead:

1. WHAT DOES YOUR BUILDING INSPECTOR REQUIRE?

As you get started, make a quick call to your town's building department to ask about local code requirements, permits and inspections. In some areas, only licensed pros are allowed to install systems.

2. WHERE WILL THE PIPE BEGIN?

In most cases, you'll want to locate the PVC pipe that sucks radon from under your concrete floor near an exterior wall so it's out of the way and easy to route outside. This is also where sump pump basins and footing drainpipes (aka "drain tile") are located in some homes—perfect places from which to suck radon. If you don't have a sump basin, you'll have digging to do (see "Make a Suction Pit," p. 149). If you use the sump basin as your suction point, be sure to seal around any pipe and wire penetrations in the lid. Special supplies for dealing with sump basin lids are available online at indoor-air-health-advisor.com, or do an online search for "radon sump lid."

3. WILL YOU RUN THE PIPE INDOORS OR OUT?

It's much easier to route the pipe outside the house, but that can cause a problem in cold climates. Condensation can form inside, causing ice to build up and stop the fan from working.

4. WHAT'S THE PIPE PATH?

If you'll be routing your pipe outdoors, it's no big deal. Just run it up along an exterior wall. But running pipe indoors can be a real nightmare. Most professional installers in cold-weather areas try to avoid condensation problems by routing the pipe up through a closet or finished garage and

How a Radon Reduction System Works

At its core, the process is simple: A fan pulls radon gas from beneath the floor and exhausts it outside. In cold climates, it's better to run the pipe inside the house rather than outside.

to a fan in the attic that blows the radon out above the roof. Be ready for a big, dusty mess if you have to route your pipe indoors. Also keep in mind that the pipe has to terminate 12 in. above the roof and be at least 10 in. away (horizontally) from any dormer windows. Ask your city's building department about any additional requirements.

5. WHERE WILL YOU PUT THE FAN?

If you'll be mounting the fan outside, put it in a place where you can get electricity to it easily. If it's indoors, the fan must be located in an unfinished attic. Never install the fan in your basement or any living space, because if there's ever a leak, the fan could pump highly concentrated radon into your home.

6. HOW WILL YOU GET POWER TO THE FAN?

The toughest part of any electrical job is getting cable from point A to point B. If there's a junction box nearby that you can extend the circuit from, you're golden. If not, you might be spending lots of time fishing cable to where you need it. Fans draw very little power—usually less than 100 watts—so you can tap any nearby circuit. You can also hardwire a fan or plug it into an outlet. In an attic, it's best to install an outlet because it makes replacing the fan easier. Outside, it's best to hardwire the fan using watertight conduit.

7. WHAT'S UNDER THE SLAB?

You may not know what kind of base material you have under your concrete slab until you actually punch a hole in the floor. (See "Make a Big Hole with Several Small Ones," p. 148.) Soil conditions affect how readily radon flows underneath the slab, so don't buy a fan until you know what you're dealing with. You'll also need to provide this information when you buy a fan. (See "Buy Your Fan from an Expert," below.)

Buy Your Fan from an Expert

Radon fans cost $140 to $250, depending mostly on size. Some radon mitigation systems require a big, powerful fan. Others work fine with a smaller model. Sizing a fan requires expertise, so we strongly recommend that you buy from an expert who will ask questions and supply you with the best fan for your situation, as well as exchange the fan for a bigger one if the smaller one doesn't fix your radon problem. One such expert is Val Riedman, a professional radon system installer who runs a website where you can get more DIY information and buy supplies. Several *Family Handyman* editors have purchased fans from him. Visit indoor-air-health-advisor.com/radon.html for more information.

FOOTING
TEST HOLE

1

Tips for Installing Your System

1. FIND THE FOOTING

If you'll be installing your PVC pipe close to a basement wall, drill a test hole in the floor and feel around for the foundation's footing. Concrete slabs are typically about 4 in. thick, so use a masonry bit that's a couple of inches longer than the thickness of the floor (our installers used a 12-in. one) to see if the footing under the foundation walls will be in the pipe's way. If you do hit the footing, try again a couple of inches farther from the wall. You can patch the test holes later with patching cement.

2. MAKE A BIG HOLE WITH SEVERAL SMALL ONES

You'll need a hole in the basement floor a little bigger than the PVC pipe to give you some wiggle room and make it easier to remove soil and gravel. You could rent a large rotary hammer drill and coring bit from the home center, but save yourself some money and try this trick instead: Just draw a 6-in. circle where the pipe will be installed. Then, using a 3/16-in. masonry bit, drill several holes close together. Now just whack the center of the large hole with a hammer to break through.

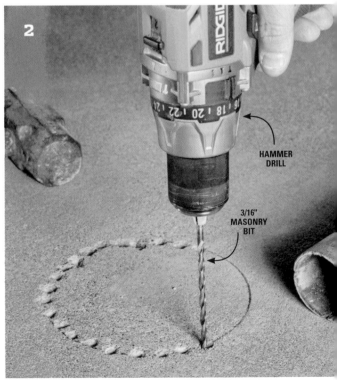

2

HAMMER
DRILL

3/16"
MASONRY
BIT

3. MAKE A SUCTION PIT

Creating a shallow pit underneath the hole gives the radon a place to collect before getting sucked up the pipe. You'll need to remove several gallons of whatever base material is under your slab. The tighter the soil, the more material you'll have to remove so the radon fan can do its job. For loose gravel, you need to remove only about 5 gallons. For tighter soils like sand, dirt or clay, plan to remove 15 gallons or more. A shop vacuum helps suck up the loose stuff. For tighter soil, you'll probably need to do a combination of hand digging and vacuuming.

4. DRY-FIT ALL THE PIPING

Doing a dry fit before gluing the PVC pipe and fittings ensures that everything will fit together properly after you apply the glue. Once you commit to gluing, you have only seconds to push and twist everything together before they're permanently fused.

5. INSTALL FIRE-STOP COLLARS IN GARAGES

If you route part of your radon piping through a garage, then you must install fire-stop pipe collars (also called fire barriers) wherever pipe goes through a finished wall or ceiling. The collars seal around the pipe, preventing—or at least slowing down—fire from spreading to other parts of the house.

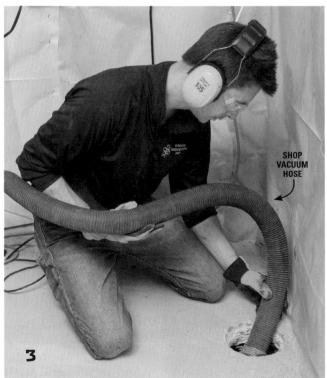

SHOP VACUUM HOSE

FIRE-STOP COLLAR

RIM JOIST

LOCATOR HOLE

CUT HOLE FROM OUTSIDE

RIM JOIST

6

PATCHING CEMENT

BACKER ROD

7

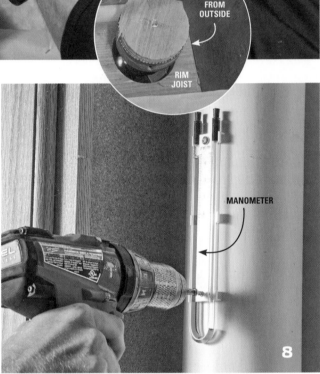

MANOMETER

8

6. EXIT THROUGH THE RIM JOIST

If you'll be running pipe directly outside from the basement or out through an attached garage, you'll need to cut a hole in the rim joist. A hole saw ($25 to $40 at home centers) is the perfect tool for this job. Buy the cheapest one you can find since you'll probably use it only once or twice in your lifetime. The installers we worked with used a 4-1/2-in.-dia. hole saw, which matched the outside diameter of 4-in. PVC pipe, giving it a very snug fit. Drill a locator hole from inside the basement first, then use the hole saw to cut the hole from outside.

7. SEAL AROUND THE PIPE WITH PATCHING CEMENT

After you've installed all the pipe, stuff some foam backer rod into the gap between the pipe and the concrete, and apply fast-setting concrete patching cement. Trowel the cement flush with the top of the concrete floor.

8. INSTALL A MANOMETER

Radon fans don't run forever (typically 7 to 10 years), so you need a warning device to tell you when it stops working. One option is a liquid-filled manometer ($10 to $30 online) mounted on the PVC pipe. When the liquid level drops, the system isn't working. Electronic monitors that measure radon in the air are another option. The Safety Siren Radon Detector, for example, sounds an alarm when radon levels become dangerous ($180 online).

DO ANOTHER RADON TEST

After installing your radon system, do another test. If that test shows you still have high levels of radon, contact the company you bought the fan from. Chances are, you'll need to install a more powerful fan. But in some cases, a second suction point (where the pipe enters the floor) is the solution. (See "Buy Your Fan from an Expert" on p. 147.)

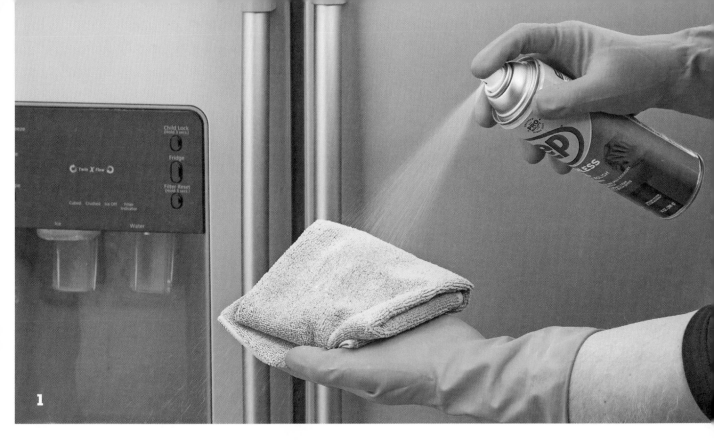

Keep Your House Running Smoothly

These home maintenance tips from the trenches will help you think like a handyman.

1. KEEP STAINLESS STEEL STAINLESS

Stainless steel appliances look great—until they get fingerprints all over them. And while no cleaner can prevent fingerprints and smudges, the way the cleaner is applied can help avoid streaks and spotting. Instead of spraying the cleaner directly onto the surface, first spray it on a microfiber cloth and then wipe it on.

2. LET YOUR FREEZER BREATHE

The vents on frost-free fridges allow air to circulate in the freezer. We suggest keeping your freezer only about three-quarter full. This allows the fan to freely circulate the cold air. It is good for the freezer and helps the refrigerator run more efficiently, saving you money on energy bills.

DON'T BLOCK THE FAN

A RAZOR WON'T HURT THE GLASS

3. CLEAN GLASS STOVETOPS WITH A RAZOR

Here's a tip for cleaning glass stovetops—use a razor! First apply Cerama Bryte Cleaner ($16 online) to the glass cooktop and let it sit. Then scrape the cooktop clean with a razor blade. Those tough baked-on spots don't stand a chance!

4. KEEP FAUCET HEADS FLOWING

Faucet spouts and showerheads can gradually clog with calcium and lime. Luckily, the fix is easy—just soak them in vinegar to loosen the buildup. Though it might seem tempting, avoid using CLR (Calcium, Lime & Rust Remover)—it can damage the finish on brass or nickel-plated fixtures.

5. LUBRICATE YOUR GARBAGE DISPOSAL

In-sink disposals get fed a lot of things, including some things they shouldn't. We suggest a monthly cleaning with ice cubes to help keep the blades free of rust. Also, pouring in a squirt of dish soap can help keep the disposal lubricated and running smoothly.

6. LUBRICATE LIGHTBULBS

If you've ever had to remove a stuck lightbulb with a needle-nose pliers,

VINEGAR

8 A GALLON OR TWO SHOULD DO THE TRICK

9 SCRATCH

10

9. RENEW YOUR VINYL FLOORS

Vinyl plank flooring is durable, easy to install and beautiful. However, it's not immune to scratches, and a little dirt underfoot can mar that beauty. Luckily, you can make these scratches disappear with sandpaper. Using a bit of water to lubricate the paper, start at 120 grit, then move on to 180 and stop at 220. Test in an inconspicuous spot at first to ensure the vinyl reacts well to sanding.

10. MAKE CARPET STAINS DISAPPEAR

Any carpet in a highly trafficked area of the house will see its fair share of stains. Here's our answer for all of them: Proxi Spray & Walk Away cleaner ($21 online). As the name indicates, you just apply it and walk away. The spray won't make every stain disappear, but it will remove most carpet stains by the time it dries.

you know it's not fun. Drop a dab of dielectric grease on a new bulb's threads to make sure it comes out easily, every time. Dielectric grease is available for about $5 at any auto parts store.

7. PATCH DAMAGED WALLS FAST

Occasional dings and dents in walls are inevitable, so it's incredibly helpful to know how to patch them quickly and reliably. We like to use Durham's Rock Hard Water Putty ($4 for a 1-lb. can) because it can be mixed quickly, it's durable and it doesn't shrink. Once you apply the compound to the repair, you can use a heat gun

to speed up the drying. The patch is usually ready for paint in under an hour.

8. DRAIN YOUR WATER HEATER

Periodically draining your water heater will extend its life and lower your energy bills. Over time, sediment collects at the bottom of the tank. On gas-powered heaters, this creates hot spots that can damage the tank and cause leaks. On an electric water heater, sediment buildup can cause the lower heating element to fail prematurely. We recommend clearing sediment from your water heater at least once a year.

One Pro's Go-To Tools

Most home repair pros have a well-organized shop full of tools; these are the items one pro said he relies on the most.

ELECTRIC STAPLER
A good electric stapler can do miles of small carpet repairs.

LASER LEVEL
Hang pictures faster and with more accuracy using a laser line instead of a tape measure and spirit level.

3-IN-ONE OIL
To keep things running smoothly, 3-in-One oil is hard to beat. It can be used on door hinges, drawer slides and tools. It's available at hardware stores for about $5.

SLIP-JOINT PLIERS
This one tool can take the place of a small or large pliers and a whole set of wrenches. It can handle plumbing fixtures, pipes and sometimes old rusty bolts.

FLIR THERMAL CAMERA
These pricey cameras can quickly find hot and cold spots.

MULTIMETER
Many common repair tasks—such as diagnosing appliance problems—require a multimeter.

RYOBI IMPACT DRIVER
For driving long bolts, an impact driver works much better than a drill.

MAGNETIC STUD FINDERS
No batteries required! These magnetic stud finders are great because they easily fit in a pocket.

ALUMINUM TAPE
Despite its name, duct tape should never be used on heating ducts. Always use aluminum tape ($8 per roll).

BALL-PEEN HAMMER
Here's a handy tip: Use the round side of a ball-peen hammer to dent nail holes in drywall so the paper facing doesn't leave a fuzzy spot in the repair.

LEATHERMAN COMBO TOOL
It's a screwdriver, file, knife, marking tool and more. This is many a pro's favorite tool. The price tag (about $100 for a model with 19 tools) may seem high, but its functionality makes it worth twice as much.

NEEDLE-NOSE PLIERS
Jobs that involve hard-to-reach places, such as working on a sink disposal, are easy with needle-nose pliers.

COMPACT DRILL
Most cordless drills are 18-volt, which means they're bigger and heavier. This 12-volt Milwaukee is small, light and powerful enough for most maintenance jobs.

Roof Stain Solutions

Remove and prevent roof algae yourself, saving a call to a pro and boosting your home's curb appeal.

Roof stains make any house stand out—but not in a good way. Luckily, these stains aren't inevitable as a roof ages. They're caused by algae growth in humid, shaded areas, usually with lots of tree cover. While algae won't damage your roof, it will hurt your home's curb appeal. Fortunately, it's easy and inexpensive to remove and prevent stubborn algae stains yourself. Here's how to clean your roof and make your home stand out in the best way.

How to Remove Roof Stains

To see an immediate improvement, you'll need to climb onto your roof, spray it with a cleaning solution and rinse it with water. A cleaning solution and water will remove most algae stains right away, but some can be especially difficult. If you have a steep roof, it's best to call a pro.

1. MIX A HOMEMADE SOLUTION

To save money, we opted to make our own solution. Commercial roof cleaners are available at most home centers, but they are expensive and won't work any better than a homemade solution. Plus, it's easy to make your own. Mix 15 oz. of an oxygen bleach powder (we used OxiClean Stain Remover, available at home centers for about $15) with 2 gallons of warm tap water in a garden sprayer. Don't use chlorinated bleach; it'll kill the lawn and plants on the ground below.

2. SPRAY THE SHINGLES

Once you're on the roof, start at the edge and spray the shingles with your homemade solution, working your way up to the ridge. A wet roof is a slippery roof, so leave a dry path back to your ladder. Allow the solution to sit for 20 minutes before rinsing. Tough stains may require an additional application and a mild scrubbing with a stiff-bristle brush.

RINSE WITH A GARDEN HOSE

After you've waited for the solution to do its work, douse the roof with a garden hose, clearing all the suds and algae off the shingles. At this point you should see a big improvement unless your stains are especially stubborn. Never use a pressure washer to clean the algae; the roof will be clean, but its life will be shortened by the loss of granules.

1

BE SAFE!
Climbing a roof is dangerous. Use a safety harness, wear boots or shoes with good traction, and consider installing a slide guard. For more information, search "roof safety" at familyhandyman.com.

2

How to Prevent Roof Stains

A great way to tackle your roof algae problem is to install zinc strips. Zinc is toxic to algae. When rainwater hits the zinc strips, zinc ions run down the shingles, killing algae. They're easy to install and inexpensive, and they do most of the cleaning work for you. You can find a 50-ft. roll of zinc strip at home centers or online for about $35.

BLACK ALGAE

CLEAN ROOF

You'll often see clean streaks in the shingles below galvanized flashing. That's because the flashing works just like zinc strips: The zinc on the flashing combines with rainwater to kill the algae.

ZINC STRIP LOCATIONS

ZINC STRIP LOCATIONS

WHERE TO INSTALL ZINC STRIPS

Zinc strips work only on areas directly downhill. So if you have dormers, ungalvanized roof vents, valleys, roofs under gables or any other sections that could obstruct the flow of zinc, install zinc strips in those locations too.

HOW TO INSTALL ZINC STRIPS

1 SLIDE UNDER THE SHINGLES Start at the beginning of the ridge and gently pry up the cap shingles with a crowbar. Roll out 2 ft. of zinc strip and slide it no more than 1 in. under the cap shingles.

2 FASTEN UNDER THE SHINGLES Fasten strip with galvanized rubber washer nails under the shingles. You can also use an exterior construction adhesive. Continue to fasten the zinc strip every 12 in. until you've reached the end of the ridge, and then clip it to length with scissors. We found cutting the zinc strip at the end saved time and kept it from flapping around in the wind.

ZINC STRIP TEST

Zinc strip is often marketed as a moss, fungus and algae preventer, but not as a remover. However, expert home inspector Reuben Saltzman installed zinc strip on a moss-covered roof to see if it would actually remove the moss over time. As you can see in the before and after photos, it significantly reduced the moss and algae. So, if you don't mind waiting, you can skip the cleaning and let the zinc strips do the job.

SHINGLES BEFORE

18 MONTHS LATER

Replace Your Roof with Algae-Resistant Shingles

If you're in the market to reshingle your roof, consider installing algae-resistant shingles. They will keep your roof looking great and cost about the same as standard shingles.

CHAPTER FIVE

FURNITURE

Stripping Furniture

Make old furniture look new again in a weekend!

If you've ever thought about stripping and refinishing an old piece of furniture that you inherited from a loved one or rescued from a dumpster, this article is for you.

Furniture refinishing is an easy and very satisfying DIY project. It's also a great way to furnish your house on the cheap. With just a little elbow grease and not too much money, you can easily remove old paint or other finish to give an old piece of furniture a new lease on life and a special place in your home. Read on for our recommended products and techniques.

Choose the Right Stripper

Most stripping products work well on just about any type of finish. So, when you're shopping for a product, it really comes down to two factors: speed and safety. Don't blindly accept marketing claims on the front of the bottle about how safe it is. Some "safe" strippers contain chemicals that are dangerous if you touch them with bare hands or inhale the fumes. Read the back of the bottle! That's where you'll find information about what chemicals are contained and what safety precautions you should take. When using any furniture stripper products, work only in well-ventilated areas and, at a minimum, follow the safety guidelines we lay out in "Strip Safely."

SAFER STRIPPERS

In 2019, the Environmental Protection Agency (EPA) banned the manufacture and sale of methylene chloride paint removers. Several paint and varnish stripper products contained methylene chloride, and they worked well, albeit dangerously. Removing that chemical, and others including n-methylpyrrolidone (NMP), was a good thing.

While safer to use, stripper products that no longer contain methylene chloride or NMP require more time to do their work. Depending on the type and quantity of paint or finish you're trying to remove, some stripper products require up to 24 hours of contact time to be effective. Luckily, the end results are worth it.

CITRISTRIP: This popular finish remover has been on the market for years and was reformulated in 2019 to remove NMP. Citristrip can

remove multiple layers of paint and varnish in one application, working on wood, masonry and metal surfaces. Brush or roll on the gel, and let it sit on the surface. With a scraper, test its effectiveness after 30 minutes or so.

As with any household solvent, when using a paint stripper, read the label on the product package and follow the manufacturer's recommendations. Because there may still be products containing methylene chloride floating around on store shelves, be sure to check the ingredients list before buying the product to avoid serious health risks associated with that chemical. The manufacturers of each such product produce a Safety Data Sheet (SDS) that outlines the product's contents and any associated hazards. You can find SDS documents on the websites of manufacturers and retailers.

3M'S SAFEST STRIPPER: 3M's Safest Stripper has no strong fumes and won't burn your skin. However, it can take up  to 24 hours to work, and it can also be hard to find in stores. Call around before you shop, or search online for it. Strippers like this that contain water can raise the grain of wood, so it might leave you with some light sanding to do. Wear gloves if you have sensitive skin.

IF YOU'RE JUST REMOVING CLEAR FINISH

Just about any stripping product on the market will remove clear finishes, but products labeled "refinisher" do it faster and are less likely to remove stain. Refinishers contain a mixture

of solvents such as methanol, acetone and toluene that allow them to dissolve clear finishes like lacquer and shellac in minutes. But you can't use them for stripping paint. When using a refinisher, be sure to follow the manufacturer's directions for application and removal, and take the recommended safety precautions.

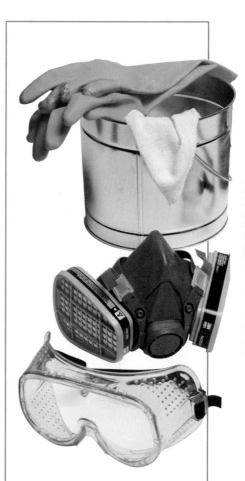

Strip Safely

Most stripping products require the use of eye, skin and lung protection. Wear splash-proof goggles, long sleeves and pants, chemical-resistant gloves and a respirator with new organic vapor cartridges. Keep a bucket of water with rags handy to wipe off stripper that gets on your skin. Work outside if at all possible. If you must work indoors, open as many windows and doors as you can.

Tools & Tips

■ METAL CONTAINER
Because some strippers eat plastic, manufacturers recommend pouring their products into a metal container (even though some are sold in plastic containers). Use a foil pan, a paint can or an old coffee can.

■ DISPOSABLE BRUSH
Use a disposable chip brush or an old paintbrush that you don't care about. When finished, allow the brush to dry completely and throw it into the trash.

■ FURNITURE-FRIENDLY SCRAPERS
Once the stripper has softened the finish, use a wide putty knife to scoop the finish off. Be sure to round off the corners of the putty knife with a file or electric grinder to prevent gouging the wood. A 3 x 3-in. piece of 1/4-in. plywood with the corners rounded off also makes a good scraping tool.

■ ABRASIVE PAD
Use plastic scouring pads to gently remove leftover stripper and residue after scraping. Avoid using steel wool, especially with water-based strippers, because it can leave rust marks behind.

ROUNDED CORNERS

■ BRASS BRUSH
A brass brush has soft bristles and is less likely than a steel brush to damage wood. Use it to remove finish from deep wood pores and turned parts like chair legs. You can also use it (or fine-grit sandpaper) to gently score the surface of hard finishes so stripper will penetrate better.

■ DENTAL PICKS
Dental picks are ideal for removing finish from small cracks and crevices. Slightly dull ones work even better because they are less likely to damage the wood.

■ ROUND SCRAPERS
A piece of dowel with a drywall screw or wood screw in it works well for getting into rounded areas where a flat putty knife won't reach. A pair of locking pliers with a round fender washer also works great as a round scraping tool.

1. CARPET YOUR WORKBENCH

A piece of used carpeting or a new carpet remnant placed on a table or workbench makes a great surface for stripping furniture. The soft carpet protects wood from nicks and scratches and also absorbs drips. You can also use a tarp, plastic drop cloth or old newspapers.

2. BRUSH IT ON THICK

Many strippers go on like a gel, so don't be afraid to put it on thick—1/8 to 1/4 in. Add a second coat if the first one dries before you have time to scrape it off or if the finish doesn't all come off the first time.

3. STRIP IN ZONES

When stripping a really large piece of furniture, do it in zones. Apply stripper to only part of the piece and scrape the stripper off before it dries.

4. KEEP IT WET

Strippers work only while they're wet. To help keep stripper from evaporating too quickly, brush it on and then cover it with a plastic trash bag or drop cloth.

5. USE A BOX

A small cardboard box works great for cleaning off your putty knife. Let the stripper residue in the box dry completely before disposing of it in the trash.

PRO TIP

Reuse Old Stripper

As long as it hasn't completely dried out, you can reuse stripper. Store it in an airtight container until you're ready to use it again.

6. IS IT REALLY WORTH STRIPPING?

Sometimes a piece of painted furniture is painted because somebody tried to hide something like a repair, ugly wood or finger-jointed boards. Try stripping a small area to see what's under all that paint before committing to doing the whole thing.

7. DON'T BOTHER STRIPPING FURNITURE YOU PLAN TO PAINT

If you're going to paint (or repaint) a piece of furniture, you probably don't need to strip it. Wash it with a TSP substitute mixed with water. Then, using medium- or fine-grit sandpaper, smooth out any bumps or flaking paint, and scuff-sand other areas so the new paint will stick better. This applies to painting over clear finishes as well.

8. STRIP HARDWARE THE EASY WAY

Got a lot of old hardware with paint on it? Fill an old slow cooker with water and a couple of drops of dish soap. Then turn it on low and let the hardware "cook" overnight. The paint should practically fall off the next day. If it doesn't, gently scrub it off with a stiff plastic brush.

9. GET RID OF STAIN (OR NOT)

Strippers do a good job of removing clear finishes, but they won't always remove stain. If your goal is to get down to raw wood, remove as much stain as you can using lacquer thinner and an abrasive pad. You might be able to remove the remaining stain with sandpaper. If that doesn't work, apply new stain that's the same color or darker than the old, or consider painting.

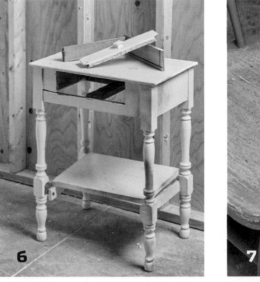

Make Your Own Barn Wood

It is easy to do, yields authentic-looking results and saves you a fortune.

Whether you're creating a rustic interior or adding aged wood accents to a modern decorating scheme, barn wood is a popular choice. And the good news is that you don't have to pick through piles of splintery old lumber or pay exorbitant prices for the look of barn wood. You can easily transform inexpensive pine boards into rustic boards that are almost indistinguishable from the real thing. In this story we'll give you a recipe for doing just that. The 8-ft. 1x6 boards we used for creating our authentic-looking "aged barn wood" cost us about $7 each.

A Foolproof Recipe

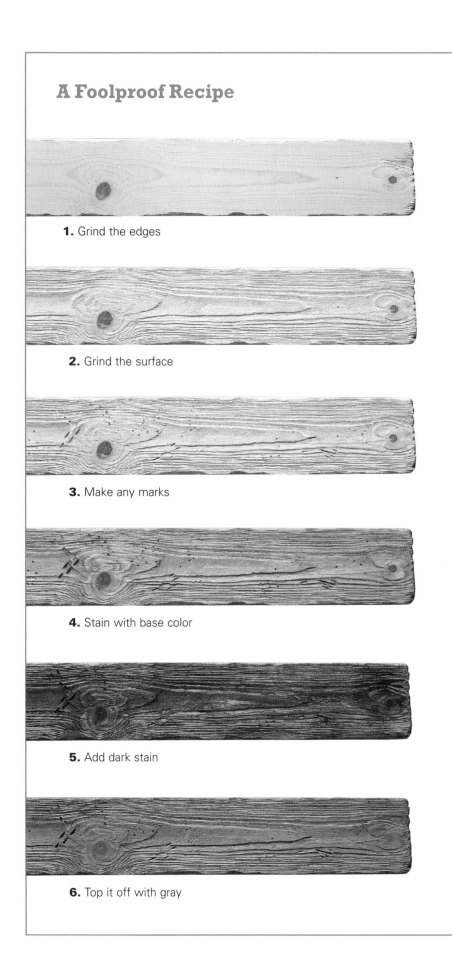

1. Grind the edges

2. Grind the surface

3. Make any marks

4. Stain with base color

5. Add dark stain

6. Top it off with gray

WHAT YOU NEED

There are a few essential tools for this project. The first is an angle grinder. It doesn't have to be expensive. The one we're using is from Harbor Freight Tools and cost only $30. The second essential tool is a knot cup brush attachment for the grinder ($8 to $24). Make sure the arbor diameter of the cup brush matches the arbor on your grinder. In addition, you'll need an awl, a utility knife and a claw hammer for further distressing.

Grinding throws a lot of dust and even an occasional wood chip, so wear safety glasses and a dust mask.

You'll also need a roller to apply the first coat of stain, and cotton rags for the remaining two coats. We used Varathane Summer Oak for the first coat, Varathane Kona for the splotchy dark layer and Varathane Weathered Gray for the final coat.

You don't have to be too picky about choosing knotty pine boards. As long as they're reasonably straight, they'll work fine.

GETTING STARTED

Since clamps would get in the way of the grinding process, tack the board to sawhorses with 6d finish nails. Then follow **Photos 1-5** to distress the surface of the wood. **Photo 6** shows an additional technique, one for making curved wire brush lines that resemble sawmill marks. You can use this technique on a few of the boards for variety. If both sides of the boards will be visible, flip the boards over and repeat the steps.

APPLY THE FINISH

When you've completed the distressing steps for all of the boards, follow the staining process shown in **Photos 7-9**.

FINISH NAIL

1 GRIND THE EDGES AND ENDS. With the grinder spinning in the direction shown above, make random gouges on the edges of the board. While you're at it, round over the sharp factory edges. Then grind the ends of the boards to make them look weathered.

KNOT CUP BRUSH

KNOT CUP BRUSH

2 ERODE THE SURFACE. Remove some of the soft wood from between the growth rings (darker wood grain) by running the cup brush along the board. Follow the grain pattern. The growth rings are harder and will remain, while the brush will wear away the softer wood between them.

Don't worry if the finish looks a little different from one board to the next. Variation will add to the authentic look. When you're done with the stain rags, hang them over the edge of a bucket or garbage can to dry before disposing of them. Wadded-up, stain-soaked rags can spontaneously combust.

Your boards will look the most authentic without a clear coating, but if you need a more durable finish, let the stained boards dry overnight before brushing on a coat or two of polyurethane. Choose a flat or matte sheen to retain the weathered look.

AWL

3 MAKE REALISTIC WORMHOLES. Punch groups of "wormholes" in random patterns with an awl. Elongate some of the holes by tipping the awl down after punching. Space groups of holes 6 to 12 in. apart.

4 ADD DENTS. You can make dents with almost any blunt tool, a metal pipe or even a chain. A hammer claw is handy and works well. Group dents in random patterns along the board.

5 CARVE OUT SPLITS. Carve out soft wood along the grain to simulate a crack. Make fake cracks on the ends of boards or along the edges. You can also simply enlarge an existing crack.

6 MAKE SAW BLADE MARKS. Sweep the grinder across the board in a series of arcs to create the look of old rough-sawn lumber. Add this pattern to a few of your boards for variety.

7 START WITH A BASE COAT. Roll on the first coat of stain. Cover the board entirely. Then wipe off the excess with a cotton rag. Let this coat dry for about five minutes before moving on to the next layer of stain.

8 DAB ON DARK STAIN. Dip a wadded cotton rag into the dark stain and apply it to the board in random patches. Spread out the patches with the rag to create an uneven layer of dark stain.

9 FINISH WITH GRAY STAIN. With a separate cotton rag, wipe on a coat of gray stain. This coat can be more consistent than the dark coat. Wipe off excess stain with a dry cotton rag until you achieve the aged look you desire. If you want the additional protection of a clear finish over the stain, let the stain dry overnight before brushing on a coat or two of flat polyurethane.

Get the Best Plywood for Your Buck

Not all plywood is created equal—learn to shop smarter with these 12 tips.

Building furniture and cabinets is an investment of both time and money. So when you're buying plywood for these projects, shop wisely. Your choices will have a huge impact on the building process and the final results. This article will help you decide exactly what you need and will help you avoid common plywood pitfalls.

1. CHECK FOR FLATNESS

Don't expect perfection—you probably won't find it. Just try to find the best of the pile. Sight down all the edges just as you would if you were buying 2x4 studs. Sometimes a sheet is warped in multiple directions, resembling a potato chip. Leave such sheets for some unlucky, less-informed buyer. If you're buying 1/4-in. plywood, don't worry about flat and straight; it won't be either, but you'll likely fasten it to structural parts, which will keep it flat.

2. INSPECT THE EDGES

Look closely at the core veneers on the edge of a sheet. They should be straight, be of uniform thickness and have few, if any, voids. If you see a lot of voids and overlapping core veneers along the edge, there will be more throughout the sheet that won't be visible until you cut it. Overlapping veneers cause undulations that aren't visible until after you've applied a finish.

3. BRING A FRIEND

Plywood in 4 x 8-ft. sheets is heavy and unwieldy. Unstacking, inspecting, restacking, loading and unloading are much easier with an extra set of hands.

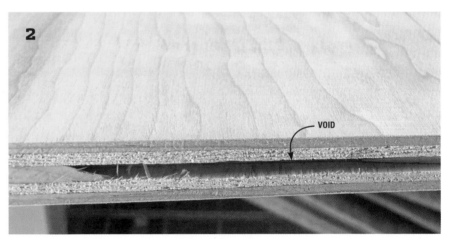

4. WATCH FOR BURIED TREASURE

The most beautifully figured face veneers will be at the lumberyard. But at the home center, try checking out the back faces of the plywood or even plywood that's meant for underlayment. Because most people look for consistency of color and grain, there are some striking veneers that get written off as ugly. Something might catch your eye that could be a really cool design element.

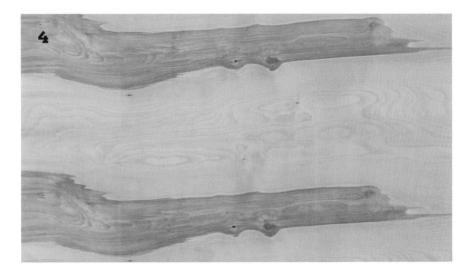

5. SPECIAL-ORDER FROM THE HOME CENTER

Some home centers will special-order many different species, core options and veneer cuts. But beware: You won't be able to look at the actual sheets before buying, and you probably won't be able to return or reject them unless they're damaged or otherwise unusable. If it's just that you don't like the grain pattern, you're probably stuck with the order.

6. USING STAIN? BEWARE OF BIRCH

Any species accepts a clear finish such as polyurethane just fine. But if you're planning to stain your piece, beware of birch, pine and maple. These species take stain very unevenly and can end up looking blotchy. If you're set on one of these species, use a prestain conditioner, which helps each take stain much more evenly. Even better, look at samples of different species with a clear finish and see if there's one that has the color you like without stain.

7. KNOW THE GRADING SYSTEM

Hardwood veneer plywood has a front and a back face and is graded by the quality of each face. The front face is graded using a letter (A-D), with A being the best. The back face is graded using a number (1-4), with 1 being the best.

8. SHOP THE HOME CENTER FOR CONVENIENCE AND SAVINGS

Baltic birch is a premium plywood found at lumberyards. A 3/4-in., 5 x 5-ft. sheet has 13 core veneers and can get quite pricey. Some home centers carry a similar product, called classic birch. A 3/4-in., 4 x 8-ft. sheet has 10 core veneers and is less expensive. It's strong, with good screw-holding capability, making it a good, affordable alternative. It's perfect for less visible

cabinet parts, drawers and shelving. As for other plywood, home centers have a more limited selection, carrying mostly veneer core (maybe MDF core), grade B2 and lower. Face veneer cuts are typically rotary cut or plain sliced, and in-stock species will usually be red oak, birch and maple. But the home center is a good option to save a little money.

9. DON'T HAVE PLYWOOD DELIVERED

If you have a way to haul sheets of plywood yourself, do it. The person pulling sheets for delivery isn't going to hand-select the nicest sheets for you. If delivery is your only option, inspect the sheets before the delivery truck leaves and reject any that are damaged or unusable. You may not have the option of rejecting a sheet because you don't like the grain pattern.

5 ⬇ **Special Order Product**

FRONT FACE – A

BACK FACE – 2

7

8

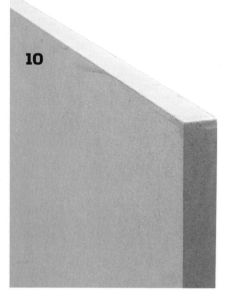

10

11

VENEER ADHESIVE
SHOWING THROUGH

10. USING PAINT? CHOOSE MDF OR BIRCH

For projects we're going to paint, we like MDF (medium-density fiberboard) or birch. B-grade birch or lower is fine. Sometimes you'll even see plywood classified as "paint grade." Birch is close-grained with a smooth texture that doesn't show through paint. With an open-grained species such as oak, the grain is visible under paint. MDF, of course, has no grain pattern, making it a good choice for painted projects. But for structural parts, we like birch veneer. For tips on building with MDF, visit familyhandyman.com and search for "MDF."

11. SAND AT YOUR OWN RISK

All plywood needs at least light sanding before finishing. Sometimes the face veneer on home center plywood is so thin that the pink veneer adhesive shows through. On several occasions, we've seen birch veneer turn translucent after light sanding with 220-grit paper. If you suspect that the veneer is ultra thin, don't use a power sander. Just sand it by hand.

12. SHOP LUMBERYARDS FOR QUALITY AND SELECTION

For the largest selection of the best-quality hardwood veneer plywood, skip the trip to your local home center and visit a lumberyard. A lumberyard that caters to cabinetmakers will give you enough options to make you dizzy. A 4 x 8-ft. sheet will cost anywhere from $80 to $120 or more depending on the species and the cut of the face veneer. Some lumberyards also stock 10-ft. sheets.

Can You Get the Bow Out?

Admit it: You've tried flattening sheets of plywood. We have too. We've tried weights, clamps, wetting down the concave side, sun-drying the convex side and gluing opposing bowed sheets together. Nothing seems to work with any reliability. If the core veneers weren't in a perfect state of equilibrium and all in harmony when they were bonded together, the sheet has little chance of flattening out. The only recourse is to save the flattest sheets for the largest parts and use the worst sheets in smaller components, minimizing any curvature.

Table in a Day

Peel-and-stick veneer makes this table stunning and simple.

When it comes to woodworking, let's face it: Many of us want masterpiece results but love shortcuts. That's where this table comes in. It's built using hollow-core doors and veneer. The method is faster, easier and cheaper than solid-wood construction, and the table is lighter and more stable. We spent about $500 on materials for the table shown in this article because we opted for high-grade zebrawood boards and veneer. But built from a species like oak or cherry, the same table could cost well under $300. Plan to complete the construction in a day, then spend a few more hours applying a finish.

Materials List

ITEM	QTY
Hollow-core door	1
1/4" x 4' x 8' plywood, MDF or hardboard	1 sheet
Solid wood for edging	as needed
4' x 8' peel-and-stick veneer	1 sheet
28" hairpin legs	4
Wood glue	16 oz. or more
Finishing supplies	as needed

EASY RECIPE FOR AN ELEGANT TABLE

A. A hollow-core door is flat, strong, lightweight and inexpensive (around $60), making it the perfect foundation for a table.

B. "Skin" glued to the door provides a tougher tabletop since the faces of a hollow-core door are super thin and easy to puncture. The skin can be plywood, MDF or hardboard.

C. Peel-and-stick veneer costs a few bucks more than standard veneer, but it gives you perfect results without special tools or skills.

D. Solid wood gives the table a durable edge. Veneered edges look just as good, but they aren't nearly as tough. Any thickness will do, but thin stock costs less and is easier to apply. This edging is 3/8 in. thick.

MATERIALS, TOOLS AND TIPS

- Hollow-core doors are available at home centers, typically in widths of 28, 30, 32 and 36 in. You can cut them down from their standard height (80 in.) for a table of a different length. You can also cut them to width, but that's a bit more work.

- We bought the 28-in. hairpin legs online for about $60. There are lots of styles and finishes available. For a dining table, we strongly recommend hairpin legs formed from three columns rather than two.

- This project requires lots of wood glue, at least 16 oz. To give yourself more working time, consider a slow-setting glue such as Titebond Extend, or add about 10% water to standard glue.

- Our plywood skin had some flaws—tiny lumps that telegraphed through the veneer and became visible only after the veneer was finished. To avoid this, examine your plywood carefully. Better yet, choose hardboard or MDF for the skin.

- When you add a skin over the door, don't cut it to fit the door; an exact match is almost impossible. By starting with an oversize skin **(Photo 4)** and then trimming it **(Photo 5)**, you'll get a perfect fit.

- When the edging is complete, make sure its top is flush with the skin. If you find any uneven spots, sand them flush, but be careful not to round the outer corner of the edging.

- Veneer requires only a light sanding before finishing. We prefer to sand it by hand only. The veneer is micro-thin and easy to sand through with a random-orbit sander.

- We finished our table with two coats of polyurethane, followed by two coats of wipe-on poly.

Endless Options

Veneer, a super-thin layer of wood, has been used by woodworkers for centuries because it eliminates hours of labor and can overlay a base material that's more stable than solid wood. More than that, it's an opportunity to use gorgeous wood without spending a fortune. We found more than 100 wood species options online, including some we'd never heard of. A 4 x 8-ft. sheet of peel-and-stick veneer can cost anywhere from $70 to $700. Our zebrawood veneer came from veneersupplies.com.

WENGE

SAPELE POMMELE

LACEWOOD

FIGURED BIRCH

BUBINGA

1

HOLLOW-CORE DOOR

STRAIGHTEDGE

2

WEBBING

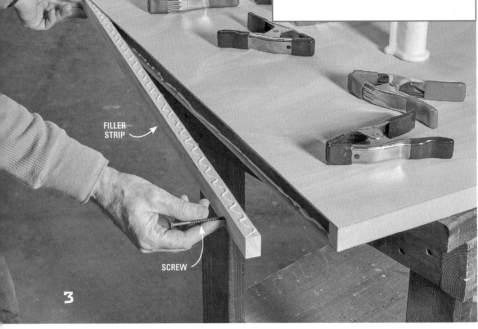

PRO TIP

Drive a screw into the strip. That way, you can pull the strip out if you've pushed it in too far.

FILLER STRIP

SCREW

3

1. CUT THE DOOR

To get a straight cut, run your circular saw along a straightedge. We used a scrap of plywood. Your table can be any length you want. Just remember to account for the thickness of the edging when you determine the door length.

2. MAKE SPACE FOR THE FILLER STRIP

Hollow-core doors have cardboard webbing inside. Use a chisel or sharp putty knife to slice through the glue that fastens the webbing to the faces of the door. Then shove the webbing inward to create room for the filler strip.

3. GLUE IN THE FILLER STRIP

Cut a strip of 3/4-in.-thick wood or plywood to fit into the door. The strip has to be perfectly straight, so choose straight stock. Fasten the strip with wood glue and spring clamps.

4. ADD A SKIN

Cut 1/4-in. material 1/4 in. larger than the door. Coat the door with wood glue and position the plywood, letting it overhang on all four sides. Nail down the perimeter of the plywood and set heavy objects on the interior area.

5. TRIM THE SKIN

Cut off the overhanging skin with a flush-trim router bit. The bearing guides the bit, leaving the skin perfectly flush with the door.

6. ADD THE EDGING

Wrap the door with solid-wood edging. Start on the short ends, then cover the long sides of the door. We skipped the clamping process and fastened the edging with 23-gauge pins instead. Note: Use a straightedge to position the edging. It has to be perfectly flush with the skin.

FLUSH-TRIM BIT

Edge Fastening Options

There are a few ways to fasten the edging. The best approach is clamping, but that's time-consuming and requires a pile of long clamps, so we went with glue and a 23-gauge pin nailer. The tiny nails are easy to hide with a smidgen of filler. An 18-gauge brad nailer would also work, but the larger nail holes are harder to camouflage.

STRAIGHTEDGE

EDGING

VENEER

PAPER

7

ROLLER

8

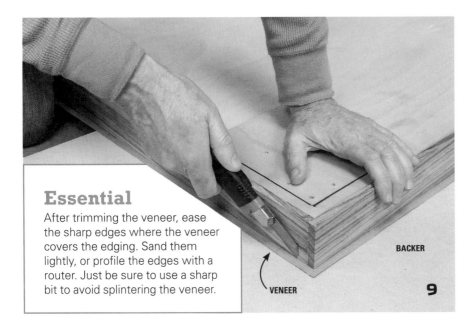

Essential

After trimming the veneer, ease the sharp edges where the veneer covers the edging. Sand them lightly, or profile the edges with a router. Just be sure to use a sharp bit to avoid splintering the veneer.

VENEER

BACKER

9

7. APPLY THE VENEER

Cut the veneer 1 in. larger than the tabletop, using a utility knife with a fresh blade. Peel off the protective paper and set the veneer in place. Don't apply any pressure until the veneer is centered on the tabletop.

8. ROLL THE VENEER

Peel-and-stick veneer uses pressure-sensitive adhesive. For a strong bond, apply lots of force and roll the whole table twice—with grain and across grain. Veneer rollers cost $20 online.

9. TRIM THE VENEER

With a helper, set the tabletop on a cutting backer such as hardboard or MDF. Be careful not to damage the overhanging veneer. Trim it with a fresh, sharp blade. To avoid splintering, cut in two or three light passes rather than one deep cut. Note: Don't use plywood as a cutting backer. The grain can pull your blade off course.

10. ATTACH THE LEGS

Screws won't hold well in a hollow-core door, so first glue on leg bases cut from 1/2 or 3/4-in. plywood. Screw the legs on and you're done!

HAIRPIN LEG

LEG BASE

10

Apply Poly With a Roller—Really!

Coating a large tabletop with a brush is a high-stress speed test. You have to move fast to coat the whole surface before the polyurethane becomes gooey. But haste often leads to missed spots, uneven coverage or ugly brush marks.

So instead, use a mini roller. Sound crazy? We thought so too until we tried it—and tried it again. Even the worst results were better than what we achieved with a brush. Here are a few tips to keep in mind when using this technique:

- Slower dry times are better, so heat is bad. You'll get smoother results at 70 degrees than you will at 80 degrees.
- Rollers work well with oil-based poly; with water-based poly, they caused a disaster.
- We've had the best results with microfiber rollers, though foam rollers are fine too.
- When the surface is perfectly smooth, finish up with two or three coats of wipe-on poly,

which is much less problem-prone than regular poly.
- Apply at least two coats, more if you want more protection. Sand lightly between coats.
- Light coats are best. Heavy coats lead to stubborn bubbles.
- The poly will look terrible at first. You'll be tempted to roll it again to fix it. Don't. Left alone the bubbles will pop and the tiny bumps will level out.
- When you've built up the desired thickness, give the finish at least a day to fully harden. Then wet-sand it to smooth out any little imperfections in the poly. We like to use 600-grit wet/dry sandpaper and soapy water as a lubricant.

Built-to-Last Viking Long Table

You can build this durable piece with basic tools and everyday lumber.

When the Vikings of yore built something—a longboat, a lodge, even a drinking horn—it was sturdy and simple, functional yet attractive. This table fits that mold with a style that still works in the modern era. It's big enough for the whole clan, yet it has a certain elegance to it. This style of table is known as a drawbore trestle. The "trestle" is the stretcher that connects the legs, and "drawbore" refers to the "bored" mortises and tenons that "draw" the legs and trestle tightly together to create a stable base. You can easily shorten (and lighten) your table by modifying the dimensions given. The benches that accompany this table are built using the same template and same basic procedures. To find out how to build them, turn to p. 189.

It's "Knockdownable"!

The table, built as shown, is enormous—long, wide and weighty. But by removing two wedges and eight screws, you can separate the legs, tabletop and trestle so you can store the table for the winter or move it to a different location.

PICK THE RIGHT WOOD

If you're building this table for inside use, you can use everyday dimensional lumber or more expensive hardwoods. But if it will be used outside, consider one of the following weather-resistant options:

CEDAR, REDWOOD OR CYPRESS. One of these "premium" exterior woods is most likely available in your area. Select boards with the most heartwood—the darker inside part of the tree that is more durable than the lighter-colored sapwood. The downside of these woods? They can be wickedly expensive and, in some cases, soft.

TREATED LUMBER. It is moderately priced and stands up well to weather, but it's often wet from the treatment process, which means it's more likely to shrink and twist, less likely to glue up well. It's also difficult to apply a good-looking finish until the wood fully dries.

DOUGLAS FIR. This is the wood we used. It's more expensive than the more widely available "standard" dimensional lumber—often labeled H-F, S-P-F or "white wood"—but cheaper than the premium woods. It's about 20% harder and stronger, heavier and more moisture resistant than standard lumber. Not all home centers and lumberyards stock Douglas fir; look for the "Doug Fir" or "DF" stamp. If in doubt, ask. In our area, Lowe's and contractor lumberyards carry Douglas fir.

If you do opt for Douglas fir, you'll enjoy the decision for a long time to come—one of our editors built a Douglas fir table with a similar design four years ago. He gives it a quick sanding and a coat of Cabot Australian Timber Oil every spring, and he covers it with a tarp during the tough Minnesota winters. The table is still as beautiful as it was on the day it was made.

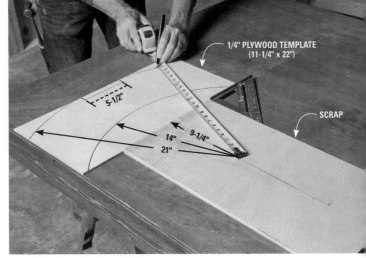

1 **MAKE THE LEG TEMPLATE.** Set a scrap of plywood against the template. Drive a screw 9-1/4 in. from the end of the scrap and use that screw as a pivot point for your tape measure. Then swing the two arcs to create the leg shape.

2 **GLUE UP THE LEG "SANDWICH."** Trace the leg shape onto two 22-in. 2x12s, lightly dampen the bottom piece, then apply polyurethane glue. Use a plastic putty knife to spread the glue slightly beyond the edges of the layout lines and across the main body of the leg.

3 **CLAMP THE LEG BLANKS TOGETHER.** Line up the "mortise" edges of the boards, then drive a few drywall screws into the scrap wood to keep the boards aligned. Clamp the perimeter to force the boards tightly together.

FIGURE A.
VIKING LONG TABLE

Overall Dimensions:
110-1/2" L x 40-3/4" W x 28-3/4" H

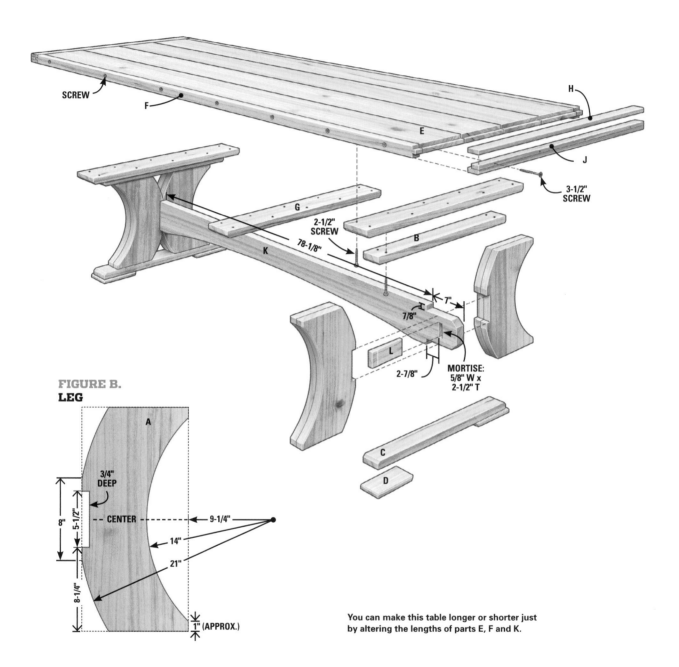

FIGURE B.
LEG

You can make this table longer or shorter just
by altering the lengths of parts E, F and K.

Cutting List

KEY	QTY.	SIZE	PART
A	8	1-1/2" x 11-1/4" x 22"	Legs
B	2	1-1/2" x 3-1/2" x 30"	Top leg plates
C	2	1-1/2" x 3-1/2" x 30"	Bottom leg plates
D	4	3/4" x 4" x 8"	Feet (white oak)
E	4	1-1/2" x 9-1/4" x 108"	Top boards
F	2	1-1/2" x 2-1/4" x 108"	Edge boards
G	3	1-1/2" x 5-1/2" x 37"	Tabletop braces
H	2	3/4" x 2" x 40-3/4"	Outside breadboard ends (white oak)
J	1	3/4" x 1-1/4" x 40-3/4"	Middle breadboard end (white oak)
K	1	1-1/2" x 7-1/2" x 92-1/8"	Stretcher
L	2	3/4" x 2-1/2" x 7"	Wedges (white oak)

Materials List

ITEM	QTY.
2x12 x 8' Douglas fir	2
2x10 x 10' Douglas fir	4
2x8 x 8' Douglas fir	1
3/4" x 5-1/2" x 4' white oak	3
2x6 x 10' Douglas fir	2
2x4 x 10' Douglas fir	1
2-1/2" exterior deck screws	1 lb.
2-1/2" exterior washer-head screws	2 lbs.
3-1/2" exterior washer-head screws	2 lbs.
Construction adhesive	1 tube

To round out our Viking table, we used white oak for the feet, the breadboard ends and the wedges. Other woods would work fine, but we liked the extra strength, hardness and contrast the white oak provided in these critical pieces. Red oak, the type you'll often find at home centers, isn't a good substitute since it's much more prone to rot. You can find white oak at specialty woodworking stores and online.

CREATE THE LEGS

Take your time at the lumberyard selecting flat, straight boards free of split ends, twists, cupping and loose knots—you'll spare yourself a lot of clamping and cussing down the road. If you have trouble finding perfect 2x12s, purchase an extra board, or longer boards, and cut around the defects. Cut your boards into eight 22-in.-long pieces, making sure the ends are square. Pair up your boards so when one is laid atop the other, there's little or no gap along the ends and edges. If you flip or rotate the boards, sometimes you'll find the perfect fit. Try to have any defects fall in the areas of the wood you'll be cutting away as you form the legs.

Mark your leg template on 1/4-in. plywood as shown in **Photo 1**. Cut just outside the line with a fine-tooth jigsaw blade, then use a belt sander to sand right up to the line. Use your template to trace the leg shape onto two leg sections **(A)**. Lightly dampen the bottom piece—polyurethane glue needs moisture to work—then apply healthy squiggles of the glue across the main body of the leg **(Photo 2)**. Use a plastic putty knife to spread the glue slightly past the edges of your template marks. Polyurethane glue is waterproof, and tightly glued seams mean less chance of moisture working its way between the boards.

Place the top board over your glued board, taking care to even up the edges. Install two or three screws in the waste area **(Photo 3)** to keep the pieces aligned, and then use clamps—lots of them—along all the edges. Drive additional screws into the waste area to help draw the pieces tightly together. The glue will foam as it goes to work. Keep your boards clamped together at least two hours or overnight for good measure. Create three more leg blanks this way.

Cut out the legs. A jigsaw with a long, coarse blade **(Photo 4)** works fine, but a band saw works better. Whichever tool you use, make a series of relief cuts as shown. These allow you to remove waste material as you cut. They also allow your blade to get back on track if it wanders and begins making angled cuts, which jigsaws in particular are prone to do. If you have a jigsaw with reciprocating action, set it at zero; it will cut slower, but your blade will wander less.

Next, use a belt sander to smooth and true up the curved sides **(Photo 5)**. Begin with a coarse belt, then progress to finer grits. If you have access to a benchtop belt sander or spindle sander, use it; you'll get results faster. Use a router with a 1/2-in. round-over bit to soften the edges of the

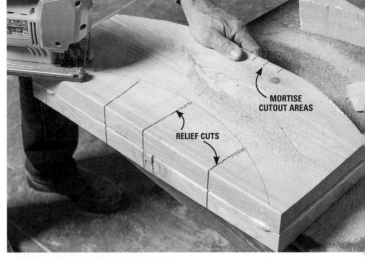

4 CUT THE LEG BLANKS. Make a series of relief cuts along the concave side of the leg, then use a jigsaw with a coarse blade (or a band saw) to cut the curves. Make a series of relief cuts for the stretcher mortise, and then use a jigsaw and chisel to make the opening.

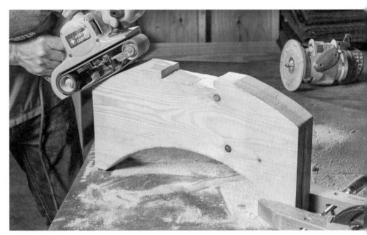

5 SAND THE LEG BLANKS AND ROUT THE EDGES. Smooth the curves and eliminate blade marks with a belt sander. Use a router with a 1/2-in. round-over bit to soften the curved edges, but leave the top, bottom and stretcher areas square.

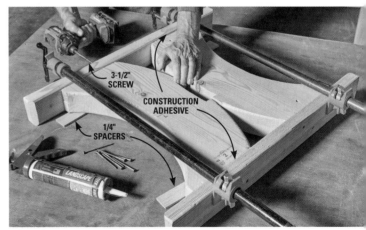

6 CREATE THE LEG ASSEMBLIES. Set the arches on 1/4-in. spacers, butt the arches together, then dry-fit the top and bottom plates. Check the stretcher opening with a 2x6 to make sure the tenon will fit. Finally, apply construction adhesive to the leg ends, and clamp and screw the parts together.

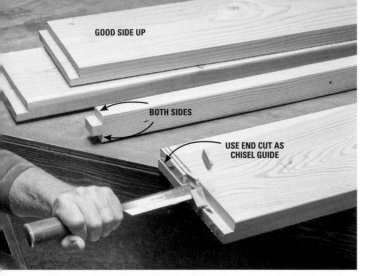

GOOD SIDE UP

BOTH SIDES

USE END CUT AS
CHISEL GUIDE

7 CUT THE TONGUES. Position the top and edge boards good side up, then with your circular saw set 3/4 in. deep, make a series of cuts starting 3/4 in. from the end. Make one of these cuts across the very end to guide your chisel. Make these tongue cuts on both sides of the edge boards.

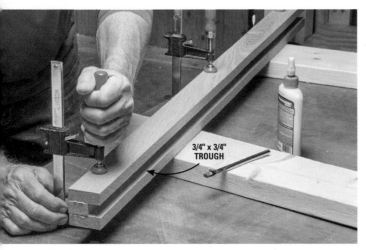

3/4" x 3/4"
TROUGH

8 BUILD THE BREADBOARD ENDS. Use waterproof glue and clamps to build the three-part breadboard ends. Make sure the center trough is 3/4 x 3/4 in. to accommodate the tongues of the top boards.

1/4" x 2-1/2" WASHER-
HEAD SCREWS
3/8" HOLES

9 ASSEMBLE THE TOP. Position the top and edge boards good side down, then screw the braces and breadboard ends to the top boards.

curved parts. Don't rout the tops and bottoms of the legs or the flat area where the mortise cutouts are.

Position two leg sections next to each other (**Photo 6**) and check to make sure the mortise cutouts (where the stretcher tenon will go) can accommodate a 2x6 test piece. It's easier to enlarge these areas now, before joining the legs. Set the legs on 1/4-in. spacers (so they'll be centered on the 2x4 top and bottom plates). Then apply construction adhesive to the ends to add a layer of moisture protection, and cinch the leg sections tightly together and to the 2x4 plates (**B, C**) with clamps. Secure the legs to the plates using 3-1/2-in. exterior screws. Repeat for the other leg assembly. Cut the feet (**D**) to size and shape, then secure them with glue and screws to the bottom plates (**Photo 10**).

BUILD THE BREADBOARD ENDS AND TABLETOP

Breadboard ends have been used by woodworkers for centuries—and for good reason:

- They help keep the ends of the tabletop boards flat and aligned.
- They help protect the end grain of the boards from moisture and wear.
- They allow the top boards to shrink and expand more freely without cracking.
- They provide a smooth edge for your stomach to rest against.

The 2-1/4-in.-wide boards along the long edges give the tabletop more mass to match the heft of the legs. Rip your two 2-1/4-in.-wide edge boards (**F**) from a 2x6. Cut these and your four 2x10 top boards (**E**) to length. To create the "tongues" that slide into the breadboard ends, set your circular saw to cut 3/4 in. deep, then make one cut 3/4 in. from each end of each board (**Photo 7**), another cut right along the end and then a couple more cuts in between. Place your chisel along the end cut and use it as a guide to remove the waste material. When you're done, each end will have a 3/4 x 3/4-in. tongue. Make the same cuts on the top and bottom of the edge boards (**F**) as shown.

Next, make your board ends (**H, J**) as shown in **Photo 8**; they're essentially three-board sandwiches with the middle board inset 3/4 in. to accommodate the tongues you've created. We made ours from white oak for strength, appearance and durability, but you can make yours from the same wood as your table. Be sure to use waterproof glue. Rout the outer edges and cut the breadboard ends to length; make them 1/2 in. longer than the width of the finished tabletop to accommodate board movement.

Place your two edge boards (**F**) and four tabletop boards (**E**) on your work surface upside down. Space your top boards 1/8 in. apart using drywall nails or shims. Even up the ends of the six boards, then tap the breadboard ends into place.

HARDWOOD FEET

10 TAKE MEASUREMENTS FOR THE STRETCHER. Position the leg assemblies, making sure they're square to the tabletop. Take inside-to-inside and outside-to-outside measurements to determine the exact measurements you need for the stretcher.

Position the braces **(G)** and make sure everything is tight and square **(Photo 9)**. Then drill 3/8-in.-dia. holes through the support braces and secure the braces to the four tabletop boards using 1/4 x 2-1/2-in. washer-head screws. Note: The slightly oversize holes give the boards wiggle room to shrink and expand to help prevent cracking. Predrill holes in the breadboard ends—one centered on each of the four wide boards—and secure them with 3-1/2-in. washer-head screws. Finally, drill holes along the center of the edge boards **(F)**; angle them slightly toward the top of the table so the screws will have plenty of meat to bite into, then drive home the 3-1/2-in. washer-head screws.

ASSEMBLE THE TABLE

Position the two leg assemblies as shown in **Photo 10**. Make sure they're square to the tabletop, then measure the distance between them. This will give you the dimensions you need to create your stretcher. We provide an exact stretcher length in the Cutting List, but your length will most likely differ.

There are a few key measurements you need to get right in order for your stretcher **(Photo 11)** and drawbore wedges **(Photo 12)** to do their jobs.

■ The shoulder measurement. This is the distance between leg assemblies. This distance is key because the shoulders hold the leg assemblies the right distance apart and "wiggle-proof" the table.

■ The tenon length and width. The tenon extends 7 in. past the shoulder and should be 5-1/2 in. wide.

■ The mortise cutout. The cutout is centered on the tenon and is 5/8 in. wide and 2-1/2 in. long. The edge of the mortise near the outside of the leg should be inset into the leg by about 1/8 in. so that when the wedge is installed, it will draw the shoulder tightly against the leg. When done properly, this joint is amazingly strong, so take your time to get it sized and positioned just right.

With all of this in mind, make the stretcher. Once you've marked the key stretcher length, tenon and mortise measurements, bend a thin piece of wood to create the arched bottom of the stretcher. Use a jigsaw to cut out the parts. Drill 5/8-in. starter holes in each end of the 2-1/2-in.-long mortises to give your jigsaw an entry point.

To make your wedges **(L)**, first cut a 3/4-in. board 24 in. long, then rip it 2-1/4 in. wide. Use a belt sander to taper each end of the board, then cut the wedges to their final 7-in. length and soften the edges.

Separate the legs and install the stretcher. Drive the wedges into place as shown in **Photo 12**. The screw driven through the tenon end helps reinforce it to prevent the wedge from blowing out the end of the stretcher when driven in tightly.

Once the stretcher and legs are locked together, secure the leg assemblies to the tabletop braces **(Photo 13)**. Sand and smooth out any rough areas, then apply your exterior finish.

MORTISE
SHOULDER
THIN WOOD STRIP
TENON

11 LAY OUT AND CUT THE STRETCHER. Use your measurements to lay out the overall length of the stretcher and establish the positions of the shoulders, tenons and mortises. Bend a flexible piece of wood and trace the edge to create the curved lower edge. Use a jigsaw to cut out all the parts, then rout the edges.

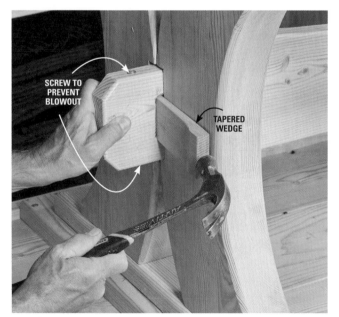

SCREW TO PREVENT BLOWOUT
TAPERED WEDGE

12 INSTALL THE STRETCHER AND WEDGE IT TIGHT. Slide the tenons through the leg openings, then tap wedges into the mortises to pull the shoulders tightly against the legs. The long screw at the end of the tenon helps prevent the wedge from splitting out the end of the stretcher.

LEG PLATE
BRACE

13 SCREW THE LEG ASSEMBLIES TO THE BRACES. Center the leg assemblies on the tabletop braces. Drill oversize holes through the leg plates, then secure the legs to the top with washer-head screws.

Built-to-Last Viking Bench

Stylish seating can be made from construction lumber.

If you think this bench looks sturdy, you're right; it's brawny enough to withstand
decades of hard use. But if you think it's complicated, take a close look at the
following pages. You'll see how simple it is to turn inexpensive framing lumber
into graceful curves.

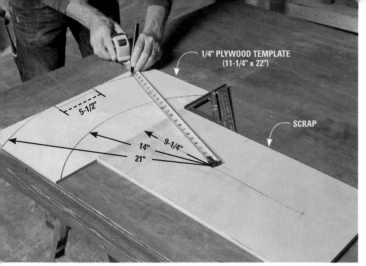

1/4" PLYWOOD TEMPLATE
(11-1/4" x 22")

5-1/2"

14"
21"
9-1/4"

SCRAP

1 MAKE THE LEG TEMPLATE. Set a scrap of plywood against the template. Drive a screw 9-1/4 in. from the end of the scrap and use that screw as a pivot point for your tape measure. Then swing the two arcs to create the leg shape.

SPREAD GLUE BEYOND LAYOUT MARKS

2 GLUE UP THE LEG "SANDWICH." Trace the leg shape onto two 22-in. 2x12s, lightly dampen the bottom piece, then apply polyurethane glue. Use a plastic putty knife to spread the glue slightly beyond the edges of the layout lines and across the main body of the leg.

DRYWALL SCREWS IN WASTE AREA

3 CLAMP THE LEG BLANKS TOGETHER. Line up the "mortise" edges of the boards, then drive a few drywall screws into the scrap wood to keep the boards aligned. Clamp the perimeter to force the boards tightly together.

CREATE THE LEGS

Start with flat, straight boards—free of splits, twists, cupping and loose knots—and you'll spare yourself a lot of head scratching and extra work down the road. We chose Douglas fir lumber, but any 1-1/2-in.-thick stock will do (for other options, see p. 183). If you have trouble finding perfect 2x12s for leg material, purchase extra lumber so you can cut around the defects.

To create a single bench, cut the four 22-in. leg blanks **(A)** to length; the ends need to be square, so cut carefully. Pair up your boards so when one is laid atop the other, there is little or no gap along the ends and edges. Try flipping or rotating the boards to find the perfect fit. Aim to have any defects fall in the areas of the wood you'll be cutting away as you form the legs.

BUILD THE LEGS

Mark out your leg template on 1/4-in. plywood as shown in **Photo 1**. Cut just outside the line with a fine-tooth jigsaw blade, then use a belt sander to sand right up to the line.

Use your template to mark the leg shape on all four leg parts **(A)**. With the marks facing up, lightly dampen one board—polyurethane glue needs moisture to work—then apply the glue in squiggles across the main body of the leg. Use a putty knife to spread it slightly beyond the edges of your template marks. Polyurethane glue is waterproof, and with tightly glued seams there's less chance of moisture working its way between the boards.

Place a second board—marked side up—over your glued board **(Photo 2)** and align the edges. Install two or three screws in the waste material area, and then apply clamps—the more, the better—around the perimeter **(Photo 3)**. Add more screws as needed. The glue will foam as it goes to work. Keep your boards clamped together for at least two hours; we left ours overnight for good measure. Repeat this procedure for the other leg blank.

Cut the legs to shape. A jigsaw with a long, coarse blade **(Photo 4)** works fine, but a band saw means less sanding. Whichever tool you use, make a series of relief cuts as shown. These allow you to remove waste material as you cut. They also allow your blade to get back on track if it wanders and begins making angled cuts. If you have a jigsaw with reciprocating action, set it at zero; it will cut slower, but your blade will wander less.

BUILD THE LEG ASSEMBLIES

Next, use a belt sander to smooth and true up the curved sides **(Photo 5)**. Begin with a coarse belt, then progress to finer grits. If you have access to a benchtop sander of some sort, use it; you'll get better results.

VIKING BENCH

Overall Dimensions:
92" L x 25-1/2" W x 16-1/4" T

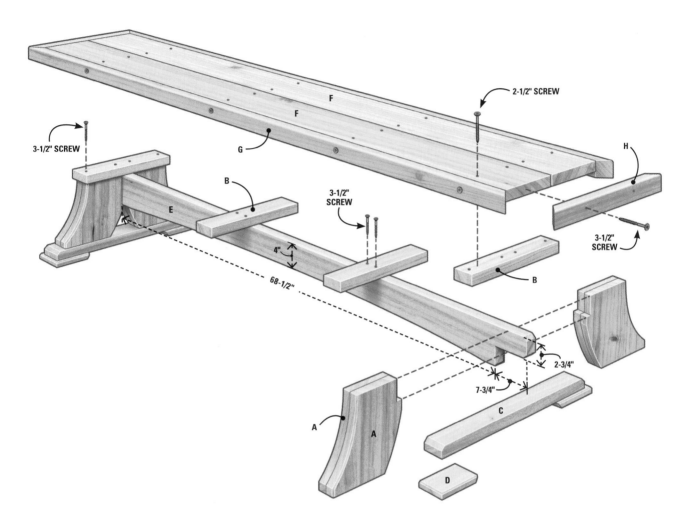

3-1/2" SCREW

2-1/2" SCREW

3-1/2" SCREW

3-1/2" SCREW

F

F

G

B

B

E

H

A

A

C

D

68-1/2"

4"

7-3/4"

2-3/4"

Materials List
(*per bench*)

ITEM	QTY.
2x12 x 8' Douglas fir	1
2x8 x 8' Douglas fir	2
2x6 x 8' Douglas fir	3
2x4 x 10' Douglas fir	1
3/4" x 4" x 3' white oak	1
2-1/2" washer-head screws	1 lb.
3-1/2" washer-head screws	1 lb.
Polyurethane glue	6 oz.
Construction adhesive	1 tube

Cutting List
(*per bench*)

KEY	QTY.	SIZE	PART
A	4	1-1/2" x 11-1/4" x 22"	Legs
B	4	1-1/2" x 3-1/2" x 14"	Seat braces
C	2	1-1/2" x 3-1/2" x 25"	Bottom leg plates
D	4	3/4" x 4" x 6"	Feet (white oak)
E	1	1-1/2" x 5-1/2" x 84"	Stretcher
F	2	1-1/2" x 7-1/4" x 89"	Top boards
G	2	1-1/2" x 2-1/4" x 92"	Long edge boards (mitered)
H	2	1-1/2" x 2-1/4" x 17-3/4"	Short edge boards (mitered)

LEG

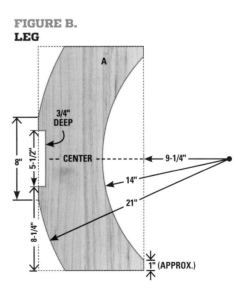

A

3/4"
DEEP

8"

5-1/2"

8-1/4"

CENTER

9-1/4"

14"

21"

1" (APPROX.)

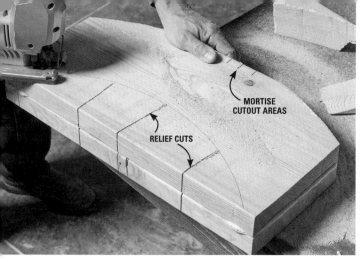

MORTISE CUTOUT AREAS

RELIEF CUTS

4 CUT THE LEGS TO SHAPE. Make a series of relief cuts along the concave side of the leg, then use a jigsaw with a coarse blade (or band saw) to cut the curves. Make a series of relief cuts for the stretcher mortise, then use a jigsaw and chisel to make the opening.

5 SAND THE LEGS AND ROUT THE EDGES. Clamp the legs to your work surface, then use a belt sander to smooth the curves and eliminate blade marks. Use a router with a 1/2-in. round-over bit to soften the curved edges, but leave the top, bottom and stretcher areas square.

6 CUT THE LEG BLANKS IN HALF. Mark the exact center of the leg blanks and use a circular saw—cutting from both sides—to cut them in half. Use a belt sander to smooth out any ridges or unevenness on the ends.

Use a router with a 1/2-in. round-over bit to soften the edges of the curved parts. Don't rout the tops and bottoms of the legs or the flat area where the mortise cutouts are.

Cut the leg blanks in half as shown in **Photo 6**. They're 3 in. thick, so you'll need to cut from both sides. Dry-fit the pieces to be sure the parts fit tightly together. Butt the tops of the legs together, then place the seat brace (**B**) and bottom leg plate (**C**) in their respective positions. Make sure the stretcher fits into the opening between the legs. Also, be sure the ends of the legs sit flat against the seat brace and bottom plate; you may need to do a little sanding or trimming until the pieces fit tight. Once all systems are a go, apply construction adhesive to the ends of the legs, cinch the tops together with a clamp, position the seat brace and bottom leg plate (**B and C**), and then secure them with 3-1/2-in. exterior screws (**Photo 7**). Repeat for the other leg assembly.

BUILD THE BENCH

Having built the leg assemblies, you've done the hardest part. Cut, shape and install the bench stretcher (**E**) as shown in **Figure A** and **Photo 8**.

Fasten the seat braces (**B**) to the stretcher, then position the two 2x8 top boards (**F**); they should run past the outer seat braces by about 6 in. Fasten the top boards with 2-1/2-in. washer-head screws. Install the 2-1/4-in. edge boards (**Photo 9**).

Apply two coats of exterior finish; we used a semitransparent deck stain. Finally, screw on the feet (**D**). We recommend using white oak for the feet because it's rot resistant. To keep your benches in tiptop shape, set them up on 2x4 blocks and cover them with a tarp before winter strikes.

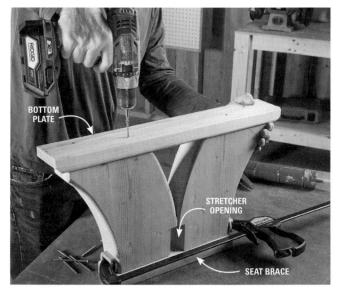

BOTTOM PLATE

STRETCHER OPENING

SEAT BRACE

7 SCREW THE LEG ASSEMBLIES TOGETHER. Clamp the leg halves together and check the size of each stretcher opening. Adjust if needed. Apply adhesive to the leg ends, and attach the seat braces and bottom plates with screws.

8 SECURE THE STRETCHER TO THE LEGS. Use clamps to pull the stretcher shoulders tight against the legs, and drive in wedges or shims to snug the tenon tight against the seat brace. Drive screws through the seat brace into the tenon.

9 COMPLETE THE BENCH. Add the two top boards, then install the edge boards along the four edges of the bench. Drill pilot holes to avoid splitting the edge boards.

Mackintosh Table

You can build this classic with inexpensive wood and two basic power tools.

No matter your experience level in the DIY space, this simple piece of furniture is right for you. It's a perfect step up for a carpentry newcomer with a modest shop and just a bit of experience building, but it's also a great design for a more experienced builder who appreciates a project that's quick and easy. Plus, the resulting table is classic, stylish and functional.

You can build the table from paint-grade yellow poplar. It's inexpensive, attractive and widely available at home centers in 1x3s, 1x4s and other standard sizes. You'll also need 1/2-in.-thick and 1/4-in.-thick material for the drawer. At our local home center, the total cost for the wood was well under $100. Aside from a drill, all you'll need to build the table are two power tools: a table saw and a plate joiner. A drill press is helpful but not necessary.

The original design for this table was developed in 1904 by the renowned Scottish architect Charles Rennie Mackintosh for a home in Glasgow. Like so many other things Scottish, it's economical in terms of time, materials and tools. Read on to get started.

■ TWO POWER TOOLS
A table saw and a plate joiner are all the muscle you'll need.

■ READY-TO-GO MATERIALS
Make the whole project from paint-grade yellow poplar.

■ A WELL-CRAFTED DRAWER
The joints are just 1/4-in. oak pegs.

FIRST MAKE THE SIDES

When you buy your lumber (see the Materials List), select pieces that are straight and flat. To make finishing easier, stay away from pieces that are green or have black streaks. Most stores have large piles to pick through—and you won't need much wood—so be choosy.

Start by cutting the legs (A) from your 1x3 material. You won't have to rip the wood; just cut the pieces to final length. Mark the top end of each leg to indicate which sides face out (Photo 1). We recommend marking each piece of a project like this. If you make your marks anywhere else, sanding will erase them, but ends usually don't get sanded.

Draw centerlines for the biscuit slots that will join the legs to the sides (B) and drawer guides (C)—see Figure A. Draw these lines across the inside faces of the legs. Position each leg so that its outside edge faces up, then place a poplar offcut under the plate joiner and cut the slots (Photo 2).

Use 1x6s to make the sides and 1x4s to make the drawer guides. Again, you won't have to rip the wood, but this time cut each piece 1 in. extra long. Glue the pieces together, making sure their top edges are flush (Photo 3). Cut some more 1x3 material to make the long stretchers (D). Also make these pieces 1 in. extra long.

After the glue dries, cut the side/guides and long stretchers to the same final length. Draw biscuit-slot centerlines on the outside faces of the side/guides, then place the pieces face up on your bench and cut slots in them (Photo 4). Use the same offcut as a spacer under the plate joiner. This method ensures that the drawer guides will be flush with the inside edge of the legs, which is essential for the drawer to work right.

Next, adjust your plate joiner to make No. 10 slots. Mark and cut slots in the legs to receive the long stretchers. Place the spacer under the plate joiner this time too. Cut corresponding slots in the ends of the long stretchers (without using the spacer, of course).

Cut vertical slots on the inside faces of the long stretchers (Photo 5). Then make a 2-5/8-in. spacer from a 1x3 for positioning the outside slots (Figure D). Make a 5-7/8-in. spacer for the middle slots.

Smooth the inside faces of the legs with 150-grit sandpaper. In addition, sand the outside faces of the side/guides and both faces of the long stretchers. Glue all these pieces together (Photo 6).

Materials List

ITEM	QTY.
1x3 yellow poplar	16 lin. ft.
1x4 yellow poplar	6 lin. ft.
1x6 yellow poplar	4 lin. ft.
1x8 yellow poplar	5 lin. ft.
1/2x4 yellow poplar	3 lin. ft.
1/4x6 yellow poplar	3 lin. ft.
1/4" oak dowel	1 ft.
No. 20 biscuits	14
No. 10 biscuits	10
Desktop fasteners	6
5/8" No. 6 screws	14
Drawer knob	1
Wood glue	as needed

Cutting List

KEY	QTY.	SIZE	PART
A	4	3/4" x 2-1/2" x 29-1/4"	Legs
B	2	3/4" x 5-1/2" x 12-1/2"	Sides
C	2	3/4" x 3-1/2" x 12-1/2"	Drawer guides
D	2	3/4" x 2-1/2" x 12-1/2"	Long stretchers
E	1	3/4" x 3" x 9-1/4"	Apron
F	1	3/4" x 5-1/2" x 9-1/4"	Back
G	3	3/4" x 2-1/2" x 10-3/4"	Short stretchers
H	2	3/4" x 3/4" x 12-1/2"	Drawer runners
J	1	3/4" x 16-3/4" x 17"	Top
K	1	3/4" x 2-3/4" x 9-1/4"	Drawer front
L	2	1/2" x 2-3/4" x 12-3/4"	Drawer sides
M	1	1/2" x 2-1/8" x 8-3/4"	Drawer back
N	1	1/4" x 12-1/4" x 8-11/16"	Drawer bottom
P	8	1/4"-dia. x 1"	Drawer pegs
Q	2	1/4" x 1" x 2-3/4"	Drawer stops

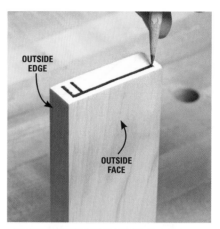

1 CUT THE TABLE LEGS. Begin by cutting the table legs from poplar 1x3s. Mark the ends of all the parts to identify the sides that face out.

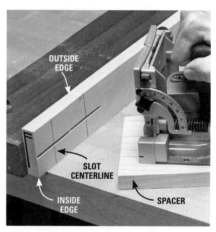

2 MAKE THE BISCUIT SLOTS. Cut a pair of No. 20 biscuit slots in the top end of each leg. Place a 3/4-in. scrap under the plate joiner to space the slots.

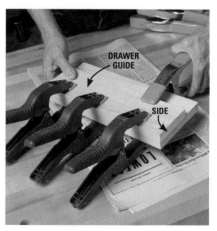

3 GLUE SIDES AND GUIDES. Glue together the table's sides and drawer guides, cut 1 in. extra long. After the glue dries, trim them to their final length.

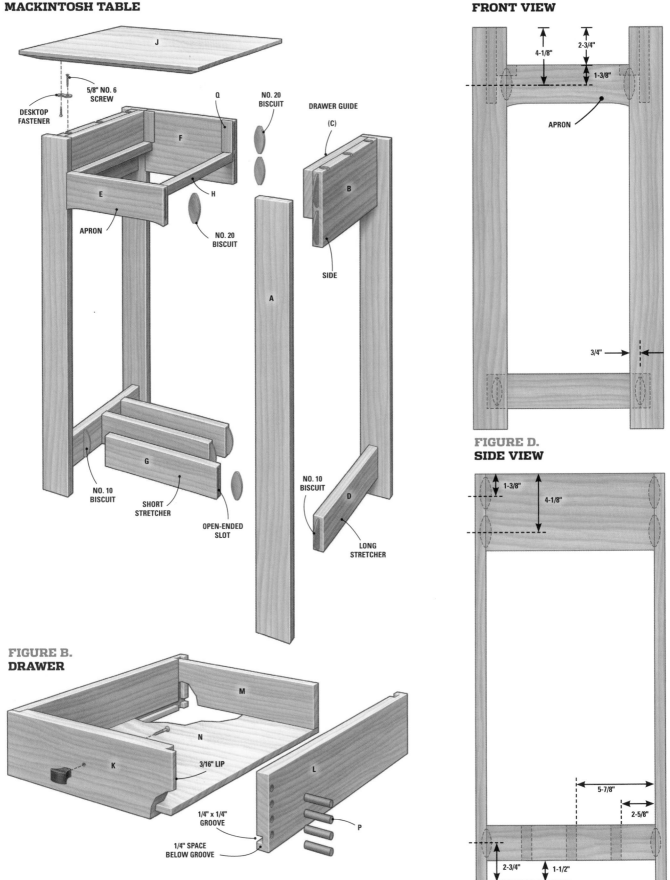

FIGURE A.
MACKINTOSH TABLE

J

5/8" NO. 6 SCREW

DESKTOP FASTENER

Q

NO. 20 BISCUIT

DRAWER GUIDE

(C)

F

B

SIDE

H

E

NO. 20 BISCUIT

APRON

A

NO. 10 BISCUIT

G

D

NO. 10 BISCUIT

SHORT STRETCHER

OPEN-ENDED SLOT

LONG STRETCHER

FIGURE B.
DRAWER

M

N

K

3/16" LIP

L

1/4" x 1/4" GROOVE

1/4" SPACE BELOW GROOVE

P

FIGURE C.
FRONT VIEW

4-1/8"

2-3/4"

1-3/8"

APRON

3/4"

FIGURE D.
SIDE VIEW

1-3/8"

4-1/8"

5-7/8"

2-5/8"

2-3/4"

1-1/2"

FIGURE E.
TOP DETAIL

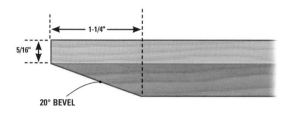

1-1/4"

5/16"

20° BEVEL

FIGURE F.
APRON DETAIL

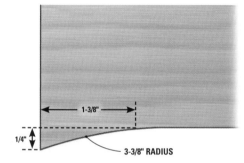

1-3/8"

1/4"

3-3/8" RADIUS

JOIN THE SIDES

The curves on the table's front apron **(E)** are a beautiful detail—and easy to make. Start by cutting the apron 1 in. extra long from a piece of 1x4. Rip it 3-1/4 in. wide. Discard the waste, then rip it again to 2-3/4 in. wide. Cut 1-3/4-in.-long pieces from both ends of the narrow offcut and glue them back to the main piece. Once the glue dries, trim 1/2 in. from one end of this piece, then trim the piece to final length. Cut the table's back **(F)** from a piece of 1x6 and trim it to the same length. In addition, cut two 1x3 spacers to this length.

Using a 1-gallon paint can as a guide, draw the apron's arches on the small pieces you cut and glued to the apron **(Figure F)**. Form the arches with a rasp and sandpaper **(Photo 7)**. Adjust your plate joiner to make No. 20 slots, then mark and cut biscuit slots in the ends

of the apron and back pieces. Mark and cut corresponding slots in the base **(Figure D)**.

Glue the base together, clamping the spacers between the legs **(Photo 8)**. After the glue dries, cut short stretchers **(G)** to fit between the long stretchers. Cut biscuit slots in the short stretchers. The lower end of these slots must be open so you can slip the parts in place **(Photo 9)**. That's easy to do—just make three overlapping cuts with the plate joiner to form each slot. Glue biscuits into the long stretchers, then apply glue to the short stretchers and slide them over the biscuits.

Cut the drawer runners **(H)** to size and glue them in place. Their front edges must be level with the top of the apron. Use a combination square to make sure the runners are parallel to the top edges of the drawer guides.

MAKE THE TOP

Assemble the top **(J)** from three pieces of 1x8. Trim pieces to final length and glue them together, making sure their ends are even. Rip the top to width after the glue dries. Sand the top to even the joints, starting with 60-grit paper. Continue with 100 grit, then finish with 150 grit. Cut bevels around the top by tilting your saw blade to 20 degrees **(Photo 10 and Figure E)**.

Using a Forstner bit, drill holes for desktop fasteners in the top edges of the table's sides **(Figure A)**. Screw the fasteners in place, then turn over the table's base and center it on the top. Fasten the base to the top **(Photo 11)**.

BUILD A WELL-CRAFTED DRAWER

Now build the drawer. Cut the drawer front **(K)** slightly undersize— 1/32 in. narrower than the space above the table's apron and 1/32 in. shorter than the distance between the table's legs. Using 1/2-in. poplar, cut the drawer sides **(L)** the same width as the front. Trim them to final length. Using a 1/2-in.-wide dado set, cut rabbets in the ends of the drawer front to receive the sides **(Figure B and Photo 12)**. (You could also make multiple cuts with a regular blade.)

Drill 1/4-in. holes in the sides **(Photo 13)**. A drill press is best, but you can do this by hand—just make sure the holes are perpendicular. Using a 1/4-in. dado set (or by making two passes with a regular blade), cut grooves for the drawer bottom in the front and side pieces. In addition, cut 1/4-in.-wide dadoes in the side pieces to receive the drawer's back **(M)**. Cut the back to width and length.

Glue the drawer together using clamps in both directions to make sure the front joints are tight **(Photo 14)**. After the glue dries, drill through the holes in the drawer's sides, making them 1 in. deep. Note: Don't drill the holes directly opposite the drawer bottom grooves.

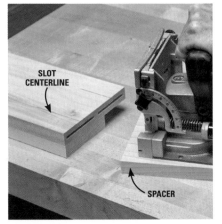

4 MAKE SLOTS IN THE GUIDES. Cut biscuit slots in the side/guides, using the spacer again. This puts the drawer guides flush with the inside edges of the legs.

5 CUT SLOTS IN THE STRETCHERS. Make vertical slots in the stretchers that go between the legs. Butt the plate joiner against a spacer to locate each slot.

6 GLUE TABLE SIDES. Glue the sides of the table, using a combination square to make sure the stretcher is in the correct position.

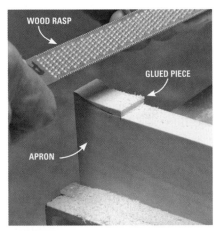

7 CREATE ARCHES. Shape arches from small pieces glued to the table's apron. With so little wood to remove, just use a rasp and sandpaper.

8 GLUE THE BASE. Glue the table's base. Clamp spacers between the legs to make sure they're parallel. Be sure the table is square.

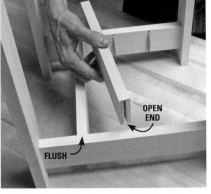

9 CUT OPEN-ENDED SLOTS IN STRETCHERS. Cut open-ended slots in the short stretchers. Slide them in place, making sure their top edges are flush.

Cut 1-in. pegs from 1/4-in. oak rods, then glue them in the holes you drilled (**Photo 15**). Glue 1/4-in.-long pegs in the other two holes (they're just for show).

Cut pieces for the drawer's bottom (**N**) from 1/4-in. poplar. Trim them to final length and glue them together (**Photo 16**). Clamping boards this thin is very difficult—we used wedges instead. Cut the bottom to final width.

Using 60-grit paper, sand the edges of the bottom until the bottom slides easily in the drawer's grooves (**Photo 17**). Fasten the bottom to the drawer's back

with screws. Remove the table's top, then slide the drawer into the table. Position the drawer's front flush with the legs, then make stops (**Q**) to fill the small gap behind the drawer's sides. Glue the stops to the base.

FINALLY, FINISH YOUR TABLE

Finish the top of the table separately. It should have equal coats of finish on both sides so it doesn't warp.

The original Mackintosh table was painted white, and if you'd like to paint your table, we recommend using

an aerosol paint. You also have the option of letting the wood darken naturally. We chose to stain our table instead. To avoid a blotchy look, we first sealed the table with two coats of water-base poly. Then we applied a coat of amber shellac, thinned 50% with denatured alcohol, to give the wood a golden color. Next we applied two coats of gel stain (General Finishes Candlelite) followed by two more coats of poly (**Photo 18**). Whatever stain approach you choose, test it thoroughly on pieces of scrap before you begin.

10 SAW BEVEL EDGES. Saw bevels around the table's top. Use a tall sliding fence to support the top.

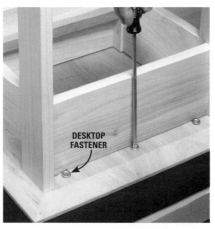

11 FASTEN BASE TO TOP. Screw the base to the top using desktop fasteners. Positioned on the outside, they won't interfere with the drawer.

DESKTOP FASTENER

12 CUT RABBETS. Begin making the drawer by using a dado set to cut rabbets in the drawer's front.

13 DRILL HOLES IN SIDES. Drill 1/4-in. holes through the drawer's sides, then cut grooves in the front and sides to receive the drawer's bottom.

DRAWER BOTTOM GROOVE

14 GLUE THE DRAWER. Glue the drawer together. Position the back of the drawer so it sits just above the groove for the drawer's bottom.

15 GLUE IN PEGS. Drill through the 1/4-in. holes to make them deeper, then glue in short pegs. This makes a very strong joint.

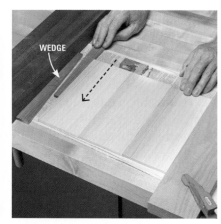

WEDGE

16 GLUE UP BOTTOM. Glue up the drawer's bottom from 1/4-in. poplar. Use opposing wedges to squeeze the pieces between two clamped boards.

17 FIT DRAWER BOTTOM. Slide the bottom into the drawer. Don't use glue, because the bottom must be free to expand and contract.

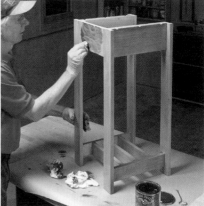

18 STAIN AND SEAL. Seal the wood with two coats of poly, then use thin coats of gel stain. Plain poplar can look quite pretty!

3-Tier Basket Stand

Build an amazingly versatile storage stand with an amazingly versatile tool.

You've seen chests of drawers, but here's a chest of baskets. It can be used in nearly any room—in the bathroom for storing towels, in the entryway for organizing hats and gloves, in the bedroom for workout clothes, even in the kitchen for veggies or hand towels.

The total materials bill for our pine stand, including the baskets, was about $50. We bought baskets at a Michaels craft store, but lots of other retailers like West Elm and IKEA also carry them. Make sure to buy your baskets first; you need to construct the stand based on their dimensions.

To keep the frame of the stand both lightweight and strong, we used biscuit joinery. It's a clever way to join wood and a technique you can use with many other projects. See p. 202 for biscuit joiner tips.

HOW TO BUILD IT

You'll first build the two ladders that form the sides of the stand, then glue and nail the crosspieces to join the two ladders.

To get started, cut all the parts to length (see the Cutting List). Mark the rung and crosspiece locations on the legs. Mark all four legs at the same time to ensure the framework is uniform and square **(Photo 1)**.

As you mark the legs, keep picturing how your baskets will sit on the runners, especially if you're using baskets smaller or larger than ours; it will help you avoid errors. Use the biscuit joiner to cut slots in the edges of the legs and ends of the rungs **(Photo 2)**. You'll need to clip the biscuits to suit the 1-1/2-in.-wide legs and rungs (see "Biscuit Tips," p. 202).

Apply glue to the biscuits and slots **(Photo 3)** to assemble each joint. Clamp the ladders together and set them aside until the glue dries.

Join the two ladders by gluing and nailing the crosspieces between them. Remember that the three front crosspieces that will support the baskets lie flat. Next, install the basket runners **(Photo 4)** even with the flat crosspieces that run across the front. Glue and nail the 3/4-in. plywood top to the stand, then apply cove molding to cover the edges **(Photo 5)**.

Materials List

ITEM	QTY.
1x2 pine board	30 ft.
3/4" x 3/4" square dowel	6 ft.
3/4" cove molding	6 ft.
3/4" plywood	1 sheet
12" x 12" x 8" baskets	3
No. 0 biscuits	16
Wood glue	as needed
2" finish nails	as needed
Watco cherry finish	as needed

Cutting List

KEY	QTY.	SIZE	PART
A	4	3/4" x 1-1/2" x 36"	Legs
B	8	3/4" x 1-1/2" x 10"	Rungs
C	8	3/4" x 1-1/2" x 12-1/4"	Crosspieces
D	6	3/4" x 3/4" x 10-3/4"	Runners
E	1	3/4" x 13" x 13-3/4"	Top
F	4	cut to fit	Cove molding

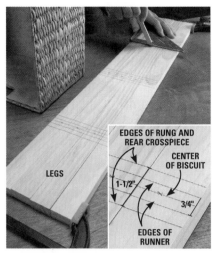

EDGES OF RUNG AND
REAR CROSSPIECE

CENTER
OF BISCUIT

LEGS

1-1/2"

3/4"

EDGES OF
RUNNER

RUNG

LEG

1 MARK THE LEGS. Clamp the legs together and mark them all at the same time. That way, all your marks will line up and you'll avoid mismatches.

2 CUT THE BISCUIT SLOTS. Cut slots in the ends of the rungs and sides of the legs. Assemble each ladder in a dry run to make sure they fit together correctly.

3 ASSEMBLE THE LADDERS. Join the rungs to the legs with glue and biscuits, then clamp the ladders together. Work fast! You have to assemble eight joints before the glue begins to set.

FIGURE A.
BASKET STAND

Overall Dimensions:
14-1/2" x 15-1/4" x 36-3/4"

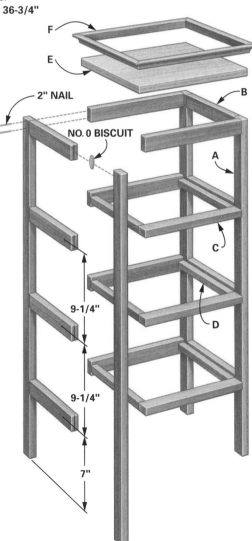

F

E

2" NAIL

NO. 0 BISCUIT

B

A

C

D

9-1/4"

9-1/4"

7"

4 CONNECT THE LADDERS. Install the front and back crosspieces with glue and nails. Then add the runners that support the baskets.

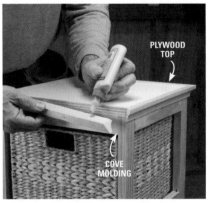

PLYWOOD
TOP

COVE
MOLDING

5 TOP IT OFF. Glue and nail the plywood top to the top of the stand, then apply cove molding to neaten up and hide the edges.

Biscuit Tips

A biscuit joiner is a superb tool for joining wood where it would be difficult to use nails or screws. The joint is strong, invisible and easy to create. The compressed wood biscuits expand on contact with moisture in the glue. Since the biscuits are placed in slots that are wider than the biscuit, you can adjust the joint a little after butting the two pieces together. Biscuits come in three common sizes: No. 0, No. 10 and No. 20. Whether you're building this basket stand or some other biscuit project, here are some of our favorite biscuit tips:

1. CLIP BISCUITS FOR NARROW STOCK

The smallest common biscuits (No. 0) are almost 1-7/8 in. long. That's too long for the 1-1/2-in. wide parts on this basket stand. But there's an easy solution: Just clip about 1/4 in. off both ends of each biscuit. Your slots will still be too long and visible at inside corners, but a little filler and finish will hide them.

2. NUMBER THE JOINTS

While you're marking the centerlines of each biscuit slot, also number each joint. That will eliminate confusion and misalignments during assembly.

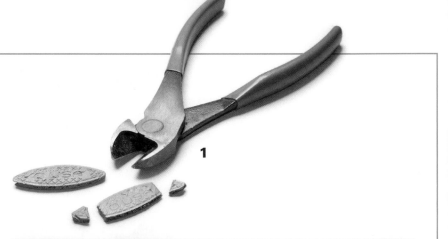

3. MAKE A GLUE INJECTOR

Spreading a neat, even bead of glue inside a biscuit slot isn't easy. You can buy special injectors online, or make your own using the cap from a marker and a fine-tooth saw.

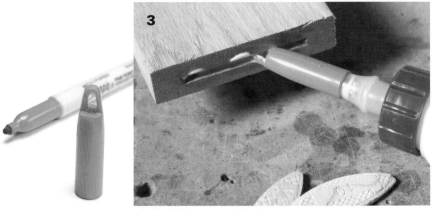

4. ALWAYS DO A DRY RUN

Biscuits grab fast. During glue-up, you don't have time to correct mistakes or dig up a longer set of clamps. So always test the whole assembly—including clamps—before you get out the glue. For complicated assemblies, give yourself more working time by using slow-setting wood glue. Titebond Extend is one brand.

Elegant & Easy Bookcases

You're not seeing double—the leftovers of one bookcase yield a second at half the price.

This is one of those rare woodworking projects that has it all: high style at a low cost and fast, easy construction that delivers sturdy, lasting results. This bookcase design is versatile too. You can easily make it shorter or taller, wider or deeper. With a little know-how, you can even adapt the building methods to other projects; we built the fireplace mantel shown here using similar techniques.

You could save a few hours of work by building just one bookcase, but there's a financial incentive to build two. By mostly using the plywood left over from the first bookcase,

you can get a second one for half price (saving $100 or more).

You'll need a table saw and a miter saw for this project. A pneumatic brad nailer will make the job faster and easier. All the materials are widely available at home centers. You may not find the solid wood panel we used for the bookshelf top (made from glued-together boards), but you can use oak stair tread material or glue boards together. Also, the home center may not carry the board widths we list, but you can easily rip wider boards to width.

A PLYWOOD BOX, DRESSED UP WITH SIMPLE TRIM

To design this project, we gave our team of professional woodworkers a tough assignment: Build a classic Craftsman-style bookcase using construction methods that any intermediate builder could handle. The result is a screw-together plywood shelf trimmed with strips of solid wood. There's no fancy joinery—no dadoes, biscuits or dowels. And that simplicity also makes this a quick project. You can easily build a pair of bookcases in one weekend and apply the finish the following weekend.

CUT THE PLYWOOD PARTS

To get started, rip the plywood parts to width on a table saw. If cutting full sheets is difficult in your small shop, cut the parts slightly oversized with a circular saw and then trim them on the table saw. Rip two 9-in.-wide planks from 3/4-in. plywood (for the shelves) and two from the 1/2-in. plywood (for the sides). Then cut them to length. To make the crosscuts with a miter saw, use a stop block **(Photo 1)**.

Next, drill the screw holes in the sides using a 3/32-in. bit **(Photo 2)**. Measuring from the bottom, mark the screw holes at 3-3/8, 16-1/8, 26-7/8, 37-5/8, 48-3/8 and 58-1/8 in. Position the holes 1 in. from the edges so the screw heads will be covered by the stiles later.

Sand all the plywood parts before assembly to avoid awkward inside-corner sanding later. Plywood usually requires only a light sanding with 150-grit paper, but watch for shallow dents or scratches that need a little extra sanding. And be careful not to sand through the micro-thin veneer along the edges.

ASSEMBLE THE CASE

When you screw the sides to the shelves, use plywood spacers to eliminate measuring errors and out-of-square shelves **(Photo 3)**. Before you cut the spacers, measure the thickness of the shelves. Although they're cut from 3/4-in. plywood, you'll probably find that they're actually a hair thinner than 3/4 in. To compensate, simply cut your spacers a bit longer (your 12-in. spacer may actually be 12-1/16 in. long, for example).

Inspect the sides before assembly and orient them so the best-looking veneer faces the outside of the case. Drill 3/32-in. pilot holes in the shelves using the side holes you drilled earlier as a guide. Also drill countersinks for the screw heads. Pilot bits that drill a pilot hole and countersink in one step cost about $5. Screw all the shelves to one side, then add the other side. Don't use glue. The screws alone are plenty strong, and any squeezed-out glue would prevent the plywood from absorbing stain later.

With all the shelves screwed into place, add the back. Measure the case from corner to corner in both directions; equal diagonal measurements means the case is square. Set the back in position and use a straightedge to mark the locations of the shelves. Fasten the back with screws rather than nails. That way, you can remove the back later to make finishing much easier.

FIGURE A.
SIMPLE BOOKCASE

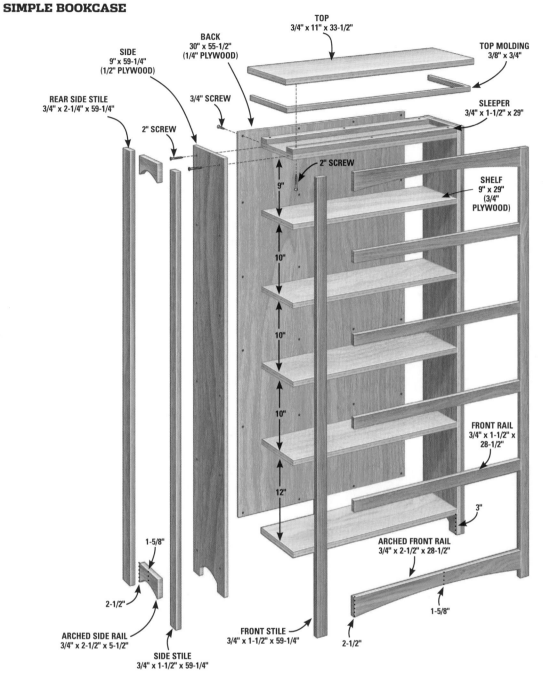

TOP
3/4" x 11" x 33-1/2"

SIDE
9" x 59-1/4"
(1/2" PLYWOOD)

BACK
30" x 55-1/2"
(1/4" PLYWOOD)

TOP MOLDING
3/8" x 3/4"

REAR SIDE STILE
3/4" x 2-1/4" x 59-1/4"

3/4" SCREW

SLEEPER
3/4" x 1-1/2" x 29"

2" SCREW

2" SCREW

2" SCREW

9"

SHELF
9" x 29"
(3/4"
PLYWOOD)

10"

10"

10"

FRONT RAIL
3/4" x 1-1/2" x
28-1/2"

12"

3"

1-5/8"

ARCHED FRONT RAIL
3/4" x 2-1/2" x 28-1/2"

2-1/2"

ARCHED SIDE RAIL
3/4" x 2-1/2" x 5-1/2"

SIDE STILE
3/4" x 1-1/2" x 59-1/4"

FRONT STILE
3/4" x 1-1/2" x 59-1/4"

2-1/2"

1-5/8"

Materials List

ITEM	QTY.
3/4" x 4' x 8' plywood (shelves)	1
1/2" x 4' x 8' plywood (sides)	1
1/4" x 4' x 8' plywood (back)	1*
1x2 x 6' solid wood (shelf rails, front and side stiles)	7*
1x3 x 6' solid wood (arched rails, rear side stiles)	3*
1x12 x 3' glued panel (top)	1*
Wood glue	as needed
No. 8 x 2" screws	as needed
No. 6 x 3/4" screws	as needed
1-3/4" finish nails	as needed

*To build two bookcases, double these quantities.
  Solid wood thicknesses and widths given are nominal.
  Actual thickness is 3/4 in. Actual widths are 1/2 in. less.

With this simple design, you can easily alter the dimensions to suit your needs. Our bookcase is 60 in. tall, 11 in. deep and 33-1/2 in. wide.

1 Crosscut the parts quickly and accurately using a stop block. The parts are too wide to cut in one pass, so flip the plank over after the first cut and make a second cut.

FIRST CUT

STOP BLOCK

2 Stack up the sides, mark the screw locations and drill through both sides at once. This cuts measuring and marking time, especially if you're building two bookcases.

CUT ARCHED RAILS

Although straight rails would look good, we cut arches in the top and bottom rails for a more elegant look. If you want curved rails, cut the top and bottom rails 28-5/8 in. long (you'll trim them to final length later). To mark the curves on the front arches, screw two blocks to a long scrap 35-7/8 in. apart. Bend a 36-in. metal straightedge between the blocks. Align the straightedge with the corners of the rail **(Photo 4)**. To mark the side rails, use the bottom of a 5-gallon bucket (or any circle that's about 10 in. in diameter).

If you end up with a small hump or two, smooth them with sandpaper. For a perfect arc, use the cutout as a sanding block **(Photo 5)**. Cut 80-grit sandpaper into 1-in.-wide strips and apply a light coat of spray adhesive to the backs of the strips.

Next, cut the stiles to length, but don't cut the rails to length just yet. Before you attach any rails or stiles to the case, position the arched bottom rails on the case sides and use them to mark arcs. Cut these arcs with a jigsaw.

ADD THE TRIM AND TOP

Fasten the rails and stiles following this sequence: Attach both of the side stiles along the front of the case. Align your nails with the shelves so they don't poke into the case. Then add one front stile. Set one front rail in place. Set the other front stile in place to check the length of the rail. If the length is right, cut the other rails to identical length. Attach the front rails and the second front stile. Don't worry if the rails and stiles aren't quite flush; you can sand them flush later. Next, add the side rails and the rear side stiles **(Photo 6)**.

Two to four nails should be adequate for each part, though you may need more if the rail or stile is badly bowed. The

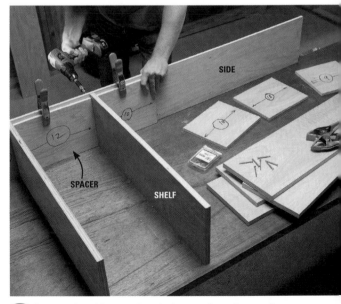

SIDE

SPACER

SHELF

3 Screw the sides to the shelves using plywood spacers to hold the shelves in precise position.

glue will provide plenty of strength regardless of how many nails you use.

Allow the glue to set for an hour before you sand all the rails and stiles using a random orbital sander. Start with a 100-grit disc to sand flush uneven joints and remove any shallow scratches. Then switch to a 150-grit disc.

To attach the top, glue 3/4-in. plywood sleepers to the top shelf as shown in **Figure A**. Then predrill and screw the top in place. The top molding is simply 3/8-in.-thick strips cut from leftover scraps. Miter the corners and glue the strips in place, again using as few nails as possible.

FINISH THE BOOKCASE

Unscrew the bookcase's back for easier finishing. We finished our bookcases with stain and three coats of polyurethane. With all the surfaces sanded to 150-grit, we applied one coat of Minwax Red Oak stain. We chose a satin sheen for the clear finish. But because three coats of satin can look like a cloudy sheet of plastic over the wood, we began with two coats of gloss, sanding lightly with a 320-grit sanding sponge between coats. We filled nail holes with color-matched wood putty after the first coat. After the second coat, we added a coat of satin polyurethane. For more finishing advice, search for "wood finishing" at familyhandyman.com. After setting the bookcases in place, we drove a 2-1/2-in. screw through the back of each and into wall studs to prevent them from tipping forward.

4 Mark arches on the front rails using a simple arc jig made from wood scraps and a metal straightedge. Cut the arches with a jigsaw.

ARCH CUTOUT

5 Sand out bumps or waves in the arches using the cutout. Stick sandpaper to the cutout with spray adhesive.

6 Glue and nail the rails and stiles to the plywood case. Use as few nails as possible—just enough to hold the parts in place while the glue sets.

CHAPTER SIX

OUTDOOR

Perfect Pergola

This high-impact project is elegant but economical.

This pergola was designed with simplicity and economy in mind, but not at the expense of good looks. It's made from standard dimensional lumber, so all you need to do is cut the parts and screw them together—no special skills required. To keep the cost down, we used pressure-treated lumber, which looked great with two coats of semitransparent stain.

This pergola is the perfect size for small gatherings. With an eye toward daytime comfort, we spaced the roof slats to block some sun but still let in enough rays for warmth.

You can build this project in about two weekends if you have an agreeable helper. We spent just under $1,300 on materials. The concrete floor, which is optional, added another $500. Your floor could be flagstones, paver bricks or even a ground-level deck.

Big, but Not Complicated

If you think this pergola is beyond your skill level, take a closer look. It takes time and muscle, but it's really just a bunch of standard lumber parts screwed together. The trickiest part of the job—positioning the posts—is almost goof-proof with simple plywood plates **(see Photo 3)**. Most sheds and even fences are more complicated than this project!

SURVEY THE SITE

Be sure you have a fairly level spot in your yard. Slopes can be subtle and a bit deceiving, so bring a level attached to a long, straight 2x4 to the yard as you check site locations. Our site sloped by about 3-1/2 in., which worked out well. We made sure the slab would be just above the grade of the yard at the higher end, which then left the lower area as a "stepping off" point on the slab. If you have a challenging yard, you may need to level an area by first terracing with a short retaining wall.

PREP THE SITE

If you're building in a grassy area, you'll need to remove the turf. You can rent a kick-style sod cutter, but if you're over 22 years old, renting a gas-powered one will be worth the extra investment. You can remove the sod in less than two hours and still have a good chance of getting out of bed the next day. If you don't have a spot that could use fresh turf, make plans to get rid of a full pickup load of sod.

1 MARK OUT THE PERIMETER. Cut the sod away and mark the perimeter of the pergola with stakes and string. Check the layout by taking diagonal measurements; if the measurements are equal, the layout is square.

2 POSITION THE POSTHOLES. Align the post bottom plates with the strings and then outline them with spray paint.

3 BUILD THE POST ASSEMBLIES. Screw plywood plates to the posts. Joining the posts this way saves you the hassle of positioning and plumbing them individually.

12"-DEEP HOLE

5 BRACE THE POSTS. Position and plumb the posts, locking them into place with horizontal and diagonal bracing. No need to buy extra lumber for the bracing; just use the 1x3s that you'll later use for roof slats.

4 SET THE POSTS. Place each post assembly in its hole. You'll need at least one helper for this job. Be careful so the sides of the hole don't cave in.

6 FILL THE POSTHOLES. Mix concrete and fill in around the post assemblies. Let the concrete harden at least one day before removing the bracing.

FRONT HEADER

TEMPORARY BRACE

7 **INSTALL THE HEADERS. Position the headers so that they'll be at least 80 in. from the floor of the pergola. Screw them to the posts, then cut off the posts flush with the headers.**

RIDGE BEAM

FRONT HEADER

8 **SET THE RIDGE BEAM. Mark the center of the front and back headers, and then screw the ridge beam to the headers.**

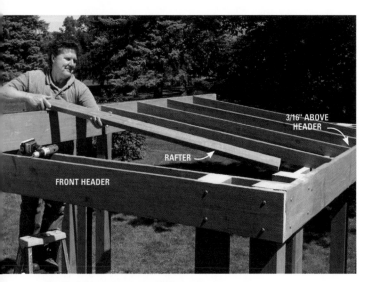

3/16" ABOVE HEADER

RAFTER

FRONT HEADER

9 **INSTALL THE RAFTERS. Cut the rafters to fit flush with the top of the ridge beam and 3/16 in. above the outer headers. Screw the rafters into place.**

PREP THE LUMBER

Every stack of treated lumber contains some beautiful wood and some ugly stuff. Take the time to pick through the pile and select good material—your project will look much better. When you get the lumber home, you'll be eager to start right away. But we strongly recommend that you let the lumber dry for a few days. Stack it with spacers so air can reach all sides of each board. Then stain it before building. Staining this pergola after assembly would be a slow, messy job. We applied two coats of Behr Semi-Transparent Waterproofing Wood Stain (No. 3533).

SET THE POSTS

You'll need to mark out a perfectly square layout for the posts. To start, position two strings exactly perpendicular to each other using the 3-4-5 triangle method (in this case, your measurements will be 9, 12 and 15 ft.). If you're not familiar with this trick, search online for "345 triangle." Once you get two lines squared, the other two will be easy. But double-check your layout with diagonal measurements **(Photo 1)** before you mark the posthole locations **(Photo 2)**.

To keep the post groupings positioned precisely, cut plates from treated plywood and fasten them to the posts **(Photo 3)**. That way, you can position, plumb and brace each assembly of three posts as if they were one post **(Photos 4 and 5)**.

Bracing the assemblies takes several trips up and down the ladder. Start by screwing some horizontal 1x3 braces onto the tops of the posts. Make sure the post assemblies are spaced the same on the top as they are on the bottom. With the spacing established, you can brace the groups diagonally to the ground with stakes **(Photo 5)**. Keep at it until the positioning is close to perfect.

Use a tub or wheelbarrow to mix the concrete, then toss it into the postholes **(Photo 6)**. The mix isn't critical because a troweled finish isn't needed. Just make sure you get it packed into the holes evenly around each grouping. We used about four bags per hole, but get a few extra bags just in case.

FASTEN THE HEADERS

The next day you can install the headers **(Photo 7)**. Overlap the corners as shown in **Figure A**. We removed our braces at the top, one at a time, as we leveled and installed each outer side header, and then we finished with the front and back. Be sure to take the thickness of your slab into consideration as you measure the distance to the bottom of the headers. Leave at least 80 in. between the slab and the header. Taller people may want to nudge it up a couple of inches.

Once the outer headers **(B and C)** are in place, cut the posts flush with the tops of the headers. We used a framing square to mark them and a circular saw to cut as deep as we could. We then used a handsaw and, once our arms felt as if they were ready to fall off, we used a 10-in. blade in our reciprocating saw. Next, cut and install the inner 2x10 headers at the front and back and then the rafter supports **(E)** cut from 2x8s. Rip the 2x8s to 6-1/2 in. at a 7-degree angle. The slightly wider 6-1/2-in. edge should go toward the inner side of the pergola. The rafters will rest on this support and extend to the outer side headers **(C)**.

BUILD THE ROOF

Measure the distance at the center of the pergola from front to back at the tops of the headers **(Photo 8)**. Cut the 2x10 ridge beam **(F)** to this length and drive screws at an angle into the headers. Measure from the top edge of the ridge to the inner edge of the side header **(C)** on each side, starting at the midpoint of the ridge and the header. Cut the rafters **(G)** to fit. Ideally it should be 7 degrees, but if your ridge is cupped slightly, you may need to adjust the cut. Because our ridge was slightly cupped, we had 6-degree cuts on one side of the ridge and 8-degree cuts on the other side. Install the rafters and fasten them with screws **(Photo 9)**.

The gable rafters **(H)** are the same as the common rafters except they sit atop the front and rear headers so they need to be scribed **(Photo 10)** to fit. Fasten these to the ridge beam by toe-screwing them at an angle or by screwing them through the opposite side of the ridge at a slight angle into the rafter (this method gives a cleaner installation and less chance of a protruding screw). Finally, screw through the side headers into the rafter ends, making sure the spacing is even.

We cut 2-1/2-in.-wide roof slats **(J)** from 1x6 material because it was better quality than the 1x3s available at the lumberyard. Start installing the slats parallel to the ridge and work your way down each side. Overhang the front and back of each course by about 5 in., then you can string a line and trim them once they're all installed. Use a 2-1/2-in. spacer as you screw each row to the rafters **(Photo 11)**. Check your progress every fifth course to make sure that you're staying perpendicular to the rafters and that you'll finish with a full-width slat at the end.

Once all the roof slats are fastened and trimmed, cut the ridge covers **(K)** and nail them over the exposed end grain at each end of the ridge beam. We mitered the ridge cover tops to fit tightly under the roof slats.

FINISH UP

If you stained the lumber before assembly, all you have to do now is coat any unstained ends of parts. Be sure to stain the top ends of each post to reduce water absorption and cracking. For extra insurance, we coated the post tops with stain followed by exterior paint. If you plan to pour a concrete floor as we did, go to familyhandyman.com and search for "concrete" to find several articles about working with concrete.

10 MARK THE GABLE RAFTERS. Tack a 2x4 to the end of the ridge beam and then align it with the header, in the same plane as the other rafters. Scribe each end of the 2x4 to create a pattern for the other gable rafters.

11 INSTALL THE SLATS. Screw the roof slats to the rafters using a spacer to position them. Make sure each slat overhangs the gables by about 5 in. After all the slats are in place, mark the ends with a string and trim them.

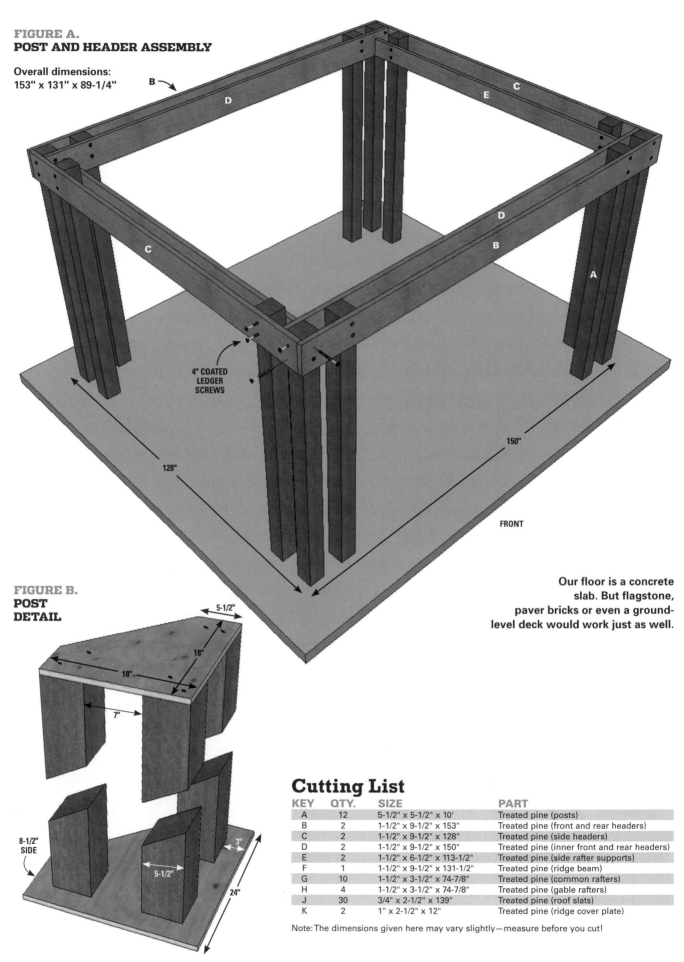

FIGURE A.
POST AND HEADER ASSEMBLY

Overall dimensions:
153" x 131" x 89-1/4"

B

D

E   C

C

D

B

A

4" COATED
LEDGER
SCREWS

128"

150"

FRONT

Our floor is a concrete
slab. But flagstone,
paver bricks or even a ground-
level deck would work just as well.

FIGURE B.
POST
DETAIL

5-1/2"

18"

18"

7"

8-1/2"
SIDE

3"

5-1/2"

24"

Cutting List

KEY	QTY.	SIZE	PART
A	12	5-1/2" x 5-1/2" x 10'	Treated pine (posts)
B	2	1-1/2" x 9-1/2" x 153"	Treated pine (front and rear headers)
C	2	1-1/2" x 9-1/2" x 128"	Treated pine (side headers)
D	2	1-1/2" x 9-1/2" x 150"	Treated pine (inner front and rear headers)
E	2	1-1/2" x 6-1/2" x 113-1/2"	Treated pine (side rafter supports)
F	1	1-1/2" x 9-1/2" x 131-1/2"	Treated pine (ridge beam)
G	10	1-1/2" x 3-1/2" x 74-7/8"	Treated pine (common rafters)
H	4	1-1/2" x 3-1/2" x 74-7/8"	Treated pine (gable rafters)
J	30	3/4" x 2-1/2" x 139"	Treated pine (roof slats)
K	2	1" x 2-1/2" x 12"	Treated pine (ridge cover plate)

Note: The dimensions given here may vary slightly—measure before you cut!

FIGURE C.
ROOF DETAIL

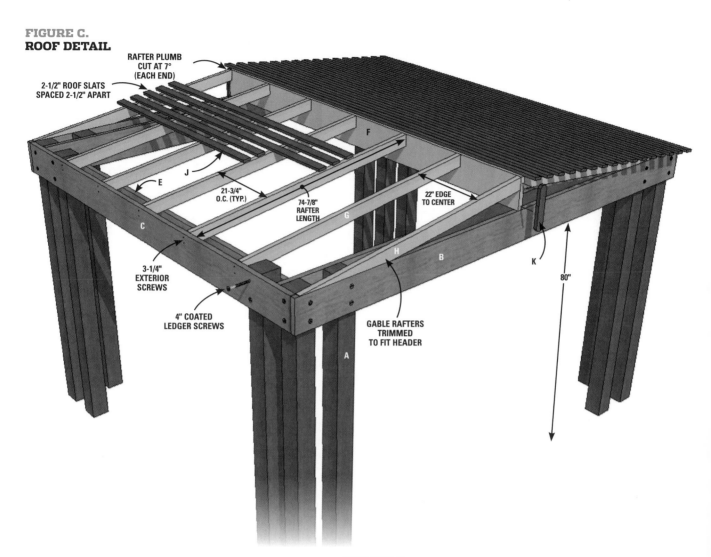

RAFTER PLUMB CUT AT 7° (EACH END)

2-1/2" ROOF SLATS SPACED 2-1/2" APART

F

J

E

21-3/4" O.C. (TYP.)

74-7/8" RAFTER LENGTH

G

22" EDGE TO CENTER

C

H

B

K

3-1/4" EXTERIOR SCREWS

4" COATED LEDGER SCREWS

GABLE RAFTERS TRIMMED TO FIT HEADER

A

80"

FIGURE D.
FOOTING AND SLAB DETAIL

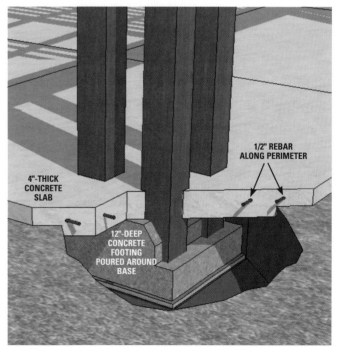

1/2" REBAR ALONG PERIMETER

4"-THICK CONCRETE SLAB

12"-DEEP CONCRETE FOOTING POURED AROUND BASE

Materials List

ITEM	QTY.
6x6 x 10' treated pine posts	12
4' x 4' sheet of 3/4" treated plywood	1
2x10 x 14' treated pine	4
2x10 x 12' treated pine	3
2x8 x 10' treated pine	2
2x4 x 7' treated pine	14
1x3 x 12' treated pine	30
5/4x6 x 2' treated pine (ridge cover plate)	1
1/4" x 4" coated deck ledger screws	48
No. 8 x 3-1/4" self-drilling exterior wood screws	60
No. 8 x 1-5/8" self-drilling exterior wood screws	210
Concrete for footings (80-lb. bag)	16
Concrete for slab	3 cu. yds.
1/2" rebar, 16' lengths	8
2x6 x 16'	4
1x4 x 2' stakes	24

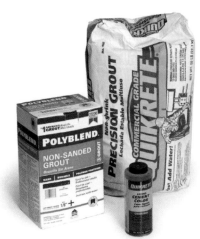

The top is made from construction grout tinted with colorant. Tile grout creates the dark veins.

Faux Stone Patio Table

Achieve the beauty and toughness of stone at a fraction of the cost.

Like a lot of other projects in this book, this one was inspired by sticker shock. A stone table caught the eye of one of our editors as he was walking through a garden center. The table was beautiful and low-maintenance, and would last a lifetime. The only trouble was the price: $650 (on sale!). As usual, we found a way to DIY it.

This version isn't real stone, but it fools most people and has all the durability of stone. Our total materials cost was just under $150—about $110 for the top and $40 for the pedestal. Everything you'll need is available at most home centers.

A DIFFERENT KIND OF GROUT

Construction grout is used mostly for heavy construction projects, such as anchoring steel columns. But it's also perfect for casting projects because it has a creamy consistency that takes on the shape and texture of a form almost perfectly. Use a smooth form and you're guaranteed a smooth, uniform tabletop. Most home centers carry construction grout in 50-lb. bags, which cost about $17 each. (Quikrete Precision Grout and Sakrete Construction Grout are two brands.) If you can't find it, go to quikrete.com or sakrete.com to find a dealer. We darkened the grout by adding cement colorant to the water **(see Photo 2)**.

BUILD THE FORM

Plastic-coated particleboard (called melamine) is perfect for form work because it's inexpensive and smooth. Cut the form base to 31-1/2 x 31-1/2 in. and then cut 2 x 32-in. strips for the form sides. Attach the sides to the base as shown in **Photo 1**. The overhanging sides make dismantling the form easier; you can just whack them loose with a hammer. Coat the form with spray lubricant **(Photo 1)**. Important: Use a lubricant that dries instead of leaving

1 BUILD AN UPSIDE-DOWN FORM. Assemble the form, spray on lubricant and wipe off the excess. Cast upside down, the tabletop's surface face will turn out as smooth and flat as the melamine form.

2 MIX ONE BAG AT A TIME. Add grout to water mixed with colorant. Turn a bucket into a giant measuring cup so you can easily use the correct amount of colored water with each bag.

3 POUR A PATTERN. Sketch a pattern on the form and fill the outlined areas with mounds of construction grout. This pattern will show up on the top of the table.

4 CREATE THE VEINS. Sprinkle dry tile grout along the edges of the mounds. The colored powder will form dark lines in the finished top.

an oily coating. The label will include language on it such as "leaves a dry film." Liquid Wrench Dry Lubricant is one brand we like.

Next, grab a pencil and sketch a random pattern on the form to outline the areas you'll cover with grout first **(Photo 3)**. The pencil lines you draw will determine where the dark veins appear in the finished top. Set the form on a sturdy work surface and level the form with shims. Construction grout is slushy and will overflow if the form tilts. Spilled grout will leave stains, so cover the floor with plastic drop cloths.

Materials List

ITEM	QTY.
Construction grout	150 lbs.
3/4" melamine	1 4' x 8' sheet
Quikrete Cement Color	10 oz.
Spray lubricant	1 can
Plastic cement tub	1
2-1/2"-wide foil tape	1 roll
2" nails or screws	as needed
Unsanded tile grout (black or charcoal)	as needed
Tile or stone sealer	as needed
Welded wire mesh	1 2' x 2' square

GET READY TO MIX

Mixing and pouring the construction grout is a three-phase process: You'll use most or all of the first bag to pour a pattern **(Photo 3)**, the second to fill in the pattern **(Photo 6)** and the third to completely fill the form.

Turning a bucket into a giant measuring cup **(see Photo 2)** will let you add equal amounts of water and cement colorant to each of the three bags without measuring each time. First, measure the correct amount of water into the bucket (we used 4.5 liters per bag) and mark the water level on the bucket. Measure in more water to locate the other two marks (at 9 and 13.5 liters).

Next, empty the bucket and dump in the cement colorant. Much of it will remain in the bottle. To wash it out, pour in a little water, shake hard and pour again. Repeat until all the colorant is washed out. Refill the bucket with water and you'll have tinted water, premeasured into three equal amounts. The colorant tends to settle to the bottom, so stir the colored water before each use.

Construction grout hardens fast. In warm weather, it will become stiff and difficult to work with in just 15 minutes. Minutes wasted cutting the wire mesh or searching for a tool can ruin the project. So have absolutely everything ready to go before you start mixing. It's best to have a helper too. To slow down the hardening, use cold water only.

Mix the construction grout in a plastic cement tub ($6). Don't pour the water directly from the bucket into the mixing tub; it's too hard to control the flow. Instead, ladle the water into the tub with a smaller container. Dump in about half the bag and mix it thoroughly. Gradually add the rest of the bag as you mix. If the mixed grout stiffens before you can use it, stir it to restore the slushy consistency. If it becomes too stiff to stir, toss it. The tabletop requires only about 2-1/2 bags, so you can afford to waste some.

5 BLOW THE GROUT. Turn down the pressure on your compressor and blow the tile grout against the edges of the mounds.

POUR, WAIT PATIENTLY AND SEAL

Photos 3-9 show how to complete the top. Don't forget to turn down your compressor's pressure to about 5 psi before you blow the tile grout **(Photo 5)**. Cut the 2 x 2-ft. section of mesh **(Photo 7)** using bolt cutters. Wire cutters won't do the job.

Resist the temptation to tear off the form as soon as the grout is hard. The longer the grout stays wet, the stronger it will get. Give it at least three days. A week is even better. To remove the form, get a helper and flip the form upside down. (Don't let the top tip out of the form!) Then knock the form sides loose with a hammer and lift the form off the top. Don't despair when you unveil the bland, gray top. The sealer will deepen the color and accentuate the black veins **(Photo 9)**.

Most sealers can't be applied until the grout has cured for at least 28 days. Before you apply sealer to the top, try it on the underside to make sure you like the look. We used a glossy "stone and tile" sealer to bring out the most color. A sealer with a matte finish will have a subtler look.

6 FILL IN THE BLANK SPOTS. Cover the bare areas of the form. Pour between the areas you covered first, not on top of them. Jiggle the form to spread and level the mix.

7 ADD THE MESH. With the form about half full, lay in the welded wire mesh for reinforcement. Then completely fill the form.

Forming a Crinkled Edge

Smooth edges on the tabletop are fine, but a crinkled edge will give it a more natural look. To start, cut four strips of aluminum foil tape about an inch longer than the form sides. Then...

Scrunch it up.

Straighten it out.

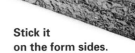

Stick it on the form sides.

FIGURE A.
PEDESTAL

The tabletop height is 30 in. The top itself is 30 x 30 in. and 2 in. thick.

- To cut half-lap joints, set the cutting depth on your circular saw to 1-3/4 in. Cut a series of kerfs no more than 1/8 in. apart. Break out the slices with a hammer and chisel.

- Fasten the top to the pedestal with eight concrete screws. Construction grout is easy to drill; you don't need a hammer drill. Wrap tape around the drill bit to mark the depth. Be very careful not to poke through the top.

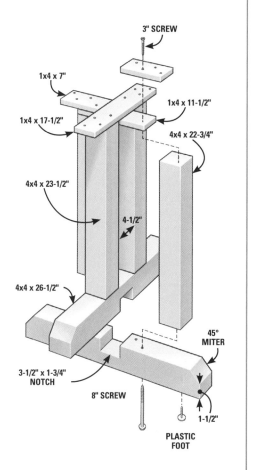

3" SCREW
1x4 x 7"
1x4 x 11-1/2"
1x4 x 17-1/2"
4x4 x 22-3/4"
4x4 x 23-1/2"
4-1/2"
4x4 x 26-1/2"
45° MITER
3-1/2" x 1-3/4" NOTCH
8" SCREW
1-1/2"
PLASTIC FOOT

Materials List

ITEM	QTY.
4 x 4 x 8' cedar	2
1 x 4 x 8' pressure-treated	1
8" construction or lag screws	8
1-3/4" concrete screws	8
3" screws	8
Furniture feet	4
Exterior stain	as needed

FAQs

CAN I MAKE IT BIGGER?
Yes, but remember the weight factor. We once made a 3 x 5-ft. tabletop from construction grout. Moving it was like a scene from *The Ten Commandments*.

WHAT ABOUT OTHER COLORS?
Home centers typically carry three or four colors of liquid colorant, and you'll find a huge range of powdered colors online (search for "cement colorant"). We have done dozens of color experiments and have learned one big lesson: Coloring cement-based products is tricky. The results we got were sometimes good, sometimes bad, but always a surprise.

WHY NOT USE STANDARD CONCRETE MIX?
You can. But don't expect to get the same look you'll get from construction grout. With concrete, you're likely to get a rougher surface with more air bubbles and craters. That's not necessarily bad, just different.

8 SCREED IT OFF. Scrape off the excess using a straight board and a sawing motion. Cover the wet grout with plastic. The longer it stays wet, the stronger it will cure.

9 SEAL THE TABLETOP. Bring out the color with sealer. Before you apply the sealer, ease the tabletop's sharp edges with 80-grit sandpaper.

Sidewalk Transformation

The look of stone without the extra labor or expense? Yes, please!

This sidewalk was just your basic concrete—in pretty good shape but with zero curb appeal. To change that, we considered tile, stone and even complete replacement. Then we discovered "overlay," a cement-based topping for existing concrete. It's used mostly by pros, but we found a supplier who provided materials and rental tools and even encouraged us to do it ourselves. We're glad we did! With a helper, it's a manageable process, and our total cost was about $800, which is less than one-fifth of the pro bid we got. Read on to learn about this transformative (and affordable) technique.

Sled-style gauge rake (3)

Cam-style gauge rake (4)

1

2

YES!
IT ACTUALLY
SMELLS LIKE
*BUBBLE
GUM!*

5

PREP YOUR SIDEWALK

Old sidewalks are seldomly perfect, but this one was in decent shape, without any cracks. If yours has cracks, you'll need to properly repair them before applying an overlay. If you don't, those cracks will promptly transfer to your new look. If your sidewalk has some heaves or uneven sections, you'll need to grind them reasonably level before applying an overlay. In this case, we just needed to thoroughly clean the sidewalk. This included edging it to remove any overgrowth, sweeping off debris and pressure-washing with a degreasing detergent.

KEY TOOLS AND MATERIALS

1. **Stampable overlay** is a high-strength polymer-modified cement. **Bond coat** is an acrylic primer that helps the overlay stick to the old concrete.

2. **Liquid release** is typically a petroleum-based liquid that helps prevent stamps from sticking to the overlay.

3. A **sled-style gauge rake** lets you skip filling control joints but leaves larger tracks to smooth out.

4. The small cams on the ends of a **cam-style gauge rake** leave a relatively track-free surface, but the cams will dip into the control joints if they're not filled.

5. We used three flexible **stamping mats** with an ashlar pattern, and a thinner, more flexible **texture mat**. The texture mat has no grout lines, so it works well for vertical surfaces and applying texture in areas where the standard stamps don't go quite deep enough. Some home centers stock them, or you can rent them from a local rental center.

1. FILL THE JOINTS

Fill the control joints to create a flat surface for the gauge rake to follow (**Photo 1**). Otherwise you'll end up with dips in the overlay. The concrete mix we had on hand filled the joints, but mortar mix would have been easier to work with. We placed markers at the joint locations so we could recut them later (**see Photo 2 inset**).

2. PRIME THE CONCRETE

For a strong bond, the overlay requires a special primer that must be covered with overlay within two hours. At first, our two-person team primed only a few feet of sidewalk. But after mixing and pouring the first bag of overlay, we realized we'd be able to move pretty quickly, so we primed the whole sidewalk.

3. ADD COLOR

We wanted to darken our overlay a little, so we added powdered pigment to the water and thoroughly mixed it before adding the overlay mix.

4. MIX THE OVERLAY

Thorough mixing is a must. Use a heavy-duty corded drill with a 1/2-in. chuck and a mixing paddle. If you don't have a heavy-duty drill, get one. After the initial mixing, allow the Brickform product to set, or "slake," for three to five minutes, and then mix it again.

CONTROL JOINT MARKER

POWDERED PIGMENT

5. SPREAD THE OVERLAY

Pour the overlay onto the primed surface. This product required a thickness of 3/8 in., so we used a gauge rake in order to get a consistent depth. A gauge rake has an adjustable cam or foot on each end, allowing you to set the depth you need. Rake carefully, pulling and pushing the product for even coverage. Don't let the cams slip off the edge of the sidewalk.

6. SMOOTH THE OVERLAY

After raking, smooth the overlay with a standard floor squeegee. At first the squeegee was a little difficult to control because the edge wanted to dig into the overlay. But it got easier with practice!

7. COAT THE STAMPS

Spray each stamp with a liquid release agent to keep the overlay from sticking to the stamp. We used a garden pump sprayer, which proved easier than a trigger-type spray bottle.

8. STAMP THE OVERLAY

Set each stamp down carefully, the whole stamp at once. Don't slide them, drag them or set one corner down first. Walk on each stamp to ensure a full, deep texture. If necessary, use a tamping tool to force the stamp down. Don't use a cast-iron tamper, though. The hard edges can dent the texture. Instead, use a soft-faced tamper.

RELEASE AGENT

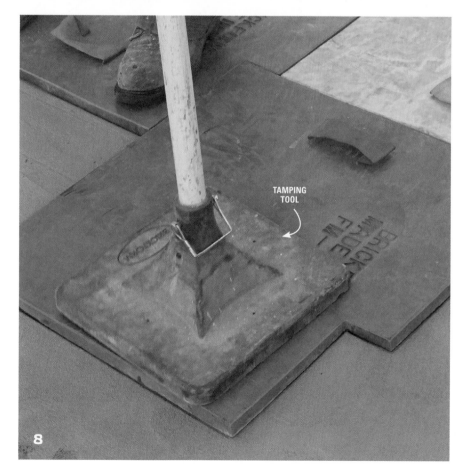

TAMPING TOOL

9. LIFT THE STAMPS

After a stamp is fully imprinted, set the next stamp and then lift the previous one. When you lift a stamp, lift straight up so you don't mess up the texture.

10. TOOL GROUT LINES

After lifting the stamps, you may have to tidy up some grout lines. A roller tool like the one shown works well for this; it creates the grout lines and adds texture to the edge of the stamped area.

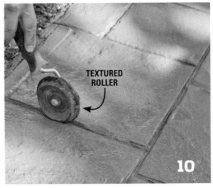

TEXTURED ROLLER

11. TEXTURE VERTICAL SURFACES

We applied the overlay to the steps as well. The horizontal surfaces are done exactly like the sidewalk. For vertical surfaces, we applied a thinner overlay— about 1/4 in. thick—and then used a texture mat to stamp them. This flexible mat also proved indispensable for getting texture right up to the house.

12. GET UP CLOSE

We used stamps to get as close as possible to the house, but where we had to use the texture mat, we added the grout lines using a brick-jointing tool.

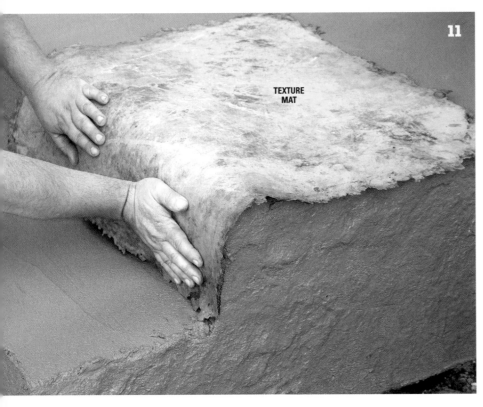

TEXTURE MAT

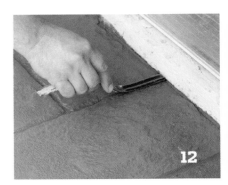

13. RECUT CONTROL JOINTS

Once the overlay has hardened, mark and recut the control joints. Caution: As we were stamping, a couple of our stamps didn't come out perfectly square with the control joints. So when we recut those, we cheated them a little bit to keep the cuts square with the pattern. But one of those cracked at the original control joint within a week. So, as you're applying the stamps, take care to keep the pattern square with the control joints.

14. APPLY STAIN

Mix the concentrated stain with water in a gallon jug, and then apply it using a hand sprayer. Apply generously, allowing the stain to pool in the low spots. Those pooled areas end up darker, giving a more natural stone look.

15. SEAL IT AND YOU'RE DONE!

When the stain is completely dry, use a paint roller to seal the overlay. Unlike when applying the stain, don't allow the sealer to puddle, because it won't cure properly. We used a brush to fully coat the grout lines and also on the stoop to get up close to the house.

One-Day Retaining Wall

Grab a buddy and build the simplest, cheapest, back-friendliest retaining wall in history.

Need to add a retaining wall but don't want to abuse your back by schlepping around landscape blocks or bust the bank buying good-looking blocks? After tapping into our editors' vast reservoir of carpentry experience, we came up with a solution: a wood foundation built as a retaining wall. Our editors have built dozens of wood foundations (yes, made from treated wood for real basements under new homes), so this was a no-brainer—super easy, attractive and cheap.

This 32-in.-high, 32-ft.-long wall was built in one fairly laid-back day by a two-person team. The materials cost $500, plus another $500 for a skid steer and its operator, gravel and some extra topsoil for fill. Having the skid steer on site sped

things along and spared our team some manual labor, but it's possible to do the digging for this project with a shovel.

The skeleton of this retaining wall is a treated wood 2x4 stud wall clad on both sides with 1/2-in. treated plywood. It's held in place with 2x4 "dead men" assemblies buried in the backfill. The dead men are 2x4 struts bolted to the wall studs and anchored to a perpendicular 2x4 sleeper **(see Figure A)**. The weight of the soil on the dead men anchors the wall against the backfill pressure. It's important to locate the bottom of the wall below grade a few inches so the earth in front of the wall will anchor the base in place.

GET THE RIGHT STUFF

Ordinary treated wood will last a good long time depending on soil conditions, although wet sites with clay will shorten the wall's life somewhat. We used ordinary treated wood from the home center, and we estimate that the wall will last at least 20 years. To build a wall that'll last forever, use foundation-grade treated wood—the material used for basements. It's usually southern yellow pine, a very strong softwood that accepts treatment better than most and contains a higher concentration of preservatives. You may find it at lumberyards where contractors shop. Or you can special-order it from any home center or lumberyard, although you'll pay a premium.

Choose nails rated for treated wood: 16d for the framing and 8d for the sheathing. Use 3-in. construction screws for standoffs and dead men connections—again, ones that are rated for treated wood. You'll also need a box each of 2- and 3-in. deck screws for the trim boards. See the Materials List on p. 230 for more needed supplies.

PREPPING THE SITE

We had a gentle slope to retain, not a huge hill. This 32-in.-high wall is designed to hold back a gentle slope, and the design is good for walls up to 40 in. tall. For walls 40 to 48 in, place the studs on 12-in. centers and keep the rest of the wall the same. Don't build the wall more than 48 in. high—a taller wall requires special engineering.

Do the digging with a shovel if you wish. The trick is to dig halfway into the hill and throw the soil on top of the hill. That way you'll have enough fill left for behind the wall. The downside is that if you hand-dig, you'll also need to dig channels for the 2x4 struts. It is much easier to hire a skid steer and an operator to dig into the hill and then cut down a foot or so behind the wall to create a shelf for resting the dead men. Expect to pay a few hundred dollars for skid steer services. The operator can also scoop out the 12-in.-wide by 10-in.-deep trench for the gravel footing and then deliver and dump a 6-in. layer of gravel into the footing. You'll need to do only a bit of raking to level off the trench. A yard of gravel will take care of 50 linear feet of wall. If you have extra gravel, use it for backfill against the back of the wall for drainage. Have the skid steer operator return to fill against the back side of the wall and do some final grading.

GET THE FOOTINGS READY

Fill the trench with gravel. Any type will do, but pea gravel is the easiest to work with. Roughly rake it level, then tip one of the footing plates on edge and rest a level on top to grade the footing **(Photo 1)**. Use the plate as a screed, as if you're leveling in concrete, and you'll get it really close to level

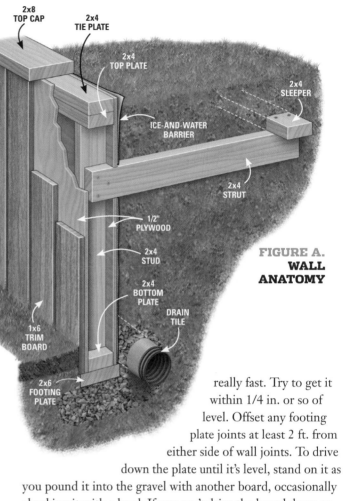

really fast. Try to get it within 1/4 in. or so of level. Offset any footing plate joints at least 2 ft. from either side of wall joints. To drive down the plate until it's level, stand on it as you pound it into the gravel with another board, occasionally checking it with a level. If you can't drive the board down to achieve level, scoop out shallow trenches on either side of the footing plate with your hand. Then there will be a place for gravel to flow as you drive down the plate.

FIGURE A.
WALL ANATOMY

Labels on figure: 2x8 TOP CAP · 2x4 TIE PLATE · 2x4 TOP PLATE · 2x4 SLEEPER · ICE-AND-WATER BARRIER · 2x4 STRUT · 1/2" PLYWOOD · 2x4 STUD · 2x4 BOTTOM PLATE · DRAIN TILE · 1x6 TRIM BOARD · 2x6 FOOTING PLATE

FRAME AND SET THE WALLS

Frame the walls in your driveway or on the garage floor. The walls are very light, so you can carry them a long way if you need to. Build them in sections, whatever length you like, and screw the end studs together at the site. Leave off the sheathing for now. Snap a chalk line 1 in. in from the outside of the footing plate to align the walls **(Photo 2)**. Place them, screw the joining studs together with four 3-in. construction screws, and screw the wall plates to the footing plates in every other stud space with 3-in. construction screws.

Plumb, straighten and brace the walls from the front side, and then add the tie plate **(Photo 3)**. Make sure to seam the tie plate joints at least 4 ft. away from the wall joints.

SHEATHE AND WATERPROOF THE WALLS

Set the plywood panels in place one at a time. Draw and cut 1-5/8 x 3-5/8-in. strut openings spaced 6 in. down from the underside of the top plate and directly next to every other stud. Nail each panel into place with 8d nails spaced every

8 in. before moving on to the next one. Cover the outside with ice-and-water barrier (**Photo 4**). The adhesive won't hold the barrier in place, so staple it as needed. Cut off the excess at the top and cut out the strut openings with a utility knife.

ADD THE STRUTS AND SLEEPERS

Slip a strut through each hole. Prop the struts so they're close to level, either by piling up dirt or supporting them on chunks of scrap wood. Screw each one to a stud with three 3-in. construction screws. (Predrill the holes to prevent splitting since it's so near the end.) Screw the sleeper to the other end of each strut with two more screws (**Photo 5**).

SKIN AND FINISH THE FRONT

Before you can finish the front of the wall and backfill behind it, you'll need to remove the front braces. So prop up the dead men to keep the wall near plumb while you finish the front. Cut the plywood and nail it on, orienting it vertically to the front so the exposed grain will match the 1x6 boards applied over them. Add the 2x8 cap, keeping a 1-1/2-in. overhang at the front. Screw it to the tie plate with 3-in. deck screws. Screw the 1x6 treated boards to the sheathing with 2-in. deck screws (**Photo 6**). We spaced our boards every 1-1/2 in. using a scrap 2x4 as a spacer. Don't trust the spacer for more than a few boards at a time. Occasionally check a board with a level and make any necessary adjustments.

BACKFILL AND FINISH

Plumb and brace the wall from the back by nailing braces to the top cap and staking them on the hill. Prop up every other strut and the sleepers with scraps of wood, otherwise the fill falling on the struts and sleepers will force the wall out of plumb. Backfill first against the front of the wall over the footing to lock the wall base into place, then fill behind it. Next, fill over the sleeper, working your way toward the wall itself (**Photo 7**). The object is to lock in the sleeper before the fill pushes against the wall. Once the backfill is in place, it's a good idea to run a sprinkler over the fill for several hours to make it settle before you remove the braces.

If you like the look of your wall, you're good to go—no finish required. The treated wood will weather from green to gray in a year or two. We applied two coats of Sikkens Log & Siding in the Butternut color.

Materials List

ITEM	QTY.
Roll of ice-and-water barrier	1
50' roll of 4" drain tile	1
Sheets of 1/2" plywood (sheathing)	8
2x6 x 16' (footing plates)	2
2x4 x 8' (studs and struts)	20
2x4 x 16' (sleeper and wall plates)	8
2x8 x 16' (top cap)	2
1x6 x 8' (trim boards)	20
Gravel	1 cu. yd.

This 32-ft.-long wall required the materials listed at left. If you're building a shorter or longer wall, just figure a percentage of these quantities and you'll get close. For the longer boards, choose them so combinations of whatever lengths will handle the length of your wall.

1 LEVEL THE GRAVEL BASE. Lay the 2x6 footing plates on edge and use a 4-ft. level to level the gravel. Pack the gravel with the footing plate to drive it down until it's flat and level.

2 FRAME AND SET THE WALL. Build the wall frames and stand them on top of the footing plates. Snap a chalk line on the footing plate 1 in. from the edge and then screw the bottom plates to the footing plate even with the line.

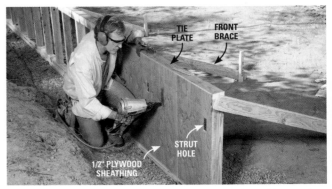

3 BRACE AND SHEATHE THE WALL. Plumb and brace the wall, then screw down the tie plate. Dry-fit the plywood to the back of the framing, mark the strut holes and cut out the holes. Then nail the plywood to the studs.

4 WATERPROOF THE WALL. Clad the back of the wall with ice-and-water barrier, and cut out the strut holes with a utility knife.

5 ASSEMBLE THE DEAD MEN. Poke the struts through the holes and screw them to each stud. Roughly prop up the struts and secure a continuous 2x4 sleeper to the end of each one with two 3-in. screws.

6 ADD THE TRIM. Nail vertically oriented plywood to the top and bottom plates and to the front of the wall. Make sure to seam plywood over studs. Screw a 2x8 top cap to the top plate, hanging it over the front of the wall 1-1/2 in. Fasten vertical 1x6s to the sheathing with 1-1/2-in. spaces between boards.

7 TIME TO BACKFILL. Plumb and brace the wall from the back. Backfill, starting at the sleeper, to anchor the wall into place as you continue filling the space behind the wall.

Deluxe Drum Composter

It's large and loaded with features—but you can build it for the cost of a bargain model.

Drum composters convert yard waste to finished compost much faster than stationary compost bins because they allow you to churn and instantly aerate the waste. Plus, drum composters are easier on your back. You can buy them online or at any garden center—small units for as little as $150 and large fancy rigs for $400 or more. They all follow the same basic design—a drum on a stand. Our version is an adaptation of that using a plastic 55-gallon drum. The drum and stand together cost about the same as a low-price model, but our composter is built stronger and has more features. It takes a full day to customize the drum and build the stand. We used rivets to speed up the assembly, but screws, nuts and lock washers work too.

FINDING AND CUSTOMIZING THE DRUM

Ask for free used 55-gallon polyethylene drums at car washes or from food processing and industrial manufacturers. Since beggars can't be choosers, you'll probably wind up with a white, green or blue drum. If that doesn't fit your backyard color scheme (paint doesn't stick well to polyethylene), contact a container firm and order the color you want. We ordered a black "tight-head" drum (top permanently sealed to the drum) for $52 from a local supplier.

Use a jigsaw to cut a door panel slightly smaller than the width of your wheelbarrow. The next step takes the most time and isn't mandatory, but it adds strength and stability to the entire door assembly: Bend 1/8 x 1-in. flat aluminum stock around the drum to form side reinforcements for the door opening. Cut the bent aluminum slightly longer than the door opening and mount it to the drum (**Photo 1**).

Then cut flat aluminum pieces for the top and bottom of the door opening and the hinge side of the door. Mount the top and bottom door opening reinforcements in the same manner. Mount the hinges at the bottom of the door opening so the door hangs down when you empty the drum. Finish the door by adding the latches (**Figure A**).

To make stirring paddles, cut an 8-ft. piece of 4-in. PVC pipe in half lengthwise using a jigsaw. Cut the halves to length so they're slightly shorter than the inside height of the drum. Arrange two halves back-to-back. Then drill and screw the pieces together to form one paddle unit. The back-to-back design is stronger than a single "scoop" and allows you to rotate the drum in either direction. Repeat for the second paddle unit.

Since the drum has a taper at the top and bottom, you'll have to sand the ends of the paddles to match (**Photo 2**). Mount the paddle units 180 degrees apart and secure them to the drum with screws, nuts and washers. Finally, mount grab handles around the drum to rotate it.

A tight-head drum comes with two threaded "bungholes." Remove the threaded caps to provide ventilation. You may need to drill additional ventilation holes if the mixture stays too wet.

How It Works

Waste becomes compost thanks to millions of hungry microbes that break waste down and convert it to nutrient-rich fertilizer. Those microbes need oxygen to thrive, and turning the drum daily creates fresh air pockets in the mix. You can accomplish the same thing by churning a pile of compost with a shovel, but a drum composter makes it easier. And more thorough mixing speeds decomposition.

ROTATE DAILY. Screw the bung caps into the holes to prevent compost from leaking out. Then grab the handles and rotate the drum several times in either direction to stir the mixture.

DROP, ROLL AND DUMP. Park your wheelbarrow under the drum and open the door. As you roll the drum downward, the compost will dump right into the wheelbarrow.

DRUM COMPOSTER

Overall dimensions: 39" W x 30" D x 58" H

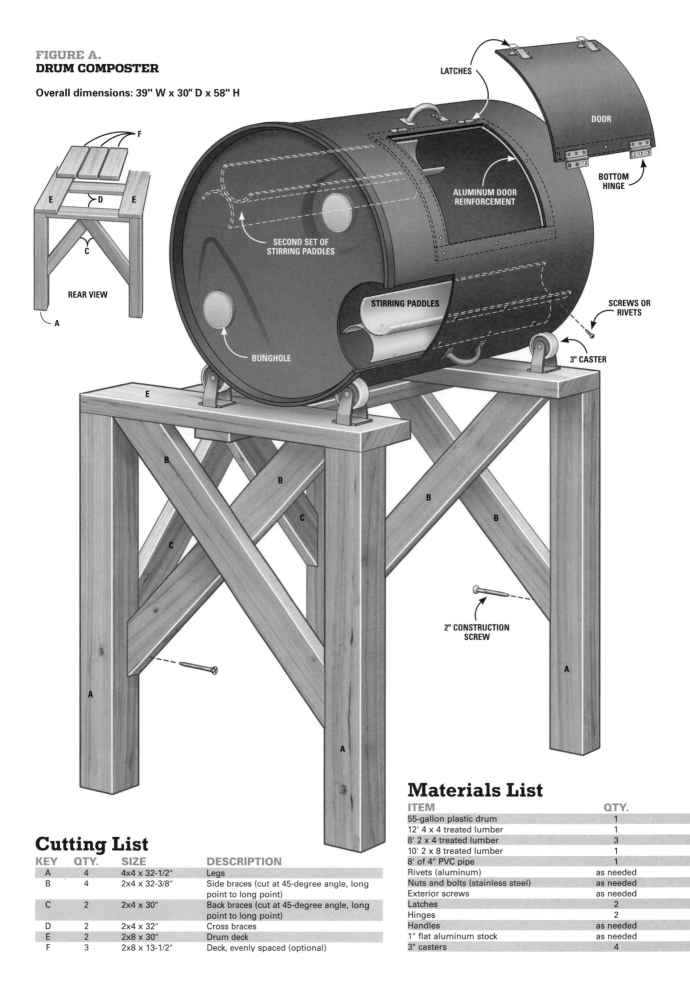

REAR VIEW

LATCHES

DOOR

ALUMINUM DOOR
REINFORCEMENT

SECOND SET OF
STIRRING PADDLES

STIRRING PADDLES

BUNGHOLE

BOTTOM
HINGE

SCREWS OR
RIVETS

3" CASTER

2" CONSTRUCTION
SCREW

Cutting List

KEY	QTY.	SIZE	DESCRIPTION
A	4	4x4 x 32-1/2"	Legs
B	4	2x4 x 32-3/8"	Side braces (cut at 45-degree angle, long point to long point)
C	2	2x4 x 30"	Back braces (cut at 45-degree angle, long point to long point)
D	2	2x4 x 32"	Cross braces
E	2	2x8 x 30"	Drum deck
F	3	2x8 x 13-1/2"	Deck, evenly spaced (optional)

Materials List

ITEM	QTY.
55-gallon plastic drum	1
12' 4 x 4 treated lumber	1
8' 2 x 4 treated lumber	3
10' 2 x 8 treated lumber	1
8' of 4" PVC pipe	1
Rivets (aluminum)	as needed
Nuts and bolts (stainless steel)	as needed
Exterior screws	as needed
Latches	2
Hinges	2
Handles	as needed
1" flat aluminum stock	as needed
3" casters	4

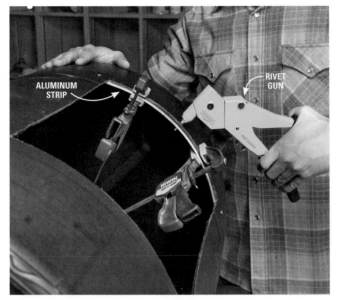

1 REINFORCE THE DOOR OPENING. Clamp aluminum strips in place so 1/2 in. extends into the door opening. Fasten the strips with rivets or nuts and screws.

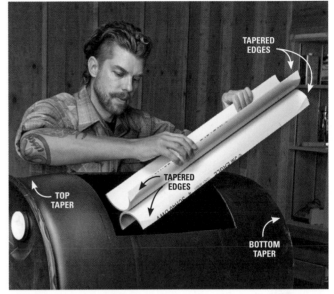

2 INSTALL THE PADDLE. Taper the ends of the paddle to match the tapered ends of the drum. Sand the paddle with a belt sander until it fits. Then install the paddle with screws.

3 ASSEMBLE THE STAND. Screw the legs to the drum deck. Then install the cross braces. Strengthen with diagonal struts.

4 MOUNT THE CASTERS. Mount two casters, then set a level on top of the drum and pry the drum up with a board. When the drum is level, position the last two casters, mark their locations and screw them into place.

BUILD THE STAND AND MOUNT THE ROLLERS

Cut the legs and deck boards to length according to the Cutting List. Then assemble the stand using a drill and exterior screws **(Photo 3)**. Add diagonal struts to prevent front-to-back and side-to-side movement when spinning the drum.

Flip the stand upright and mount two casters so they ride in the recess around the drumhead. Then level the drum and mount the remaining two casters **(Photo 4)**.

LOAD, SPIN AND DUMP

Load the drum with yard waste and add a compost starter to get the batch cooking (you can buy a package of compost starter for about $15 online or at any home or garden center). Rotate the drum composter at least once every day to mix and aerate the batch. When the compost is ready, just dump it out into a waiting wheelbarrow. You're then free to use it as desired throughout your yard and to get started churning the next batch of compost.

North Woods Bench

Made from lumberyard pine, this inexpensive, easy-to-build bench is an instant classic.

This bench is simplicity itself. You can easily build it with hand tools, but we used a miter saw to cut the stretchers to length and to cut the 10-degree angles on the ends of the center stretcher, and we used a circular saw for all the other cuts. If you don't own a miter saw, you can use a circular saw or jigsaw for all the cuts. To make the holes for the clover shapes, you'll need a 1-in. hole saw mounted in a corded drill, or a powerful cordless drill.

We used No. 2 knotty pine to build this bench; you'll need one 6-ft. 1x12 and one 10-ft. 1x4. Select boards that are straight and flat, with solid, not loose, knots. We assembled the bench with countersunk 2-in. trim screws and then filled the holes with wood filler. If the bench is going outdoors, be sure to use corrosion-resistant screws.

CUT OUT THE PARTS

Using the Cutting List on p. 238 as a guide, cut the two legs and the top from the 1x12 **(Photo 1)**. The legs require a 10-degree bevel on the top and bottom. Be careful to keep both bevels angled the same direction. Then cut the stretcher and aprons to length. The stretcher has a 10-degree angle on each end.

Next, mark the legs and aprons for drilling and cutting, using the dimensions in **Figures B and D** as a guide. Draw the grid layout as shown in **Photo 2** to locate the holes. Use a nail or a punch to make starting holes for the hole saw at the correct intersections.

Drill 1-in. holes halfway through the boards **(Photo 2)**. Make sure the pilot bit on the hole saw goes through the board so you can use the hole to guide the hole saw from the opposite side. Flip the boards to complete the holes.

Make the remaining cuts on the legs and aprons with a circular saw **(Photo 3)**. Finish up by sanding the parts. We wrapped 80-grit sandpaper around a 1-in. dowel to sand the insides of the holes. Sand off the saw marks

and round all the sharp edges slightly with sandpaper. If you plan to paint the bench, you can save time by painting the parts before assembly.

BUILD THE BENCH

Start by marking the location of the stretcher on the legs. Arrange the legs so the bevels are oriented correctly, and screw through them into the stretcher. Next screw the two aprons to the legs **(Photo 4)**.

The only thing left is to screw the top to the aprons. It'll be easier to place the screws accurately if you first mark the apron locations on the underside of the top and drill pilot holes for the screws **(Photo 5)**. Stand the bench upright and align the top by looking underneath and lining up the apron marks. Then attach the top with six trim screws.

We finished this bench with old-fashioned milk paint (available online and at some paint stores). If the bench is going outdoors, rub some exterior glue on the bottom ends of the legs. That will prevent the end grain from soaking up moisture and rotting.

Inspiration Is Everywhere

Our editor saw this charming red stool while visiting a cabin in the Wisconsin wilderness. The simple piece had an ingenious design detail: a cloverleaf, clearly made with three overlapping drill holes. Our piece is a little longer and stronger, but it keeps the same folk art detail.

1 CUT THE LEG BLANKS. Set the saw to cut a 10-degree bevel. Mark the 1x12 and align the saw with the mark. Then use a large square to help guide the cut.

2 DRILL OUT THE CLOVER SHAPE. Mark out a grid with lines spaced 1/2 in. apart. The centers of the holes will be on four of the intersections. Drill all four holes halfway through the board. Then flip the board and drill from the other side to complete the holes.

3 CUT THE LEG ANGLES. Mark the "V" in the center and the two outside angles on the legs. Then cut along the lines with a circular saw. Accurate cutting is easier if you clamp the leg to the workbench.

4 SCREW THE APRONS TO THE LEGS. Drive trim screws through the legs into the stretcher. Then attach the outside aprons with trim screws.

5 POSITION THE SEAT SCREWS. Here's a goof-proof way to position the screws that fasten the seat to the bench frame. Center the frame on the seat and trace around the aprons. Then drill pilot holes through the seat to mark screw locations. Drive screws through the seat and into the aprons.

FIGURE A.
EXPLODED VIEW

Overall dimensions: 38" L x 11-1/4" W x 16-1/2" H

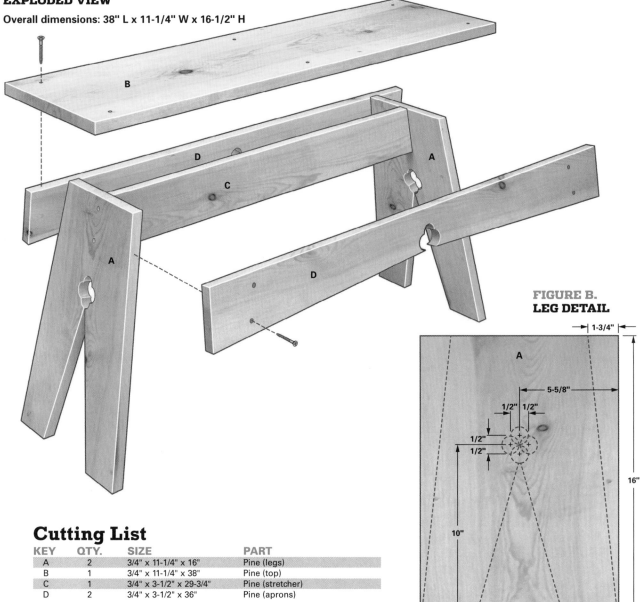

FIGURE B.
LEG DETAIL

Cutting List

KEY	QTY.	SIZE	PART
A	2	3/4" x 11-1/4" x 16"	Pine (legs)
B	1	3/4" x 11-1/4" x 38"	Pine (top)
C	1	3/4" x 3-1/2" x 29-3/4"	Pine (stretcher)
D	2	3/4" x 3-1/2" x 36"	Pine (aprons)

FIGURE C.
STRETCHER DETAIL

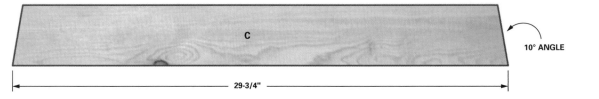

FIGURE D.
APRON DETAIL

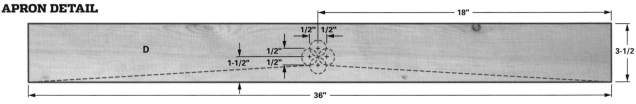

Arched Planter

Bend wood to create this graceful plant stand. You can make it with only two boards!

With this elegant curved deck planter, you can have a splash of garden anyplace you like. Deck it out with flower pots to accent your patio, deck or front steps.

In this article, we'll show you how to build the whole project in a leisurely weekend. Bending wood strips into laminated arches may seem challenging, but we'll walk you through the process step by step. After you build your first planter, you'll have the hang of it, and the next one will be a cinch to build. The key, as you'll see, is a simple plywood "bending" jig that you can use over and over again.

You can complete this project if you're handy with basic carpentry tools. However, you'll need a table saw equipped with a thin-kerf blade for ripping the strips and other parts—a circular saw just won't do the job no matter how steady you are. However,

you'll still need a circular saw, as well as a belt sander and at least four 3-ft. pipe or bar clamps **(Photo 4)**. Our total materials cost for each planter was less than $40. The jig plywood cost about $30.

SELECT WOOD WITH SMALL, TIGHT KNOTS

You need only two 8-ft.-long 2x8s for the entire project. Our planter is made from western red cedar, chosen for its beauty and natural decay resistance. But any wood you choose will be fine as long as you select straight boards with small, tight knots. The long, thin strips will break at large knots during the bending process. You'll be using nearly every inch of each board, so pick ones without splits or cracks at the ends. It may take some sorting at the home center, but the effort's worth it.

While you're at the home center, pick up 2 qts. of exterior woodworking glue along with a mini paint roller **(Photo 6)**, a 4 x 8-ft. sheet of 3/4-in. plywood and a 10 x 20-ft. roll of painter's plastic (3 mil). Also buy brads for your air nailer **(Photo 11)**, if you have one, or a small box of galvanized 1-in. brads if you intend to hand-nail.

CUT THE PARTS

Cut each 2x8 to the lengths called for in **Figure A** and then start the ripping process. Ripping 5/16-in.-wide strips can be hazardous, so be sure to use a push carriage **(Photo 1)**. Make your carriage from 1/4-in. and 3/4-in. plywood, custom-sized to match the height of the table saw fence. We cut 15 strips from each board, but you may get fewer depending on the thickness of your blade. Don't worry if you wind up with fewer or unusable ones; you can build each arch with as few as 13 strips. Just be sure to use the same quantity for each arch so they'll match. If any of the strips break at knots, keep the pieces together because you can still use them (more on this later).

Rip the platform slats next and then the 1/2 x 3/4-in. platform cleats. Rip the pieces first to 3/4 in. wide from a chunk of 2x8, then turn the 1-1/2-in. strips on their sides and rip them into 1/2-in. strips. Cut the cleats to length with decorative 22-degree angles on the ends.

MAKE THE BENDING JIG

Cut the plywood for the bending jig to size **(Photo 2)** and use one of the knot-free strips to form the curve. Use 3-in. screws partially driven into the plywood at the locations we show and push the center of the strip 13-1/2 in. out from the edge while you scribe the curve. Don't beat yourself up striving for a perfect curve; small variations won't be noticeable. It may seem odd to make this curved cut with a circular saw **(Photo 3)**, but it's surprisingly easy

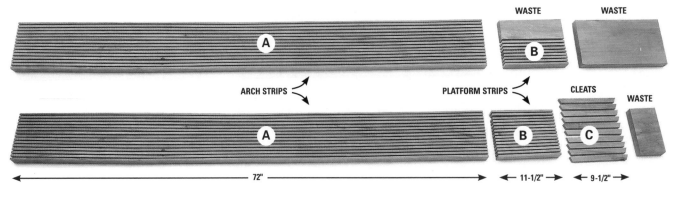

and safe on a gentle curve like this. The curve will be smoother than any you can achieve with a jigsaw. Just make sure to set your blade depth at 7/8 in. Any deeper and the blade may bind and kick back.

The two curves on the two sections of the jig are slightly different, and you'll have to recut the top part of the jig to match the bottom. To find this difference, lay 15 strips in the jig and tighten the clamps until the arch is completely formed (**Photo 4**). You'll have to tighten the clamps in "turns" as the strips gradually bend, i.e., tighten two clamps until they run out of threads. Then leave them in place while you completely unscrew the other two, slide those jaws tight to the jig and continue tightening those. Work on pairs, tightening the outer two, then the inner two. You'll get the feel for the clamping process on this "glueless" dry run and it'll make the actual glue-up easier. When the clamps are tight, the strips will be tight to the jig at the bottom and there will be a gap between the arch and the jig at the top. Trace around the top with a 3/4-in. spacer to re-mark the top curve (**Photo 4**). Then unclamp everything and recut that part of the jig.

BLOCK UP THE CAULS AND GLUE UP THE ARCHES

During glue-up, the strips have a tendency to lift away from the clamps while the glue is wet and slippery because of the stresses in the curves. "Cauls" are simply blocks of wood that hold the strips flat and prevent this. Make the cauls from six 2x4s (three on both the bottom and the top) and space them evenly with blocking sized so the cauls will be flush with the top of the arch (**Photo 7**). Have these ready to go before the glue-up—you won't have time to spare later.

Mark a centerline on the strips and keep them aligned with the bending jig centerline when you start gluing later (**Photo 6**). Lay painter's plastic directly below the jig to keep your workbench and clamps clean, and then start gluing the strips. A mini paint roller greatly speeds up the process, and time is of the essence. Glue both sides of each strip and push the glued surfaces lightly

together to delay glue setup. Slip in any broken strips near the middle of the arch, matching up the breaks after they're coated with glue. Use flawless strips for the first and last strips of each arch. After you spread the glue, pull the jig together, bending the strips as far as you can while a helper slides the clamps closed. That'll speed up the clamping process. Then lay plastic over the caul locations, screw the cauls into place, screw the top 2x4s into place and tighten the clamps. Again, work on pairs, progressively tightening them. Work quickly. If you still see gaps between any strips, close them by driving a wedge between the jig and the arch or add more bar clamps from above. Ignore the clamping instructions on the glue bottle—leave the clamps in place for at least three hours.

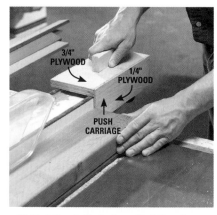

1 Cut the 2x8s to length following **Figure A**. Rip 5/16-in.-wide strips for the arches and the slats. Build a push carriage sized to fit your fence to safely cut thin strips.

Labels: 3/4" PLYWOOD, 1/4" PLYWOOD, PUSH CARRIAGE

Label: 6' x 5/16" ARCH STRIPS

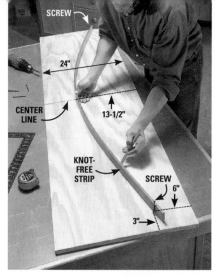

2 Draw the arch on the bending jig plywood using one of the knot-free strips of wood and a pair of 3-in. screws.

Labels: SCREW, 24", CENTER LINE, 13-1/2", KNOT-FREE STRIP, SCREW, 6", 3"

Label: CUT 7/8" DEEP

3 Set the blade of the circular saw to cut 7/8 in. deep and cut the curve. Clamp the plywood to the workbench and hold your saw with both hands.

Labels: GAP, 3/4" SPACER

4 Clamp 15 strips in the bending jig and re-mark the top curve with a 3/4-in. spacer block. Then remove the strips and recut that curve only.

You don't have to wait until you've removed the clamps to start cleaning up glue and flattening the arch. As the glue starts to "gel up" (dry to the touch but gooey beneath the surface, about one hour into clamping), remove the cauls (leave the clamps tightened) and start scraping away the glue from the top side of the arch. A paint scraper works great for most of it; use a small chisel or screwdriver to get into the crevices.

The key is to remove as much glue as possible. Hardened glue is nearly impossible to remove and any leftover glue will clog and ruin sanding belts in no time. After you've scraped off the glue, wipe off any other glue smears with a damp (not wet!) rag. Don't worry about the bottom side yet; you can get it after the three-hour clamping period. The glue there will stay softer longer because it's against the plastic.

FLATTEN THE ARCHES AND CUT THE ENDS

Start belt-sanding diagonally with 60-grit belts to knock off the high spots (**Photo 9**). After the surface is flat, remove cross-grain sanding marks by sanding following the curve. Then belt-sand with 80- and then 100-grit belts. Finish up with 100-grit paper in a random-orbital sander. Remove the arch from the jig, scrape off the glue,

5 Screw together three clamping cauls, adding blocks as needed so they'll be even with the top of the laminating strips (see **Photo 7**).

6 Roll glue onto both sides of each strip (one side of top and bottom strips) and position them, keeping the jig and strip centerlines aligned.

and flatten and sand the opposite side. Then repeat the whole process for the other arch.

If you have a benchtop planer, use it for the whole flattening process. Feed in one end and you'll be able to gently push the arch sideways and follow the curve as it goes through the machine. Make sure all the glue on the surface is removed. Hardened glue will dull the cutting knives.

Mark and cut off the bottom and ends as we show in **Photo 10**. Cut one end first, then measure over 68 in. and cut the other end. Ease the sharp edges of each arch with a round-over router bit or sandpaper.

MOUNT THE CLEATS AND THE PLATFORMS

We show you an easy way to mount the cleats on both arches using a mounting template made from plywood (**Photo 11 and Figure B**). Cut it to 68 in. and lay out the cleat positions as shown. Then position and fasten the cleats (**Photo 11**).

Separate the arches with temporary platform strips and lightly clamp the arches together (**Photo 12**). Make sure the arch ends are even, then glue and nail the platforms to the cleats.

At this point you can head off to the nursery to buy some new plants, but if you'd like a finish on your planter, you can use any stain designed for exterior siding. To further protect your planter against rot, spread a layer of exterior wood glue on the feet of each arch.

FIGURE B. CLEAT TEMPLATE

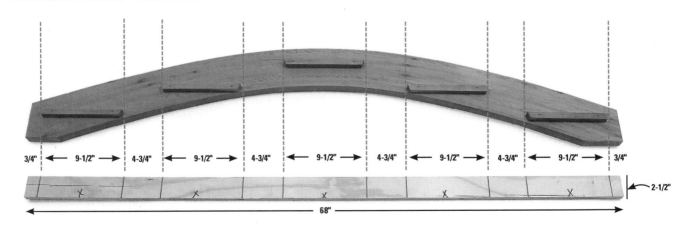

7 Pull the jig together as far as possible and snug up the clamps. Then screw the cauls down and finish tightening the clamps.

CAUL

PAINT SCRAPER

8 Remove the cauls after one hour and scrape off the excess glue from that side. Remove the clamps after three hours and scrape the glue from the other side.

9 Belt-sand both sides of the arch flat with 60-grit paper, then 80-grit. Smooth the surface with a random-orbital sander with 100-grit paper.

68" TO THE OTHER END

VERTICAL LINE

HORIZONTAL LINE

10 Clamp the arches together and draw vertical lines just short of the ends. Then scribe the bottom horizontal lines with a 2x4 spacer. Cut the ends with a circular saw.

CLEAT MOUNTING TEMPLATE

FLUSH WITH ARCH BOTTOM

11 Lay the cleat-mounting template (**Figure B**) flush with the arch bottoms. Then glue and nail the end cleats. Rest the template over the first set of cleats and mount the next two cleats, then move it again to mount the top cleat.

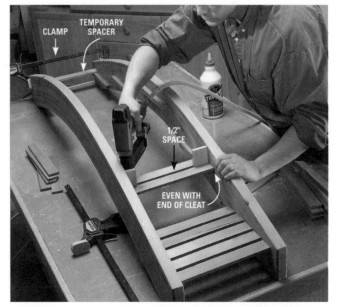

CLAMP

TEMPORARY SPACER

1/2" SPACE

EVEN WITH END OF CLEAT

12 Space and clamp the arches. Then glue and nail the platform strips on the cleats, keeping them even with the cleat ends and spacing them 1/2 in. apart.

SPECIAL SECTION

SAVE BIG ON HOUSEHOLD BILLS

Avoid Insurance Surprises

Stay informed with these 10 critical lessons most homeowners learn only after a claim.

With something as complicated as homeowners insurance, there's nothing better than having an insider tell you what's what. We recently met an expert who's spent half his life working with insurance claims—as a contractor for homeowners, and later as a claims adjuster. What he told us has completely changed the way we look at our policies. And even more important, we now understand the limitations of our coverage.

1. YOUR GARAGE MAY NOT BE FULLY COVERED

Policies are set up to insure your main structure and whatever is physically attached to it. This would include an attached garage but NOT a detached garage. Structures such as stand-alone garages and sheds are typically covered at only 10% of your main dwelling coverage. So, if you carry $200,000 of coverage on your house, your detached garage would be protected only up to $20,000.

Our expert says this is a perfect situation for an "endorsement" to add coverage (see "Insurance Vocabulary"). Typically, the upcharge is nominal for the increased coverage.

2. TERMS FREQUENTLY CHANGE

Occasionally, letters arrive from your insurance company. If you're like most people, you don't read them. But understand this: Insurance companies are constantly fiddling with your contract. And those letters legally inform you of changes—usually new exclusions. In the fine print, the company puts the onus on you to call if you want to restore the coverage through an endorsement. Often, that's a call worth making.

3. BEWARE OF STORM CHASERS

Storms attract traveling contractors who follow damaging weather. They may be reputable—or not. You're safer with a local, established contractor who will be around if repairs aren't done right or if there is a warranty issue. What good is a 10-year warranty if you can't find the contractor?

Before signing anything, consult the Better Business Bureau, Angi and the secretary of state to see if contractors are registered, and the Department of Labor and Industry to be sure their licenses are up to date.

Insurance Vocabulary

■ **ENDORSEMENT:** An insurance endorsement is an amendment that changes the terms of the original policy. Endorsements are also called riders.

■ **EXCLUSION:** An exclusion limits or eliminates coverage for things that the insurance company is unwilling to insure.

---

4. GET REPLACEMENT COST COVERAGE

Something you don't want to change in your insurance policy is your replacement cost coverage. Insurance companies would much rather cover you for actual cash value (ACV) or market value. That's because market or ACV pays for only the depreciated value of what's insured—meaning what an item is worth after calculating its diminished value over time. For example, on a 15–year-old roof, you may get only $3,000 even though the cost to replace it would be closer to $7,000.

That's why our expert loves replacement cost coverage, which pays the entire cost. Often, adding this coverage to your policy increases your bill by only a couple of dollars per month.

The Case of the Crushed Garage

Pulling into the yard of the home pictured above, our expert could plainly see that a large tree had fallen and damaged the detached garage beyond repair.

The owners held a typical policy with coverage of $130,000 on their house. Because the garage was detached, it was considered an "other structure"— limiting it to only 10% of the coverage of the main structure.

The estimate to rebuild the garage came to $23,000, but the insurance payment could not exceed $13,000. Our pro says it was terrible to explain this to people who had no idea they were underinsured. They were (obviously) not happy.

5. YOUR FINISHED BASEMENT MIGHT BE AT RISK

Standard policies typically don't cover a sewer backup or sump pump failure. If this occurs in your finished basement, you could be looking at a costly cleanup and remodel. Even if you did purchase a sewer backup endorsement, a limit of $5,000 is standard. That may be enough to pay for the cleanup and dry out, but it leaves nothing for rebuilding. Our expert recommends coverage of at least $10,000 for a finished basement.

6. CONSIDER A PUBLIC ADJUSTER

Not all adjusters are alike. You likely are familiar with insurance adjusters who work for the insurance company. But there are also independent adjusters (also known as public adjusters) who work on behalf of the homeowner. For example, if you had a lot of damage from a smoky fire that required many complex repairs, hiring an independent adjuster might be a good idea.

Independent adjusters handle the contractors and the insurance. They also use their understanding of the industry to increase your claim payout, which may make their fee of 5 to 10% of the total claim worthwhile.

7. SOME ADJUSTERS DON'T KNOW WHAT IT TAKES

A good adjuster understands how houses are built, but few have actually worked in the trades. That means when writing up the claim, they often miss legitimate materials needed to replace your damaged property. That's where a good contractor comes in.

8. DON'T LET A STORM CHASER TOUCH YOUR HOUSE

During the frantic hours post-storm, everyone wants to prevent further damage. A common tactic of storm chasers is to put a tarp on your damaged roof to prevent a roof leak.

If you can't get up on the roof yourself, hire a trusted handyman to do it. "Tarping" can be a tactic of storm chasers to attempt to lock you into hiring them because they have already done work to your home.

9. A GOOD CONTRACTOR CAN GET YOU MORE MONEY

A skilled contractor knows not only how to repair the damage but also how to speak insurance. Ideally, they've had experience persuading adjusters to include missed expenses needed to do the job right. A contractor can add up to 25% to your claim payout. The goal is to make sure your claim pays enough to let your contractor properly install your new roof without cutting corners.

Hail-Damage Disappointment

When our expert got a call about a roof claim, he reviewed the policy and wasn't surprised to see a "roof over 15 year exclusion." Since the roof was more than 15 years old, this meant that only the actual cash value (ACV) was covered. Just like a car, an asphalt roof wears out and depreciates, or loses value, over time.

Here's what the payout looked like:

Replacement cost	$9,600
Minus depreciation	$5,760
Total ACV	$3,840
Minus deductible	$1,000
Total net payment	$2,840

Money-Saving Strategies

- **GET A LIST OF DISCOUNTS** Insurers offer discounts to homeowners for improvements that make their homes a better risk. These include safety features such as indoor sprinklers, smoke detectors and dead bolts. Discount programs change frequently. If you haven't spoken to your agent within the past year or you've made a major home improvement, you may be missing out on significant discounts.

- **INFORM YOUR AGENT ABOUT UPGRADES** Insurance companies like to insure homes with newer plumbing and electrical systems as well as burglar alarms and sprinkler systems because these features reduce the risk of fire and water damage. If you upgrade any of these systems in an older home, tell your insurance agent. One homeowner we spoke with called her agent to report recent plumbing upgrades, and after a short conversation, the agent raised her overall coverage by $50,000 and cut her yearly premium by $400.

- **THINK TWICE BEFORE FILING A CLAIM** Every time you file a claim, you risk higher insurance rates in the future. So in the long run, filing a claim can actually cost you more than you'd receive in a payout. Paying for a smaller loss yourself will almost always cost less than the premium increase you'll face later. A good rule of thumb: Don't file a claim if it's worth less than $1,000 more than your deductible. Statistically, if you file two claims in a three-year period or make claims related to maintenance issues such as a chronic leak, you risk triggering a rate hike or worse. Your insurance company may even drop you. Just inquiring about a claim (without even filing it!) could raise your rates.

Too Much Water, Not Enough Coverage

One spring, our pro encountered a flooded-basement claim involving a breaker that had tripped during the winter. When the wet season came, the pump failed to turn on.

After his inspection, he sat down with the homeowners and explained that they had an endorsement for "limited water backup and sump discharge or overflow coverage." This is a good endorsement to have if you have a finished basement. But in this case, the coverage was limited to the standard $5,000, while their loss topped $15,000. It was a tough conversation because the homeowners thought they were fully covered.

If you live in a home with a finished basement, consider increasing your endorsement coverage limit to at least $10,000.

10. WHEN YOU HAVE PROPERTY DAMAGE, DO SOMETHING

As the homeowner, you have the responsibility to mitigate problems. If, for example, you have a plumbing or roof leak, don't let it cause more harm to your home. The insurer can refuse to pay for a loss you could have prevented. If you can show you took action that saved the company a larger payout, the company will be more accommodating with your claim.

It's worth reading the section of your policy titled "The Duties of the Insured." It spells out your obligations to prevent further damage. Keep your receipts, as you'll be reimbursed for costs incurred to avoid further harm. Also, photos are essential—before, after and in between!

10-Step Plan to Save Electricity

Slash your electric bill up to 40%!

With electricity prices on the rise, opening your utility bill can sometimes be a sobering experience. So we interviewed top energy experts to find manageable ways to lower that bill as much as possible. Following these 10 tips can cut your electric bill by up to 40%.

In this story, we'll show you the best ways to save electricity. Everything you need to start saving is available at home centers or online. But before you start, find out about rebate programs by contacting your local utility company and reading "Websites That Can Save You Money" on p. 252. You might just get a check for saving electricity!

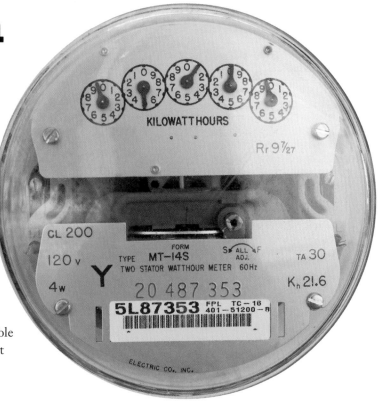

You can expect to pay less than $5 for a CFL bulb that will provide 10,000 hours of light and use $10.40 of electricity (at 8¢ per kilowatt hour). To get the same output with incandescents, you would have to use seven bulbs, and the electricity would cost $48.

1. SWITCH TO CFLS

Replacing incandescent bulbs with compact fluorescent lightbulbs (CFLs) is one of the quickest, easiest ways to save money—and a place everyone can start. CFLs use about 75% less energy and last up to 10 times longer than incandescent bulbs. This can save you more than $30 in electric costs over the lifetime of each bulb. Switching to CFLs in the five most frequently used fixtures in your house will save about $60 per year, according to Energy Star.

Choose CFLs with the Energy Star label to get the greatest savings. Energy Star products have to meet energy-efficiency guidelines set by the EPA and the Department of Energy. When you shop, keep in mind that light fixtures with dimmers require special CFLs—always read the label.

When your CFLs are finally spent, recycle them (to find locations, visit lamprecycle.org).

2. INSTALL SMARTER SWITCHES

Motion sensors (occupancy sensors) automatically turn lights on and off so you get (and pay for!) light only when you need it. Using motion sensors can save you $100 per year. Some motion sensors need to be manually turned on but turn off automatically. These are great for bedrooms because they won't turn on when you move in your sleep.

Some switches are installed in junction boxes; others are wireless. You can also buy light fixtures with built-in motion sensors. You'll need special motion sensors for electronic ballasts that control CFLs (Leviton's ODS10 is one type). Special-order them at home centers or buy them at grainger.com (800-472-4643).

Use timers to control bathroom fans so that a fan will run for a preset time to air out the room and then automatically turn off. (To install a timer, visit familyhandyman.com and search for "install switch.") You can set the length of time you want the fan to run. Purchase timer switches at home centers or online for around $20. Be sure the timer you buy is rated for motors, not just lighting (check the label).

Motion sensors are the perfect solution for left-on lights. They turn off automatically so you don't waste electricity.

A timer lets you turn on the fan and walk away. You don't have to remember to come back later and turn it off.

3. BUY ENERGY STAR APPLIANCES

When you shop for appliances, look for the Energy Star label. It means the appliance meets certain energy-efficiency guidelines. The average household spends $2,000 each year on energy bills. Energy Star says that appliances bearing its label can cut those bills by 30%, for an annual savings of about $600. But you don't have to replace everything to see a savings. Just replacing an eight-year-old refrigerator with a new Energy Star model can save $110 or more per year in electricity.

Not sure what to do with your old appliance? Recycle it. Don't salvage and resell it—that only passes the electricity-hogging appliance along to someone else. Check with your utility company or local home center for programs for appliance pickup and recycling. Or visit dsireusa.org.

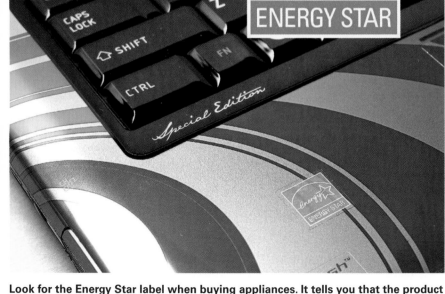

Look for the Energy Star label when buying appliances. It tells you that the product meets strict standards for energy efficiency.

4. SERVICE YOUR AIR CONDITIONER

Roughly half of an average home's annual energy bill (gas and electric), about $1,000, is spent on heating and cooling. Air conditioners placed in direct sunlight use up to 10% more electricity. If yours sits in the sun, plant tall shrubs or shade trees nearby—but don't enclose the unit or impede the airflow. Place window units on the north side of the house or install an awning over them.

Keep your window or central air conditioner tuned up so it runs at peak efficiency (search for "air conditioners" at familyhandyman .com to find out how to do it yourself). Every two or three years, call in a pro to check the electrical parts and the refrigerant.

If your central air conditioner is more than 12 years old, replacing it with an Energy Star model can cut your cooling costs by 30% and save you from doling out cash on maintenance costs. The payback for replacing a 12-year-old system is typically about eight years. An air conditioner's efficiency level is measured by the seasonal energy efficiency ratio (SEER). The higher the number, the more efficient the unit. A 13 or 14 SEER rating is considered high efficiency.

The best way to keep your air conditioner running at peak efficiency is to spend a couple of hours each year on basic maintenance—cleaning and straightening the fins, changing the filter and lubricating the motor.

Websites That Can Save You Money

As we've shown throughout this story, saving money on electricity isn't just about turning off the lights when you leave the room. Even before an appliance reaches your home, you can pocket some serious cash. Several rebate programs pay consumers to buy energy-efficient products and appliances. To find a program that works for you, to pick the right appliance or to learn more energy-saving tips, check out the sites below.

- **ENERGY.GOV** The Department of Energy's site provides information on how to use energy more efficiently in your home.

- **DSIREUSA.ORG** This database of state incentives for using energy-efficient products allows you to search by ZIP code.

- **ENERGYSTAR.GOV** Energy Star offers advice for buying energy-efficient products and appliances as well as cutting electrical and energy costs.

5. KILL ENERGY VAMPIRES

According to the Department of Energy, 75% of the electrical use by home electronics occurs when they're turned off. These energy vampires suck electricity all day long—costing you an extra $100 each year. So unplug your electronics when they're not in use, or plug them into a power strip and turn off the strip.

Don't worry about losing the settings on new computers and TVs.

Each has a memory chip that resets everything when you power back up. If you have an old VCR or other device that flashes when the power goes out, keep it plugged in. Some power strips, like the BITS Smart Strip shown, have a few outlets that always have power even when you flip off the switch. This type of strip has a main outlet for the computer. When you turn off the computer, the strip also shuts down other devices, such as your scanner, printer or modem.

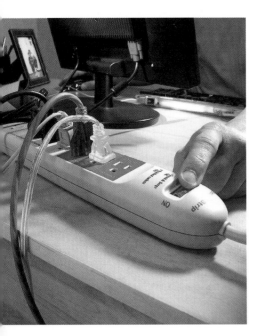

Electronics guzzle power even when turned off. Stop wasting electricity: Plug them into a power strip, then turn it off.

BRUSH

6. CLEAN OUT THE LINT FOR DRYER EFFICIENCY

A clogged lint screen or dryer duct drastically reduces the efficiency of your dryer, whether it's gas or electric. Clean the lint screen after each load and clean the exhaust duct once a year (to see how, search for "dryer" at familyhandyman.com). The LintEater, shown in the photo above, has an auger brush that attaches to a drill to clean out the ducts. It's available at Lowe's for about $35.

Electric dryers use about $85 of electricity annually. A dirty lint screen can cause the dryer to use up to 30% more electricity ($25 per year), according to the Consumer Energy Center. Cleaning and maintaining your dryer is also an important safety measure—lint buildup is a common cause of fires.

Dry loads of laundry back-to-back so the dryer doesn't cool down between loads (a warm dryer uses less energy). And run the dryer only until the clothes are dry. Overdrying damages your clothes and runs up your electric bill. If you're in the market for a new dryer and already have a gas line in the house, go with a gas dryer. A gas dryer is more efficient.

7. CHANGE YOUR FURNACE FILTER

Keeping your furnace (gas or electric) tuned up has two important benefits: It makes the furnace run efficiently and it prolongs the furnace's life span. And better yet, you can perform the annual tune-up yourself in about three hours (for complete instructions about how to do this, search for "furnace" at familyhandyman.com).

Change the furnace filter every month of the heating season (or all year round if the filter is also used for air conditioning). Be sure you insert the new filter so that it faces the right way. The filter protects the blower and its motor; a clogged filter makes the motor work harder and ultimately use more power.

8. SAVE ON ELECTRIC WATER HEATING

If you routinely use an electric water heater at only certain times of the day, you're wasting electricity keeping the water hot 24/7. To solve that problem (and save some money), install an electronic timer switch. Timers are available for 120- and 240-volt heaters. They can be programmed for daily or weekly schedules so you heat the water only when you need it. Installing a timer can save you around $25 per year.

To make your water heater even more efficient, drain the tank and flush out the sediment at the bottom (for step-by-step guidance on how to do this, go to familyhandyman.com and search for "flush a water heater"). Otherwise, your water heater could be expending energy heating through inches of sediment before it ever even heats the water.

If your electric water heater is warm or hot to the touch, it's losing heat. Wrap it with an insulating blanket (about $30 at home centers).

A timer turns on the water heater only when you need it, so you don't waste electricity heating and reheating water that sits in the tank.

Sediment lowers the efficiency of your water heater. Turn off the power, hook up a hose to the drain valve and drain the tank every 6 to 12 months.

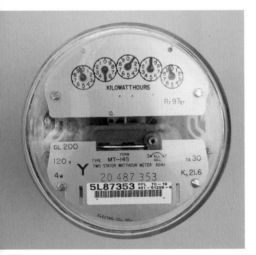

Time-of-use meters replace the existing meter and attach to the meter box. They enable you to pay less for electricity used at certain times of the day.

9. GET SMART METERING

Smart metering programs vary among utility companies, but the basic idea is the same: The utility installs a special "smart" meter that tracks how much electricity you're using. The utility uses that data to make sure its power grid doesn't get overloaded and cause blackouts. If the grid nears capacity, the utility can shut off major appliances in customers' homes for short periods of time (such as 15 minutes per hour). Not all utility companies offer smart metering, but some do and many others are considering it.

What's in it for you? Oftentimes, money! Some programs provide users with a monthly credit for signing up. Others let you view your home's usage online in real time so that you can better manage your electrical consumption. Others let you choose "real-time" or "time-of-use" pricing that allows you to pay less for electricity used during off-peak hours (for example, on weekdays from early afternoon until 8 p.m.).

These plans reward you for using electricity when it's cheapest. Smart metering makes the most sense if you're away from home all day—you won't notice or care if things get turned off—although it's a good idea for everyone else too! According to SRP, a power utility company, the plans cut 7% off your bill, which is $140 for the average $2,000 yearly energy bill. Check with your local company to find out what smart metering programs are available in your area.

10. RUN YOUR REFRIGERATOR FOR LESS

Your refrigerator uses more electricity than all your other kitchen appliances combined. To keep its energy costs down, clean the coils twice a year, which will improve efficiency by 30 to 50%.

Your fridge and freezer run more efficiently when they're full. Put water containers in the fridge and ice bags in your freezer to keep them filled. Keep the refrigerator setting between 35 and 38 degrees and the freezer between 0 and 5 degrees F.

Refrigerator door seals wear out over time. Test your seal by closing a dollar bill in the door. If it pulls out easily, replace the seal (go to familyhandyman .com and search for "refrigerator seal").

If your fridge was made before 2001, it's using at least 40% more electricity than new Energy Star models. If you're replacing your

Brush and vacuum the coils at the bottom or the back of the refrigerator. A coil cleaning brush (about $7 at appliance parts stores or amazon.com) is bendable and can fit in tight areas.

fridge, buy an Energy Star model and recycle your old one. Don't hook up the old one in the basement or garage—an inefficient refrigerator costs as much as $280 a year in electricity, according to the Consumer Energy Center. Any money you save buying food in bulk and storing it is lost in the electric costs of an inefficient second fridge.

Monitor Your Usage and Change Your Habits

Knowing how much electricity you're using is the first step toward using less. Electricity monitors, like the ones offered by Blue Line Innovations ($179 at bluelineinnovations.com), pair with your smartphone to give you a real-time readout of how much electricity you're using at the moment and your electrical use for the month to date. This helps you understand when and how you're using power so you can reduce your energy consumption.

Program your local utility rates into the monitor to determine your energy costs. Seeing the dollars and cents prompts you to save by making you more conscious of the electricity you're using. When you see the tally rising, you'll be reminded and encouraged to turn things off. According to Blue Line Innovations, studies have shown that real-time feedback causes people to change their habits, which results in their using 10 to 20% less electricity. The monitors are also available at amazon.com and Target.

Hire Contractors Off-Season and Save

The right timing can help you pay less for better results.

Choosing the right time to hire home contractors can save you money, get you better quality work, ensure you'll get the job done on schedule and make the whole process less frustrating. All types of contractors have slow seasons when they're more willing to negotiate lower costs and shorten lead times, and when they're less likely to rush through a job. If your job isn't an emergency, it's often worth waiting for a slow period.

ROOFING

The busiest season for most roofers is the fall as homeowners scramble to prepare for winter. Spring is also hectic because there is a push to address problems that occurred in winter and early spring. The standard rule is to schedule your roofing project between the Fourth of July and Labor Day. If your roof covering is other than asphalt shingles, such as metal, rubber or tile, then you have more flexibility and could strike a good deal for a winter job.

EXTERIOR PAINTING

Summer is the busiest season for house painters, in part because some homeowners prefer to have messy work done while they're on vacation. January and February are slow months for most contractors, so if it's possible to apply paint at that time in your area, start then. Otherwise, the trade tends to lag in September and October.

INTERIOR PAINTING

Most people paint when they have just purchased a house (which spikes a bit during spring) or are preparing for the holidays. Across the board, January and February are considered the slow seasons for interior painting.

CONCRETE WORK

Spring and summer are the peak seasons, so consider colder months. Concrete work is less subject to cold weather than other exterior jobs because you can pour concrete even at low temperatures. For major projects that require a concrete truck to traverse your driveway or yard, frozen ground is preferable.

HEATING AND AIR CONDITIONING

When the weather changes—becoming hot in late spring or cold in fall—systems break down and HVAC people get busy. Have your air conditioning system serviced or replaced in the off-peak times. Early fall and spring are good periods.

INTERIOR REMODELING

If you can work around the mess and inconvenience of a kitchen or bathroom remodeling project during November or February, the months on either side of the holiday season, there's a good chance you'll find more and better choices of contractors and be able to strike a better deal.

Put the Brakes on High Auto Insurance Costs

Keep your coverage and lose the big bill with these cost-saving tips.

Everybody wants to save on car insurance. But most people can't figure out how to do it without either reducing coverage or increasing their deductibles. We got some better advice from a seasoned insurance expert who's worked with dozens of major insurance companies.

Insurance laws vary by state, so some of these cost-saving methods may not apply in your area. But if you follow these tips, you should be able to save an average of $300 per year, or possibly more, on your car insurance. We'll work with a model of a two-car household with two 57-year-old adults and one college-age driver. This household's annual premium is $2,300 based on one accident and one speeding ticket.

1. PAY IN ADVANCE

You generally pay extra if you're paying your car insurance bill month-to-month. If you have the cash on hand, paying the premium in advance can earn you a discount (check with your agent). Find out the least expensive pay period from your insurer—it's often six months.

2. PAY PROMPTLY

Some companies offer attractive incentives for paying the invoice within 10 days, rather than taking the full 30 days. We're not telling you to pay your mortgage late so you can

pay the insurance company early. But if your insurer offers a "prompt pay" discount (ask for one), it may be worth your while to reprioritize your bill payment schedule. If you're temporarily short on cash, it may even make sense to pay with your credit card.

3. COMPLETE A "SENIOR DRIVER" TRAINING (AND REFRESHER) COURSE

Most car insurance companies offer a discount for each driver on the policy aged 55 and older who takes an authorized driver safety education program (some states mandate this discount). The initial course is eight hours, and some companies (and states) allow you to take a four-hour online version ($20 per driver). Classroom rates vary. You'll be a safer driver and can pocket the savings every year. For more information, contact your insurance agent, AARP, AAA or your local adult education center, or search online for "senior driver education."

4. KID AT COLLEGE?

This one's a no-brainer. If your kid is away at college and isn't driving the family car, your insurance rates will be lower. Tell your agent that your child is at school and work out arrangements for those few days when he or she is home. If your student has a car at school, you should still notify your agent. The rates may be lower based on the school's location.

5. CHANGE JOBS OR RETIRE?

If you drive 20 miles on your commute to work every day, you're going to be paying a higher premium than people who drive only 5 miles. So if you get a new job closer to home, tell your insurance agent immediately. Also, if you're lucky enough to retire, tell your agent so that they can reclassify you as a "pleasure driver." You'll see a welcome drop in your premiums in both cases.

6. TRACK YOUR TICKETS

Insurance companies check your driving record regularly and increase your premium on the very next bill if they find a traffic violation. But they're not always so quick to reduce your premium later when the violation falls off your record. So keep track of the dates of your tickets and ask for a reduction once your record is "clean" (usually three years, but check with your state's Department of Motor Vehicles).

7. SHOP EARLY

Everyone should shop around for new insurance rates every few years. This helps ensure that you're always getting the best rate and coverage available in your area. Insurance companies reward early shopping (30 days before renewal is perfect) by giving better rates. Last-minute shopping (less than 10 days before the policy expires) makes insurance companies think you're irresponsible, and that can be reflected in a higher quote.

8. AVOID SMALL CLAIMS

If you get a small dent or other minor damage on an older car, think twice about filing a claim and getting it fixed. To avoid rate hikes, it might be worth your while to just live with it if there are no safety issues. And if you have towing coverage on your policy and use it to get your jalopy towed every six months, be ready for a 10% rate increase on your next renewal. Buy a roadside assistance plan (available from AAA, AARP and other vendors) instead. It's much more cost-effective.

9. DROP COLLISION AND COMPREHENSIVE COVERAGE WHEN IT MAKES SENSE

Let's face it—old cars (10-plus years) often aren't worth much. So at a certain point in time, it doesn't make sense to keep paying for collision and comprehensive (C&C) coverage. Find the "book" value of your vehicle on the internet (check edmunds.com, nada.com, or kbb.com) or at the library. Then add up the annual premiums for C&C. Chances are you're paying for the full value of the vehicle every three years. If you're comfortable accepting a low level of risk, cancel your C&C coverage and put that money away. At the end of the day, you'll probably come out ahead.

10. INSTALL AN ALARM

You can often earn a discount from your insurer by taking steps to make your car more secure. The discount amount will vary by location, the make and model of the alarm, and the theft likelihood of your particular vehicle model. But insurers tend to give the largest discounts for installing a "stolen vehicle recovery" system like LoJack or GM's OnStar. These systems can locate a stolen vehicle within a few minutes and prevent a total loss. The discount alone may pay for one of these systems in just a few years.

You can learn more about such systems and their security features by visiting lojack.com.

Avoid These Insurance Mistakes

■ Don't let your car insurance lapse. If you're up against the payment deadline, overnight the check or contact your agent's office to see if you can drop off the check, or put it on your credit card. Renewal of a lapsed policy can cost you an extra 20% for several years. That's IF the company even agrees to reinstate you (it doesn't have to).

■ Don't reduce your liability coverage to save money. It won't save you much and may actually cost you more in premiums. You risk your home, savings and a garnishment of future earnings if you injure someone and you're underinsured.

■ You can settle fender-bender claims on your own, but you still have to report the accident to your insurance company. You probably won't see a premium increase because you paid for the damage yourself. But if you don't notify your agent and the other person makes a delayed claim for injury, your company can deny coverage.

■ Check out all the details of "first accident forgiveness" policies to be sure you're not paying more up front. Also check out whether a second accident or a driving violation on this type of policy results in far higher premiums than a traditional policy.

■ Never cancel an existing policy until you receive the new policy paperwork. Insurance companies can refuse to underwrite you even after they have accepted your check and issued a binder. If that happens, you may not be able to reinstate the policy.

1

Airtight fireplace doors fasten to the masonry opening like other door systems, but they seal the area to keep heated air from leaking up the chimney.

Cut Your Winter Heating Bills

Use less energy without sacrificing comfort.

Every year as winter approaches, you see the same old recycled news stories on how to cut your heating bill. Some of the ideas in these articles are good and some are bad, but they all contain the same advice you've been hearing for decades.

So for this article, we went looking for new approaches. We talked with experts and found some new, some innovative and some tried-and-true ways to tame your heating bills. These tips will save you money—while still keeping you warm.

1. STOP FIREPLACE HEAT LOSS

Wood-burning fireplaces can warm up a room, but more often they rob a house of heat by letting it escape up the chimney. If you have a modern fireplace with a cold-air intake from outside, make sure you equip it with an airtight door. If you have an older fireplace that uses room air for combustion, equip it with a door that has operable vents. And be sure to keep those vents open only when you

have a fire in the fireplace. Otherwise, heat will constantly be sucked out of the house.

Airtight doors have gaskets that seal the doors to stop air leaks. They're pricier than other door systems, but the energy and heat savings are worth it. Enter "fireplace doors" in a search engine to find local retailers. One online retailer is fireplacedoorsonline.com. In addition to new doors, consider installing a chimney-top damper, which will also help reduce heat loss.

Quilted curtains cover drafty windows, making your room feel warmer at a lower temperature.

2. INSTALL INSULATED CURTAINS TO BLOCK DRAFTS

If you're turning up the heat in the house to compensate for drafty windows, consider insulated or quilted curtains, which can increase your comfort and let you keep the temp down. The curtains are available in various colors, patterns and sizes. Enter "insulated curtain" in a search engine to find retailers. Online sources include amazon.com and wayfair.com. Prices start around $30, and a curtain can be installed in less than 10 minutes on your existing curtain rod.

3. TURN DOWN THE HEAT AND STILL BE COMFORTABLE

We all know the mantra by now—turn down the thermostat during the winter months and you'll save money. And it's true. According to the Department of Energy, for every degree you lower the thermostat, you'll save 1% on your energy bill. But turning down the heat has a big drawback—you have to wear extra clothes to stay warm. Another solution? Use a space heater to stay comfortable in the room where family members gather, like the living room. Fireplaces and fireplace inserts can provide space heating, but electric heaters are the easiest way to warm up a room.

Baseboard, fan-forced air and oil-filled electric heaters all have roughly the same energy efficiency, although oil-filled units are the quietest (but also larger and heavier). You'll have to turn down the heat enough (usually 5 degrees F or more) to offset the cost of the electricity used by the space heater and still pocket a savings. Space heaters range in price from about $35 to more than $100, depending on benefits

Space heaters cut heating bills only if you turn down the temperature in the entire house. The heaters work best in walled-in rooms, where the heat can be contained, rather than in open spaces.

like a remote control, a programmable thermostat and safety features. You can buy them at home centers, discount stores and amazon.com.

A towel warmer ($60 and up) can act like a small space heater for your bathroom and provide you with a toasty towel after bathing. There are freestanding units and units that mount to the wall, and those that are plugged in or hard-wired. Towel warmers are available at amazon.com and other online retailers. Towel warmers don't save energy, but they can keep you warm in the bathroom when the house thermostat is turned down.

Towel warmers take the edge off a chilly bathroom and give you a toasty towel to use for drying off after a bath.

4. MAKE YOUR WINDOWS WORK FOR YOU

Keep open the blinds or drapes on windows with direct sun exposure (usually on the south side of the house) to let the sunlight heat the room. Heating doesn't get any cheaper than this! At night, close the blinds or drapes to cover the cold glass.

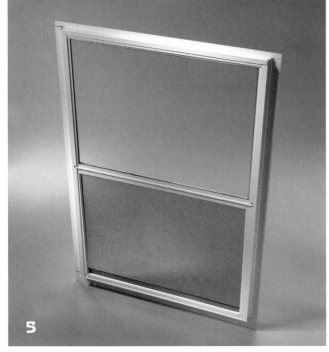

5

If you have single-pane windows, installing storm windows is one of the most cost-effective improvements you can make to reduce heat loss.

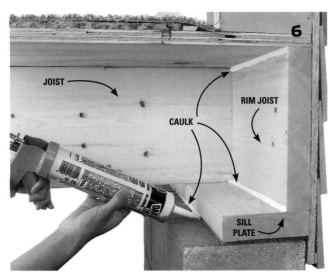

Caulking the sill plate and the rim joist stops air leaks along the foundation.

7

Point the Thermal Leak Detector at windows, walls and ceilings. When the detector finds a cold or warm spot, the LED light changes from green to red (for warm) or blue (for cold).

5. CUT HEAT LOSS WITH STORM WINDOWS

Storm windows aren't new, but they're definitely improved: New ones open and close and can be left on year-round. Some offer low-emissivity (low-e) coatings to further cut heat loss. You can use low-e versions even if your windows already have a low-e coating.

You'll see the biggest payback when they're used over single-pane windows. But don't use storm windows over aluminum windows—heat buildup between the two windows can damage the aluminum, and drilling holes for installation can cause leaks.

You can buy or special-order storm windows at home centers, but you may have trouble finding low-e models. One source is ProVia (provia.com). Storm windows start at $90. Measure the height and width of the window (from the outside) before ordering. Do-it-yourself installation takes about 30 minutes per window.

6. SEAL BASEMENT AIR LEAKS

Sill plates and rim joists are usually poorly insulated (if at all) and very leaky. So if you have an unfinished basement, grab some silicone or acrylic latex caulk to seal the sill plate. If you simply have fiberglass insulation stuffed against the rim joist, pull it out. Run a bead of caulk between the edge of the sill plate and the top of the foundation wall. Use expanding spray foam anywhere there are gaps larger than 1/4 in. between the sill and the foundation. For hollow-block foundations, stuff fiberglass insulation in the holes, then seal it with expanding foam.

Caulk along the top and bottom of the rim joists, and use expanding foam to seal around holes for electric, water and gas lines. Then cut rigid foam insulation to size and place it against the rim joist (go to familyhandyman.com and search for "insulate rim joist"). Caulk around all four sides of the foam insulation.

7. USE A LEAK DETECTOR TO FIND DRAFTS

If your home is drafty, use the Thermal Leak Detector from Black & Decker ($35 at amazon.com). The battery-operated handheld tool uses infrared sensors to identify spots that are warmer or colder than the surrounding area, signifying an air leak or poor insulation. Of course, once you locate the source of the draft, you'll have to do some detective work to figure out the problem and how to fix it. The detectors are also available at Home Depot and Menards.

Add loose-fill insulation if your attic is underinsulated.

8. ADD ATTIC INSULATION

In most homes, but especially in older homes, adding insulation in the attic will cut heat loss. At a minimum, homes should have attic insulation between R-22 and R-49 (6 to 13 in. of loose fill or 7 to 19 in. of fiberglass batts). Check with the local building department to find the recommended level for your area, or visit energystar.gov and search for "insulation R-values."

Stick your head through the attic access door and measure how much insulation you have. If your insulation is at or below the minimum, adding some will lower your heating bills.

If you need to add more, go with loose-fill insulation rather than fiberglass batts, even if you already have fiberglass. Loose fill is usually composed of cellulose or fiberglass and lets you cover joists and get into crevices. Pros charge about 70¢ per sq. ft. to blow in 7 to 8 in. of insulation. You can rent a blower and do the job yourself for less than half that cost, but it's a messy job and you have to watch your step so you don't go through the drywall floor in the attic.

9. GET AN ENERGY AUDIT

A surefire way to find air leaks and identify insulation problems is to have an energy audit. The audit, which takes two to three hours, uses a blower door test and an infrared camera to pinpoint leaks and will identify ways to improve energy efficiency. It costs $250 to $400 (schedule the audit through your utility company and ask about rebates). To learn more, go to familyhandyman.com and search for "energy audit."

An energy audit is worth the investment because it's almost impossible to find certain sources of energy loss on your own. You'll get a detailed report listing upgrades you can make to cut heat loss and use less energy.

The auditor closes all doors and windows, then inserts a blower in the doorway to test for air leakage.

Dispelling Common Energy-Saving Myths

Some energy-saving myths have been repeated so many times that people believe they're true. We're here to set the record straight.

MYTH 1: REPLACING WINDOWS IS A GOOD INVESTMENT

New windows can increase security and comfort, but they'll take 20 to 30 years to pay for themselves. Replacing single-pane windows with double-pane low-e windows will save energy and money—about $340 per year for a 2,000-sq.-ft. house in cold climates, according to Energy Star (energystar.gov). In a house with 20 windows, you'll save $17 per window in energy costs each year by replacing single-pane windows with double-pane, but it'll take you almost 24 years to recoup the cost of new windows at $400 apiece.

MYTH 2: EXTERIOR CAULKING IS THE BEST WAY TO SEAL LEAKS

Done correctly, exterior caulking keeps out water. But if you want to make your house more energy efficient, work inside not outside. Seal attic air leaks (go to familyhandyman.com and search for "air leaks") and spray expanding foam in basement leaks, such as around cables coming into the house.

MYTH 3: CLOSING REGISTERS SAVES ENERGY

Most heating duct systems have so many leaks that closing a register won't force more warm air into other rooms—it will force more air out of the leaks.

In addition, forced-air heating systems are designed to operate with all of the registers open. The fixed-speed blower won't perform as well with registers closed and can create a whistling in the ducts.

If in the winter you want to close off a portion of your house, like the upstairs, talk to a rep from your furnace company or a heating specialist to determine the best way to save energy with your furnace.

Stop Drafts Cold at Electrical Boxes

Keep warm air where you want it.

The small air gaps around electrical boxes on exterior walls and ceilings leak more air than you might imagine. In fact, a mere 1/8-in. gap around just six ceiling boxes is the equivalent of cutting a 4-in. hole in your ceiling. Think of the amount of heat you'd lose! When you combine that with the leaks around all the electrical boxes in outside walls in your house, it's no wonder your house feels drafty.

Many homeowners install plain foam gaskets between the cover plate and the switches/receptacles. However, those gaskets don't always seal well. Infrared thermograph images of those outlets will show cold air still entering (which means warm air escaping) the house.

We'll show you more effective methods that permanently seal those leaks. Sealing is easy to do and you can complete the entire house in about four hours. The materials are inexpensive, and the project will be one of the best investments you'll ever make! All you need is a caulk gun, caulk and aerosol foam. Here's how to do it.

BUY THE MATERIALS

Gaps around ceiling boxes must be sealed with an "intumescent" fire-blocking caulk or foam. Ordinary spray foam burns too quickly, opening the gap and creating a chimney effect that feeds the fire. Intumescent caulk or foam, on the other hand, swells when heated so it prevents that airflow. Regular caulk or foam can be used on wall-mounted boxes.

If the electrical boxes aren't mounted flush with the drywall, adding a box extender will make them easier to seal. Extenders are available at most home centers for single, round and multiple-gang boxes.

SEAL CEILING BOXES

Intumescent foam works best to seal large gaps (larger than 1/8 in.) around ceiling boxes. But the foam drips out as it expands and is difficult to remove after it cures. So turn off the power and double-check with a voltage sniffer. Then remove the light fixture, spread a drop cloth and inject the foam **(Photo 1)**. Intumescent fire caulk doesn't drip like foam, so you don't have to remove the light fixture or cover the floor.

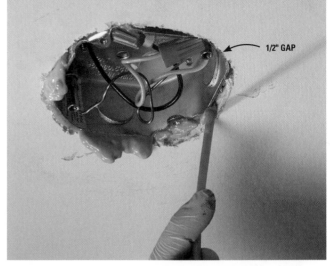

1 FILL CEILING BOX GAPS WITH FIRE-BLOCKING FOAM. Invert the spray foam can and shove the tube up into the gap. Gently squeeze the trigger and slowly pump foam into the gap. Let it cure for about two hours. Then cut off the excess and reinstall the light fixture.

1/2" GAP

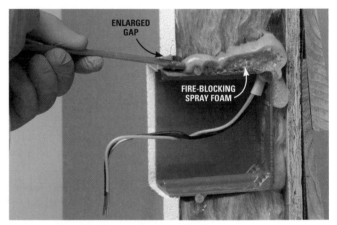

ENLARGED GAP

FIRE-BLOCKING SPRAY FOAM

2 SEAL THE WIRE INTRUSIONS. Align the tube with the wire intrusion(s) and squeeze the trigger to shoot a small dollop of foam around the box opening. Don't overdo it or the foam will force its way into the electrical box and you'll have to remove the excess later.

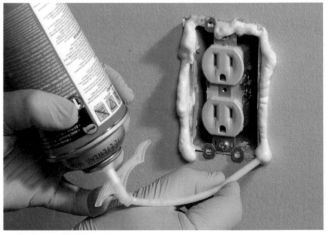

3 SEAL AROUND A FLUSH-MOUNTED BOX. Apply foam or caulk into the gap around the flush-mounted box. After the foam hardens, slice off the excess with a serrated knife.

4 ADD A BOX EXTENDER. Unscrew the switch or receptacle and twist it at an angle. Then slide the box extender over the device and into the wall box. Remount the device, straighten it and then tighten the screws.

BOX IS SET BACK TOO FAR

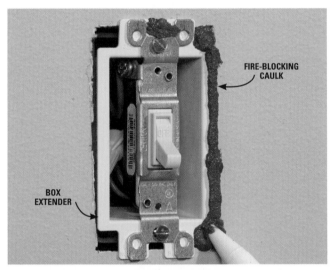

FIRE-BLOCKING CAULK

BOX EXTENDER

5 SEAL AROUND THE BOX EXTENDER. Squirt caulk between the box extender and the wall. Smooth the caulk bead with a wet finger.

Cover the Mess with a Bigger Plate

If your caulking/foaming job got out of hand and extends beyond the cover plate, you don't have to repaint the wall to cover your tracks. Just buy a "jumbo" cover plate (about $1.50).

REGULAR PLATE

"JUMBO" PLATE

SEAL FLUSH-MOUNTED WALL BOXES

Sealing wall boxes is a two-step process: First, seal the cable intrusions and then the gap around the box. To locate open box knockouts, shine a light inside to see where the cables enter the box. That way you'll know where to inject the foam. If you can't spot the entry points, turn off the power and pull the switch or receptacle out far enough to see.

Next, enlarge the gaps above and below the box (if needed) to provide room to insert the foam's tube deep into the wall cavity. Seal the wire intrusion openings with foam **(Photo 2)**. We used intumescent fire-blocking foam to seal the wire intrusions as an added measure of safety, but it's not required by code. You can use regular spray foam. However, never seal the intrusions from inside the box—that doesn't meet code and you'll have to remove the sealant if it's ever inspected. Finish the job by shooting ordinary foam around the box **(Photo 3)**.

SEAL RECESSED WALL BOXES

Sometimes wall-mounted electrical boxes are recessed because of an installer error or new tile installed over the old layer. You can seal around the gap with caulk, but that doesn't solve the problem of the box not being flush with the wall. That's where a box extender comes in handy. It provides solid mounting for the switch or receptacle and makes the box easier to seal.

Start by sealing the wire intrusion following the procedure above. Then turn off the power (check it with a voltage sniffer) and slide on a box extender **(Photo 4)**. Next, seal the gap around the box extender **(Photo 5)**.

Fix Leaky Can Lights

If you have older recessed lights in a ceiling under an attic space, you're likely losing a lot of heat through the holes in the housing and around the base of the fixture. Caulking those openings or covering the fixture with an airtight box can create a fire hazard. The easiest and best solution is to buy an airtight LED retrofit light/baffle kit (one choice is the Halo No. RL560WH-R; shown below). Just remove the bulb, screw in the threaded adapter and snap the LED unit in place—no more air leakage.

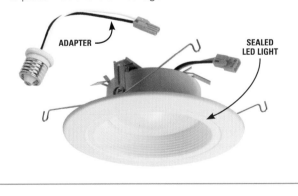

ADAPTER

SEALED LED LIGHT

Don't Waste Your Money on These 15 Things

Avoiding unforced spending errors will let you save for the stuff you really want.

It's easy to get into a spending rut in regard to household purchases, buying the same stuff you've always bought out of habit. But sometimes the same old, same old can cost you, whether we're talking about everyday purchases, monthly bills or occasional big-ticket items. In many cases, making a simple swap can save you money, time and even headaches. We checked with experts in more than a dozen fields—from interior design and automotive pros to insurers and horticulturists—to find out what we should stop wasting our money on (and what we should spend it on instead).

1. RUNAWAY AC AND HEAT

According to energystar.gov, a typical U.S. household spends around $2,000 a year on energy bills, with nearly half going to heating and air conditioning.

"A programmable thermostat can save you 10% a year on your cooling and heating bills," says Mary Farrell, senior editor at Consumer Reports. Set your thermostat 7 to 10 degrees higher on warmer days and the same amount lower on chilly days and see whether the money you save doesn't feel better than being slightly warmer or cooler than you're used to. Even easier, make these adjustments when you plan to be out of the house.

2. A NEW STICKER-PRICE CAR

You should get a good discount on a new car without having to rely solely on your negotiating skills. One secret is timing: Watch for low- or zero-percent interest on loans, cash-back offers and special lease terms. "Cash-back offers can even be as high as $10,000," says Ivan Drury, senior manager of insights at the automotive research site edmunds.com. "Every month there are new incentives available from every automaker," he says. "It's pretty rare that someone looking for a car has no incentives available." You can check current rebates by make and model at edmunds.com and jdpower.com.

The best time to buy a new car is at the end of the model year (usually August or September) or at the end of the calendar year. The regular deals didn't happen in 2020 because of the pandemic and the resulting auto shortages, but, generally, "buying at the end of the month does yield a bit better deal," says Drury. The reason: Many dealerships receive monthly volume bonuses, meaning they get additional money back from the automaker if they sell a certain number of vehicles in a month. You probably won't get a giant discount, but you can likely get another $200 or so knocked off the sticker price.

Don't be lured by a holiday sale at the beginning or middle of the month. Drury says, "Those holiday deals are usually the incentives you can get all month, so it still makes sense to wait until the end of the month to save a bit more."

3. HOMEOWNERS INSURANCE ...

One with a low deductible, that is. Raising a $500 deductible to $1,000 can cut your annual premium up to 25%, according to Mark Friedlander, director of corporate communications for the Insurance Information Institute, a nonprofit consumer education group. Have a monitored burglar alarm or fire alarm system? Some insurers will knock 10 to 20% off your annual homeowners premiums for that. Ask your agent about any other discounts you might be missing.

4. ... AND CAR INSURANCE

There's a similar savings step with your car: Increase the $250 deductible to $1,000 and you could save up to 40% on your premiums. At the same time, sniff around to see whether you have earned any discounts that could save you even more. "If you're driving less than you used to due to the COVID-19 pandemic, ask your insurer whether you qualify for a low-mileage discount, which might cut your auto premiums by 10 to 15%," says Friedlander.

Bundling your home and auto policies with the same company, if you haven't already, could save you an additional 15 to 20% on each policy. Then pay your premiums in full up front instead of using a payment plan and you might save another 10%.

Even if you are maxing out all your available discounts, it still pays to shop your insurance coverage around every year or two, getting at least three quotes, to see if you can get a better deal. In a study by the Texas Insurance Department, people saved an average of $125 per year on auto policies just by comparing rates.

An independent agent can help you with those comparisons; find one through the Independent Insurance Agents & Brokers of America, or check comparison-shopping sites such as insure.com, netquote.com and selectquote.com.

Chances are you're being sold faster internet than you need.

5. EXTRA-FAST INTERNET

Companies such as Xfinity and Google offer home internet speeds of up to 2,000 Mbps (or 2 Gbps), but unless you are a hard-core online gamer, that blazing-fast service is probably a waste of money. The Federal Communications Commission recommends internet speeds of 12 to 25 Mbps for most families, even those who stream games or videos. You won't see a big difference in your everyday browsing speed, but you will see a difference in your bank account. For example, for service in White Plains, New York, Xfinity charges as little as $40 per month for download speeds of 100 Mbps, $80 for 1,000 Mbps, and a whopping $300 for 2,000 Mbps.

7. A REPAIR-PRONE AUTO

Before you choose your next ride, check the True Cost to Own calculator at edmunds.com to find out how much different models would cost you over time. Information includes purchase price, repairs, depreciation, insurance, fuel and more based on your ZIP code and five years of ownership. For example, Houston buyers purchasing a 2020 Honda Civic two-door LX coupe can expect to pay $12,339 over those five years ($4,541 for fuel, $7,127 for insurance and $671 for repairs), while a BMW 330i could run $17,444 ($6,584 for fuel, $8,275 for insurance and $2,585 for repairs). Of course, check with your insurer to see rates for particular models.

8. SPRING FLOWERS

"When you buy in the spring, you're paying full price for all your plants," says Renee Marsh, a designer and teacher at the New York Botanical Garden. "Buy in summer or even fall because nurseries don't want to manage those plants through the summer heat or have to overwinter them." By waiting, you can easily save 20 to 50% or more. "Don't get carried away by the spring flower bling," Marsh says.

9. ENERGY-GUZZLING APPLIANCES

Older dishwashers, refrigerators and other essential appliances use a lot more energy and water than newer models, especially newer ones with an Energy Star certification from the Environmental Protection Agency (EPA). For example, a dishwasher with an Energy Star label uses 3.5 gallons of water or less per cycle, compared with the more than 10 gallons used by some older models. Energy Star-certified washing machines clean clothes using 33% less water and 25% less energy than standard washers, while certified clothes dryers use 20% less energy than other models. So if your existing model is on its way out or you're looking to upgrade, choose an energy-efficient replacement for long-term savings.

10. STORAGE BINS

Organizing guru Marie Kondo suggests using shoeboxes to organize items such as T-shirts, socks and tools in your drawers and closets. If you're decluttering, these freebies can save you quite a bit, considering that shoebox-sized bins from the Container Store cost $5 (or more) apiece.

11. FULL-PRICE FURNITURE

The biggest sales at furniture stores typically take place on certain holidays—Presidents Day, Memorial Day and Labor Day—and also at the end of the year, according to Chris Gaube, head of brand marketing at the home furnishings retailer Raymour & Flanigan. A smart strategy is to shop before those holidays to check prices and then wait to buy at the holiday sales, when much of the inventory could be at least 10 to 20% cheaper.

6. Large Rugs

A lot of work goes into weaving good-quality handmade rugs, and the price can skyrocket when you go up in size. For example, a 4 x 7-ft Turkish rug might be $300, while an 8 x 10-ft. version could cost $2,000. To save money but get the look, Rebecca Hawkins, president and head buyer for furniture retailer Celadon Home, suggests trying a decorator's technique called layering. Buy a large rug in an inexpensive material such as sisal, jute or seagrass for around $200. Then place a smaller, more expensive rug on top, like that 4 x 7 Turkish model. Result: You've spent $500 instead of $2,000. "Designers and home stagers use this a lot to save a bundle," Hawkins says.

And if you want to save even more, ask about buying floor samples. Says Gaube, "Typically our floor samples are discounted 30 to 50% during holiday sales."

12. LARGE OUTDOOR PLANTS

"A plant in a three-gallon pot looks nice and big, but it has usually been repotted a number of times, so the root structure has been compromised," says Renee Marsh of the New York Botanical Garden. When you're looking for plants to grow in your yard, think smaller. "A one-gallon potted plant has a healthier root system that will allow it to catch up to the bigger plants in a season or two, plus it is a fraction of the cost."

Or go even smaller and buy plant plugs—tiny plants with deep root systems. "Within a growing season or two, they will be the equivalent in almost every case of a plant you paid five times as much for that comes in a one-gallon pot," says horticulturist Kim Eierman. For example, a Lindera benzoin, or northern spicebush shrub, can cost $29 in a one-gallon pot, while five plugs of the same shrub cost $25.

13. REPLACEMENT TIRES IN PAIRS

Tires don't usually go flat in pairs, but the salesperson at the tire store will tell you that you need to buy them two at a time. Unless the tire on the opposite side of the one being replaced has less than 75% of its tread, you don't necessarily have to change it at the same time.

14. BOX SPRINGS

If you're shopping for a new mattress but your box spring isn't broken, don't let the salesperson talk you into buying one. That'll save you roughly $150 to $300 if you're buying a queen mattress, the most popular size, according to Consumer Reports testers.

Those testers also say that you should be able to get a good quality mattress for less than $700, including innerspring models, which tend to be more popular than cheaper foam mattresses—and cost far less than the thousands of dollars many brand-name manufacturers charge for some models.

15. A Big Lawn

Spend a lot less on yard care by getting rid of some of your lawn or never growing one to start with. By growing native plants instead of the usual grass, you can save two kinds of green. "After they're established in your garden, they don't need constant watering, they don't need any fertilizers, and they're more pest- and disease-resistant, so you save on pesticides," says Kim Eierman, a certified horticulturist and the founder of ecobeneficial .com, a gardening education website. One study by the EPA found that the costs of maintaining an acre of native prairie or wetland plants such as grasses totaled about $3,000 over 20 years. Maintaining the same size lawn covered in traditional turf would set you back around $20,000—and even more for a larger lawn.

Save Water (and Buckets of Money)

If your home was built before 1994 and still has the original plumbing fixtures, you're using 30 to 40% more water than a comparable new home.

Shrinking supply and growing demand are driving up water bills. Add the cost of heating water and rising sewer fees and you can see how thousands of wasted gallons turn into hundreds of wasted dollars. You can save water by fixing drips and leaks. But in most homes, replacing water-wasting fixtures results in the biggest savings. Those savings depend on your local water costs; the estimates given here are based on average costs.

EFFICIENT (BUT EFFECTIVE) TOILETS

A toilet manufactured before 1994 wastes almost $100 per year, compared to a modern, efficient model. A toilet made before 1980 wastes almost twice as much. The cost of a new toilet, plus installation, is typically $200 to $400—so your return is 25 to 100% per year, guaranteed. Unlike earlier models that often required double-flushing, most of today's water-saving toilets do their job in one flush.

LOW-FLOW SHOWERHEADS

Showerheads are not only the second-heaviest water user but also major energy eaters. That's because 70% of the water flowing through the head comes from your water heater. By reducing both water consumption and water heating, a low-flow showerhead can pay for itself in just one month! And an efficient showerhead no longer means settling for a drizzle instead of a downpour. Many water-efficient showerheads change the shape and velocity of the water stream—even the size of the drops—to provide the high-flow feel.

WATER-SAVING BATH FAUCETS

Like showerheads, efficient faucets save both water and energy. So—for a family of four—an efficient faucet will typically pay for itself in just a year or two and continue to save you money for many more years. Most water-saving faucets use special aerators that increase airflow to compensate for decreased water flow, giving you the same feel as other faucets.

WHAT ABOUT KITCHEN FAUCETS?

Efficiency in kitchen faucets is a matter of debate. Some say more efficient is always better. Others say that in the case of kitchens, low-flow is bad; it just takes longer to fill the sink or a pitcher. For now, the naysayers have the upper hand. WaterSense doesn't rate kitchen faucets and few low-flow models are available.

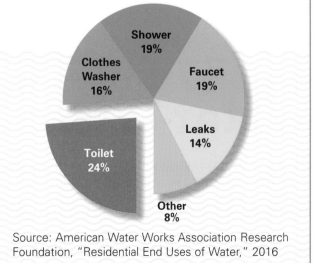

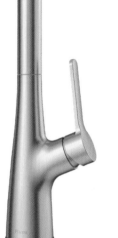

PRO TIP

The Badge of Efficiency

Look for the WaterSense logo. To earn this label, products must use at least 20% less water and still perform as well as or better than other products in that category. Go to epa.gov/watersense for more information.

Where's the Water Going?

Bathrooms use more water than any other room. About a quarter of household water is literally flushed down the toilet.

- Shower 19%
- Faucet 19%
- Leaks 14%
- Other 8%
- Toilet 24%
- Clothes Washer 16%

Source: American Water Works Association Research Foundation, "Residential End Uses of Water," 2016

7 Ways to Be Water-Wise

Quench your garden's thirst—and save time and money on watering too.

It's possible to reduce your household's outdoor water use by 20 to 50% with a few easy changes. To keep the water bill low and plants in their prime—while being kind to the planet—try these tips from the National Garden Bureau and Gardener's Supply Co.

1. CONSIDER COMPOST

Using organic matter, such as compost, shredded leaves or composted manure increases the water-holding capacity of soil. Add 1 inch of compost per year.

2. GIVE YOUR PLANTS A SOLID SOAK
Sprinklers will work, but a soaker hose applies water directly to the soil at the roots, making up to 90% available to plants.

3. SPREAD MULCH

Mulch prevents weeds that would soak up all the water you add to the planting area. Organic types are best; try grass clippings free of weedkillers, evergreen needles and shredded leaves.

4. USE RAIN WATER

Capture free water by placing a rain barrel or a cistern at a downspout. A 1,000-sq.-ft. roof collects about 625 gallons of water from 1 inch of rain.

5. KNOW YOUR PLANTING SITE
Determine a given area's sun and shade levels, soil type and wind conditions, then group plants with similar needs for more efficient watering.

6. BUY DROUGHT-TOLERANT PLANTS

Some plants get all the water they need from rain. For perennials suited to drought conditions, look for native plants that are adapted to your climate and soil type.

7. KEEP UP WITH GARDEN CHORES
Healthy plants mean less work. When you regularly weed, thin and prune, you add to the health of your plants and, in turn, need to water less frequently.